D0213038

The Uncertain Friendship

Recent Titles in
Contributions to the Study of World History

Uneasy Alliance: Relations Between Russia and Kazakhstan in the Post-Soviet Era, 1992–1997
Mikhail Alexandrov

The Maori and the Crown: An Indigenous People's Struggle for Self-Determination
Dora Alves

Shamanism and Christianity: Native Encounters with Russian Orthodox Missions in Siberia and Alaska, 1820–1917
Andrei A. Znamenski

Neville Chamberlain and British Rearmament: Pride, Prejudice, and Politics
John Ruggiero

Philanthropic Foundations in the Twentieth Century
Joseph C. Kigor

The Politically Correct Netherlands: Since the 1960s
Herman Vuijsje
Translated and annotated by Mark T. Hooker

Continuity during the Storm: Boissy d'Anglas and the Era of the French Revolution
John R. Ballard

Ambivalent Embrace: America's Relations with Spain from the Revolutionary War to the Cold War
Rodrigo Botero

Paper Liberals: Press and Politics in Restoration Spain
David Ortiz, Jr.

Triumph and Downfall: America's Pursuit of Peace and Prosperity, 1921–1933
Margot Louria

Philadelphia's Enlightenment, 1740–1800: Kingdom of Christ, Empire of Reason
Nina Reid-Maroney

Finance from Kaiser to Führer: Budget Politics in Germany, 1912–1934
C. Edmund Clingan

The Uncertain Friendship

The U.S. and Israel from Roosevelt to Kennedy

HERBERT DRUKS

Contributions to the Study of World History, Number 80

GREENWOOD PRESS
Westport, Connecticut • London

Library of Congress Cataloging-in-Publication Data

Druks, Herbert.
The uncertain friendship : the U.S. and Israel from Roosevelt to Kennedy / by Herbert Druks.
p. cm.—(Contributions to the study of world history, ISSN 0885–9159 ; no. 80)
Includes bibliographical references and index.
ISBN 0-313-31423-3 (alk. paper)
1. United States—Foreign relations—Israel. 2. Israel—Foreign relations—United States. 3. United States—Foreign relations—1933–1945. 4. United States—Foreign relations—1945–1953. 5. United States—Foreign relations—1953–1961. I. Title. II. Series.
E183.8.17 D78 2001
327.7305694—dc21 00-034141

British Library Cataloguing in Publication Data is available.

Library of Congress Catalog Card Number: 00-034141
ISBN: 0-313-31423-3
ISSN: 0885-9159

First published in 2001

Greenwood Press, 88 Post Road West, Westport, CT 06881
An imprint of Greenwood Publishing Group, Inc.
www.greenwood.com

Printed in the United States of America

The paper used in this book complies with the Permanent Paper Standard issued by the National Information Standards Organization (Z39.48–1984).

10 9 8 7 6 5 4 3 2 1

Contents

Preface

The years from Franklin D. Roosevelt to John F. Kennedy, 1933 to 1963, represent thirty crucial years in American and world history. For the Jewish people and Israel they were thirty years of a struggle for survival. Seldom in history did a people lose so much and later, despite it all, achieve so much. This is a history of the relations between that people and the United States from 1933 to the present. This book will examine that history from the Franklin D. Roosevelt years in the White House to the first two years of Kennedy's presidency.

The United States and Israel shared many things in common, not the least of which was a heritage of civilization and a mutual interest and love for the principles of democracy. In the course of the past fifty years, the United States was a friend of Israel and Israel was one of America's most reliable friends and allies. But that friendship had its limitations, for the United States likewise maintained good relations with various Arab states and peoples. And the United States had always to consider that which was in its best interest from a domestic as well as a global perspective.

Roosevelt voiced his support for Zionism and the Zionist ideal of establishing a Jewish state in the Land of Israel, but he never went out of his way to help the Jews establish that state. He even failed to help the Jews find refuge in Palestine or any where else. Ultimately, his concern was with geopolitical factors rather than humanity. On reading the history of his relations with the founders of the Jewish state and with Arab leaders and British officials, one can see contradictory remarks and statements. While on the one hand Roosevelt would promise support for the establishment of a Jewish state, on the other hand he would inform the monarchs of Syria and Saudi Arabia that nothing would be done without consulting them. He was always considerate of the imperial interests of

Great Britain and the aspirations of the Arab leaders. The Jews did not find asylum in the Land of Israel or anywhere else in the world. Six million Jews were murdered by the German Nazis and their collaborators.

When Roosevelt died on April 12, 1945, Vice President Harry S Truman became president. He seemed more sympathetic to the Jewish people and he called on the British to make good on their 1939 promise to admit one hundred thousand Jews to Palestine. But they refused.

While Truman was the first to recognize the Jewish state once it was proclaimed on May 14, 1948, he was most reserved when it came to helping Israel obtain weapons with which to defend itself.

From 1949 various American presidents supported Israel's call for peace negotiation with its Arab neighbors and the United States provided loans and grants. From the time of the Yom Kippur War of 1973, those loans and grants were increased to some two billion dollars per year. Similar large loans were made to Egypt and Jordan. While Israel and the United States developed respect and friendship for one another, there were stressful and difficult times in that relationship.

Throughout this history one can see that the United States and Israel disagreed with one another. At times one party made demands or requests that the other could not fulfill. But that was only natural in view of the complexity of international relations and the conditions of the Middle East as well as the range of American interests. The United States was the first to recognize Israel. That was President Truman's decision. It had been a decision opposed by most of the top officials in the State and Defense departments. Truman felt an affinity towards Israel and believed that the Jewish state might some day become a bulwark of democracy against the spread of totalitarianism in the Middle East and Africa. Once Israel proved itself in the field of battle, some individuals like Secretary of State George C. Marshall and Secretary of Defense James Forrestal were more inclined to agree with the president, but others like Undersecretary Robert Lovett continued to display an aversion to the Jewish state of Israel.

Recognition was important, but it was not everything. Israel still needed weapons with which to maintain its independence. The United States would not sell those weapons to Israel, and Truman upheld a UN arms embargo against the Middle East even though it had lapsed once the British Mandate had come to an end on May 14, 1948. The British continued to supply their Arab clients with all manner of weapons, in disregard of the UN embargo and later the Tripartite (British, French, and American) agreement. There were many Arab states and their advocates that strove to see the end of Israel and it was left in a militarily disadvantageous position.

It seemed that by upholding a Middle Eastern arms embargo the

United States hoped to help mediate differences and lower tensions in the Middle East, but that did not happen, especially not after the United States decided to provide Egypt with loans and arms during the early years of the Dwight D. Eisenhower administration. Eisenhower and his secretary of state, John Foster Dulles, entered the White House deprecating Truman's presidency. Dulles toured various Arab states and maintained that Truman had been partial to Israel and he promised that the Eisenhower administration would pursue a more even-handed approach to the Middle East condition. Ultimately, the Eisenhower administration would endorse Prime Minister Anthony Eden's call upon Israel to surrender its Negev to Egypt and Jordan in return for peace. The formula was "Land for Peace." Prime Minister David Ben-Gurion's response was: no. Somehow they realized that Ben-Gurion not only said no, but he meant it.

The United States, under UN auspices, invested its powers as of June 25, 1950, to stopping the North Korean–Chinese Communist- and Soviet-backed aggression against South Korea. Not only was the future of Asia at stake but so was the freedom and independence of Western Europe, the Middle East, and Africa. In April 1951, President Truman had intelligence reports that Russia was helping to amass some one hundred thousand Chinese Communist troops each week in Manchuria, building up its air force very rapidly, and that it had stationed seventy-five subs in the Kamchatka peninsula. As President Truman put it, "I shudder to think what will happen if they use all those forces against us, for we will be in World War III." At the same time that he dispatched American troops to Korea, in support of the United Nations, he sent American reinforcements to Berlin and Western Europe so as to advise the Russians that he would not allow them to move against the free world.

Israel found itself in a precarious situation. It did not wish to be overtly against the Soviet Union, for fear of jeopardizing Soviet Jewry, but it found itself isolated and surrounded by Arab states that refused to conclude peace agreements or treaties. Most of the Arab states had treaties of alliance and treaties of friendship with one another or with the major powers. Israel had no such understandings or security arrangements. Moreover, it had no steady source of defense supplies. Britain and the United States had encouraged the development of the Baghdad Pact as a way to stop Soviet expansion into the Middle East, but Israel was not invited to join.

It was during the Korean War that Prime Minister Ben-Gurion advised the United States that Israeli troops would be made available to the Western Alliance in case of a Soviet threat to the Middle East. In return, Ben-Gurion sought to purchase weapons from the United States with which to do the job. But the Truman and Eisenhower administrations would not come to such an understanding with Israel. As rivalry between the

Russians and the Americans increased in the Middle East and Africa, the United States concentrated its main efforts and resources at "containing" the Soviet Union. In 1951 Truman asked Israel's friends not to press for the proposed $150 million grant-in-aid. Truman said that he "had to be allowed to drag his feet for a while on this matter since his greatest efforts were to be directed toward financing the war in Korea." Ultimately, the United States did make good on its loan commitment to Israel despite the huge demands of the Korean War.

By 1954 Russia had provided Egypt and other Arab states with more than $500 million worth of arms, but the United States and Western Europe made little effort to balance the situation by selling Israel the weapons it needed. President Eisenhower in 1953, even echoed the British suggestion that Israel yield the Negev, 60 percent of Israel proper, to Egypt and Jordan in return for "peace."

Egypt's blockade of Eilat and the Suez Canal against Israeli and Israel-bound ships, its fostering of terrorist attacks against Israel, and its massive buildup of Soviet and western arms in the Sinai placed Israel in a most precarious position. The very existence of Israel as a sovereign and independent state was in question. Through the developing crisis, the United States continued to maintain a posture of friendship with all the parties concerned. But American policy was not as "even-handed" as its architects had hoped for or claimed.

Prime Minister Moshe Sharett observed in October 1954 that Israel watched "with profound dismay and mounting anxiety the policy of the American government to arm the Arab states—Iraq today, Egypt . . . and Syria the day after tomorrow." As he saw it, Israel was forced to use its meager resources to buy arms and counterbalance the massive infusion of Soviet, British, and American weaponry sold to the Arabs. Sharett was "at a loss to understand how the U.S. could reconcile that policy with her declared concern to see Israel prosperous and secure?" He observed that the Russians and the Americans competed for the "friendship of the Arab states," to Israel's detriment.

In the face of Arab acts of aggression, Israel was advised by President Eisenhower, in April 1956, to abstain from "retaliatory acts which may result in very dangerous consequences." Prime Minister Ben-Gurion thanked the Americans for their declared opposition to any attack in the Middle East, but he advised them that such a declaration did "not relieve" Israel's "grave anxiety" for its security. He recalled how the world had failed to help save the Jews of Europe in the 1930s and 1940s and it seemed to him that history was repeating itself in the 1950s.

For some time Israel had been unsuccessful in obtaining a steady flow of arms, but because the British and French felt threatened by Soviet-backed Egyptian moves in the Middle East and Africa, they formed a temporary alliance with Israel. Because of Egypt's military buildup in the Sinai and its countenancing of terrorism against Israel, as well as its illegal blockade of the Suez and the Straits of Tiran to Israel, the Israel Defense Forces met and defeated the Egyptians. This was done within one hundred hours, between October 29 and November 2, 1956. The United States, like the Soviet Union, sided with Egypt, while France and Britain sided with Israel. But it would not countenance any unilateral Soviet intervention in the Middle East.

Once the 1956 war was over, Egypt, Syria, Jordan, and Iraq continued building their armed forces, but Eisenhower still refused to supply Israel with the necessary equipment to help offset that imbalance of power. Repeatedly, Secretary of State Dulles would proclaim that the United States wanted to mediate Arab-Israeli differences, and if it sold weapons to Israel it would lose its influence with the Arab world. Dulles insisted that Israel could never match the armaments accumulated by the Arabs since it was a much smaller and far less wealthy state. Israel insisted that it did not wish to match them quantitatively, but it did wish to establish a qualitative edge. Faced with possible annihilation by the vast Arab military buildup, Israel directed its efforts toward the development of scientific and technological innovations, and even nuclear research. Six million Jews had been killed by the Nazi Germans; Israel would not permit itself to be sacrificed by the diplomatists. Both the Eisenhower and Kennedy administrations would be concerned with this turn of events.

Kennedy realized that Israel needed American arms in order to survive. While he worked on developing the friendship with all the nations of the Middle East, he was greatly disturbed by Russia's expansion and its interventionism in Yemen and the Arabian Peninsula through its client, Egypt. It was during the Kennedy administration that the United States agreed to sell Israel the Hawk defensive missile system. President Kennedy's vision of America's commitment to Israel represented a major departure and crossroads in U.S. relations with Israel. He was the first president to sell arms to Israel and the first to guarantee Israel's security, not once, but on at least three different occasions. He said to Foreign Minister Golda Meir in 1962: "The United States has a special relationship with Israel in the Middle East really comparable only to that which it has with Britain over a wide range of world affairs." But at the same time he advised Israel that the United States had to maintain its ties of friendship with Arab countries throughout the world and if the United States "pulled out of the Arab Middle East and maintained our ties only with Israel this would not be in Israel's interest." While Kennedy tried to maintained that friendship with all parties in the Middle East, he did approach America's relationship with Israel from a more realistic and pragmatic perspective.

The turmoil in the Middle East would continue. There would be at least three more wars between the Arabs and Israel, and there would be various endeavors to establish a peace between Israel and its Arab neighbors. The United States would play a critical role in all of those events. While the United States would be supportive of Israel in at least some of the years following the Kennedy administration, it likewise sought to keep its friendships and commitments to the Arab countries. This balancing act would be a most difficult task and would seldom be appreciated by the parties to the dispute.

Acknowledgments

This is a study of the diplomatic relations between the United States and Israel from the days of Franklin D. Roosevelt to John F. Kennedy. It is based upon published works and documents, archival materials of such presidential libraries as the Harry S Truman, John F. Kennedy, and Dwight D. Eisenhower libraries; the Library of Congress, the National Archives, Yale Library and Archives, the Israel State Archives, and various collections such as the Zionist Archives in New York and Jerusalem.

In addition to consulting the archives, interviews were conducted with various participants in the making of this history. Among those interviewed were Moshe Arens, Eytan Bentsur, Benjamin V. Cohen, Roger P. Davis, Simcha Dinitz, Eliahu Elath, Mordechai Gazit, Israel Goldstein, Mordechai Gur, Raymond A. Hare, W. Averell Harriman, Avraham Harman, Dr. Reuben Hecht, Samuel Katz, Dr. Emanuel Neumann, Richard H. Nolte, Benjamin Netanyahu, Yitzhak Rabin, Gerhard Riegner, Samuel I. Rosenman, Yitzhak Shamir, Ovadiah Soffer, Robert Szold, Harry S Truman, and Ezer Weizman.

Many thanks to the many people who helped me in this endeavor.

1

FDR, the Holocaust, and the Promised Land

As the Nazis took power in Germany, the future for the Jews looked dim. Observers like James G. McDonald, chairman of the Foreign Policy Association, 1933–1936, and League of Nations High Commissioner for Refugees, 1938–1945, were very pessimistic. In an address before a New York town hall meeting on May 4, 1933, he said: "I personally know nothing which the Jews can do *en masse* publicly as a group, which will help Jews in Germany and . . . I know nothing which the Jews in Germany can do to help themselves." As far as McDonald could see, there was no place for the Jews to go. "Where will they go? What would happen to their accumulation of their life-time . . . what would happen to the heritage they have built up . . . during the centuries?"[1] Bernard S. Deutsch, who aspired to be ambassador to Germany, expressed his concern in May 1933 that at any moment there would be "a general massacre in which many thousands of Jews would be slain." He did not anticipate that the American government would help the Jews since America was greatly interested in economic relations with Germany. But while he warned that there would be a coming slaughter, he did not speak one word "in condemnation of Germany or of hitlerism." Apparently, Deutsch had an interview with Adolf Hitler, and he wanted to be the American ambassador to Germany.[2]

There was one place that could have received the Jews. That place was the Land of Israel, or Palestine as the British and the Romans before them had called it. By May 1939, the British closed it to Jews. Only seventy-five thousand plus another twenty thousand Jews could enter between 1939 and 1945. The British closed the Land of Israel to the Jews, and Roosevelt's administration went along with that policy. The British violated the pledges they had made to the Jewish people since the time of

Lord Arthur Balfour's Jewish homeland declaration of November 1917, and President Roosevelt collaborated in that violation.

Americans and their government had displayed a traditional interest in the establishment of a Jewish homeland in the Land of Israel since the days of Presidents John Adams, Thomas Jefferson, and James Monroe. Every president from Woodrow Wilson's time declared his support for the establishment of such a state.

In November 1917, many had hoped that the Balfour Declaration, which was issued by the British government and confirmed by the Allies and which supported the establishment of a Jewish homeland on both sides of the Jordan River, might signal the end of the Diaspora. And it was this declaration that formed the basis for the League of Nations Mandate over the Palestine area. In his letter to Lord Walter Rothschild, the British foreign secretary Arthur Balfour declared:

> His Majesty's Government view with favor the establishment in Palestine of a national home for the Jewish people and will use their best endeavors to facilitate the achievement of this object, it being clearly understood that nothing shall be done which may prejudice the civil and religious rights of existing non-Jewish communities in Palestine, or the rights and political status enjoyed by Jews in any other country.[3]

That declaration might never have been issued had President Wilson not encouraged the British government to issue it.

Presidential support for a Jewish homeland continued even during the isolationist period of the 1920s and 1930s. In 1922, Henry Cabot Lodge, a leading isolationist senator, led the Senate in support of a joint congressional resolution favoring the establishment of a Jewish homeland, and President Warren G. Harding signed that resolution. On October 29, 1932, President Herbert Hoover praised the work of the Jewish community of Palestine: "I have watched with genuine admiration the steady and unmistakable progress made in the rehabilitation of Palestine which . . . is renewing its youth and vitality through the enthusiasm, hard work and self-sacrifice of the Jewish pioneers." But while American presidents and the Congress maintained a traditional sympathy for Zionism, State Department officials consistently opposed even mere expressions of sympathy for Zionism, presumably because they feared possible Arab disapproval.

Franklin D. Roosevelt's policy towards the question of a Jewish homeland or Jewish state in the Land of Israel was two-faced. To the Jews he would say that he supported the idea, and to the Arabs he would say that nothing would be done without their consultation; he thereby gave the Arab sheiks a veto over this matter. This was similar to his policy towards the rescue of European Jewry. Roosevelt would declare his sympathy for the plight of the Jews, but would not make a move to open the gates of the United States to those Jews who might escape the Nazi German murderers. In the spring of 1938, Roosevelt conferred with Rabbi Stephen S. Wise, Bernard M. Baruch, and Louis Kennedy and confided that he found Hitler "an undoubtedly great personality." Those present were astonished by what Roosevelt had said. Rabbi Wise was particularly "sorry to hear the President refer to the evil maniac in such terms."[4] It was then that Roosevelt said that "we will have to relax the regulations with regard to affidavits" and "if we really want to be of help, we will have to permit the incoming of refugees without affidavits."[5] But those were only words, and ideas. Roosevelt and his administration never even tried to ease the immigration restrictions. On the contrary, when it came to Jewish refugees he made it more difficult for them to enter the United States.

In the early 1930s President Roosevelt issued many statements and proclamations in support of Zionism. By promising to "watch with deep sympathy the progress of Palestine," he recalled how American presidents and the Congress had supported the idea of making Palestine into a Jewish homeland. He maintained that the Jews had the right to rebuild their land based upon the principle that all people had the inalienable right to life, liberty, and the pursuit of happiness. He found it "a source of renewed hope and courage" that, through international understanding, Jews could return to their promised land "to resettle the land where their faith was born and from which much of our modern civilization has emanated."[6]

Roosevelt's words were many and persuasive, but his deeds were few and empty.

President Roosevelt was unwilling to inhibit British ambitions in the Middle East, and he refused to upset the Arabs for fear of undermining Allied military efforts during World War II. He had a Balfour Declaration to uphold, a Balfour Declaration issued by Britain thanks to the support of President Wilson, and which was upheld by American presidents since 1917. While Roosevelt issued proclamations in support of a Jewish homeland and expressed the hope that the Jewish people could return to the Land of Israel, he, at the same time, reassured the Arabs that nothing would be done without their consent and he suggested to Zionist leaders that the Jews look elsewhere for a homeland.

When the Peel Report of 1936, followed by the White Paper of 1937, called for the partition of west Palestine and proved unacceptable to Arabs and to various Zionist groups, there were definite indications that the British planned to impose severe restrictions on Jewish immigration to Palestine. President Roosevelt revealed his usual favorable attitude towards the Jewish homeland idea by declaring that the Jewish people could make the Land of Israel into the "eastern Mediterranean." But when it came to implementing that idea into specific steps, all that Roosevelt did do was to advise the British that America wished to be informed of any changes in policy involving Palestine.[7]

By the fall of 1937, it was no secret that the British planned to limit Jewish immigration to Palestine to less than twelve thousand a year. When the British asked the State Department for information regarding Jewish attitudes towards Palestine, Wallace Murray, chief of the State Department's Near East Division, told them that the Jews were badly split. Rabbi Wise and his supporters wanted complete freedom of Jewish immigration to Palestine while non-Zionist Jews, such as Felix Warburg, were opposed to the establishment of a Jewish homeland in Palestine for fear that it might damage their position in the non-Jewish world and lead to widespread anti-Semitism. Still another faction accepted partition in the hope that more favorable terms might be achieved through further negotiations with the British.[8] Murray observed on September 17, 1937, that in

> view of this clear division of opinion among the representatives of American Jewry it seems to me that we are in a strong position to request that they come to some agreement among themselves before they approach us with a view to our taking any particular line of action. In other words we seem to be in a good position to ask Rabbi Wise to produce some proof that he speaks on behalf of all of American Jewry before we comply with any specific requests that he may make.[9]

That was an impossible demand.

American Jewry, and for that matter Jewry throughout the world, was divided on the future goals for Palestine. Some favored partition and the creation of an independent Jewish state, while others opposed partition because they wanted all of the Land of Israel, and yet still others were entirely opposed to a Jewish state. The Jews were as divided on the question of the future Jewish state as they were on the rescue of European Jewry, as they had been divided throughout history. This division enabled Roosevelt and certain State Department officials like Murray to find further excuses for not taking effective measures to fulfill American commitments. It was easy for Murray to say "first come to some agreement amongst yourselves and then come to us with your problems."

Throughout the war years, the anti-Zionist Jews presented their views to the Roosevelt administration. On September 25, 1943, Morris D. Waldman, executive vice president of the American Jewish Committee, wrote to Murray that

> the promise of a Jewish political nationhood flies in the face of 2,000 years of Jewish history; that it is a denial of the rights won by Jews since their emanci-

pation; that the theory and existence of a World Jewish Congress is a singular innovation in international affairs that threatens to work damaging effect upon the status of Jews in all countries; that it is especially obnoxious to American Jews because it is repugnant to the spirit of American democracy.[10]

Four days later Waldman pleaded his case personally to Murray. Waldman was convinced that it was time to organize and express the viewpoint of the great majority of American Jews who felt, "opposed and feared Jewish nationalism in any form because of the danger that the position of Jews in the United States was becoming seriously undermined."[11] Furthermore, "the American Jewish Committee would take a highly important decision to organize American Jews for the purpose of actively opposing all manifestations, whether on the part of Zionists, the American Committee for a Jewish Army, or others, which would tend to set off American Jews from other American Citizens."[12]

Waldman, in conversations with Murray and other State Department officials in January 1944, maintained that within a year or two the majority of Jewish opinion in America would be anti-Zionist. According to a Near East memo found in the Breckinridge Long papers, he planned to bring about this conversion through publicity in Jewish papers, and local representatives in Jewish communities. Waldman claimed that "the first generation eastern European Jews in the United States were now a dwindling minority and that their children were, in his opinion, good Americans who were not likely to be carried away by notions of extreme Jewish nationalism."[13] He believed that if the Zionist activities were permitted to continue, "a greatly increased anti-Semitic movement in the country would arise after the war, with far reaching and disastrous consequences."[14]

Waldman's views reflected the position on Palestine taken by the American Jewish Committee at that time. While it favored an end to the restrictions imposed by the White Paper policy of 1939, it was opposed to a Jewish state idea. Its leadership was afraid that a Jewish state might cause American Jews some embarrassment. They were afraid that the anti-Semites might have more fuel for their furnaces of hate. They were afraid of being asked: "Are you Americans or are you members of the Jewish State?" As the American Jewish Committee stipulated in its summary position on November 8, 1943: "There can be no political identification of Jews outside of Palestine with whatever government may be there established."[15] That position would change once Israel became a reality. To date, the American Jewish Committee supports Israel.

When Richard E. Gutstadt, director of the anti-Defamation League, wrote to Justice Louis D. Brandeis on August 16, 1940, of his fears concerning charges of divided loyalties as a result of Zionism,[16] Justice Brandeis had an answer for such fears:

> Let no American imagine that zionism is inconsistent with patriotism. Multiple loyalties are objectionable only if they are inconsistent. A man is a better citizen of the United States for being also a loyal citizen of his state, and of his city. . . . Every American Jew who aids in advancing the Jewish settlement in Palestine though he feels that neither he nor his descendants will ever live there, will likewise be a better man and a better American for doing so.[17]

The American Jewish community was badly divided on the questions of Palestine and rescue. American Jews were afraid to speak up lest they might be accused of warmongering and disloyalty, thereby making it much easier for Washington officials to disregard the plight of European Jewry and to go along with British colonial ambitions in the Middle East.

One of the most tragic aspects of this history was that American Jews like James Rosenberg, Lawrence Steinhardt, and Morris Waldman were leaders within the American Jewish community. Some of these individuals revealed the same kind of bias towards the persecuted Jews of Europe as did some Jews in Austria and Germany when Jews from Poland entered their countries after World War I. Those Austrian and German Jews of the 1920s exhibited nothing less than Jewish anti-Semitism and their anti-Semitism added to the anti-Semitism of such misfits as Eugen Duhring, Houston S. Chamberlain, Julius Streicher, Karl Lueger and Hitler. Individuals like Waldman seemed to have conveniently forgotten that they had been immigrants, the sons of immigrants, or at the very most the grandsons of immigrants. And their biased attitudes contributed to the abysmal failure that was the "diplomacy of rescue."

Perhaps Roosevelt did not want to upset the shaky British Empire and then have to bail it out; or perhaps it was because he did not think Palestine was suitable for mass Jewish immigration? Whatever his reasons may have been, Roosevelt suggested to Rabbi Wise that the Jews look elsewhere. He felt that if war could be postponed "for another two or three years at the most, we will have a world conference on the reallocation of territories. . . . and then we might find some large areas as a second choice for the Jews." Roosevelt did not seem to understand the importance of the Land of Israel to the Jewish people. The president realized that it was so small an area, a country so tough and difficult to cultivate, and that it was so sensitive politically. He thought that it would be much more sensible to locate in a land with fewer difficulties and greater potential. Rabbi Wise asked the president if he would care to swap the few hundred acres he had at Hyde Park for the one and a half million acres of the King Ranch in Texas. "No, I would not," said Roosevelt, but being a practical man he realized the need to have alternative plans. He was not suggesting that the Jews give up Palestine "but Palestine possibilities are going to be exhausted so you ought to have another card up your sleeve."[18]

According to a letter Brandeis sent to Robert Szold on November 16, 1938, the president posed a similar question to Brandeis: "You don't object to satellites?" "No," replied the justice, "but Palestine alone can provide the remedy." Brandeis advised Roosevelt that at one time he believed that the world's indignation at Hitler's atrocities would eventually compel Great Britain to permit Jews to enter Palestine, but he gave up on that idea and became convinced that only if the Jews were strong and well populated in Palestine would the British keep their promises with respect to Palestine. The world had to realize that the Land of Israel could absorb the Jewish refugees. If there were other countries that offered refuge, very well and good, but the Land of Israel was the foremost goal.[19]

In October 1938, Chaim Weizmann advised leading Americans to persuade the president to prevent the British from blocking Jewish immigration and establishing an Arab state in Palestine. "Do not submit to the fate of the Assyrians and give up Jewish Palestine," warned Weizmann.[20] As far as David Ben-Gurion was concerned the great menace to world Jewry came from Hitler and Benito Mussolini. Hitler was "not the only enemy and destroyer of Jewry the world over," but that Mussolini marched in "his footsteps." He considered both Hitler and Mussolini to be "our death enemies" and because of this it was of "seven-fold" importance to expand the immigration of Jews to the Land of Israel. But then the British were "definite" in their decision not to permit any further Jewish immigration to Palestine in the event of war. This was part of their appeasement policy towards the Arabs. He believed that the British would not pursue such a policy if the threat of war would vanish.[21]

In early March 1939, Weizmann appealed to Roosevelt directly and asked him to stop the British from breaking their solemn trust. Such a breach, warned Weizmann, was bound to produce a catastrophe in Palestine and would "completely undermine all confidence in international pledges given small nations." He believed that at this "zero hour" for the Jews, only the president's influence could stop British plans to establish a new state where Jews would remain a permanent minority and only the president of the United States could keep the doors of the Land of Israel opened.[22] About a month later, Weizmann cabled Brandeis to intervene with the president: "Induce President urge British government delay publication their proposals. . . . If new policy imposed Jews will conduct immigration disregard legal restrictions. Will settle land without permission even if exposed British bayonets. Please impress President . . . only extraordinary emphatic step can possibly produce effect."[23]

Brandeis, Wise, and others went to see the president in 1938 and again in 1939, but they were unable to change the thinking of Roosevelt's men and on May 15, 1939, the British issued their White Paper, which provided that after a five-year period, when seventy-five thousand Jews had entered Palestine, the Arabs would be consulted about future Jewish immigration. Acquisition of lands by Jews was to be severely restricted. The British had in this way officially declared their opposition to the creation of a "Jewish state against the will of the Arab population of the country." No restrictions were apparently imposed on the number of Arabs that could enter the Land of Israel. And many thousands of Arabs did immigrate to the Land of Israel at this time. The British went along with Arab terrorist leaders of the area like Haj Amin el-Husseini, whom they had appointed to be the Mufti of Jerusalem with a yearly salary. British officials used their diplomatic umbrella again, this time over the Land of Israel. By scrapping Lord Balfour's promise to the Jews, they closed the only place of refuge for millions of European Jews. Ultimately they did not even permit the seventy-five thousand Jews to enter the Land of Israel. International politicos and their diplomacy had condemned the Jews of Europe to the gas chambers of Nazi-occupied Europe.

U.S. ambassador to London, Joseph P. Kennedy, was instructed to inform the British that thousands of Americans had voiced their strong protests against the alleged plans to keep Jews from entering Palestine, but at the same time he was to say, almost apologetically, that America was not trying to run the British Empire. Soon after the British published their White Paper of 1939, President Roosevelt seemed unwilling to accept Britain's interpretation that the Palestine Mandate framers had not intended to make Palestine into a Jewish state, but he did not fight it. Said Roosevelt:

> Frankly, I do not believe that the British are wholly correct in saying that the framers of the Palestine Mandate could not have intended that Palestine should be converted into a Jewish state against the will of the Arab population of the country.
>
> Frankly, I do not see how the British government reads into the original Mandate or into the White Paper of 1922 any policy that would limit Jewish immigration.[24]

Roosevelt promised Wise that he would do all he could,[25] but when the rabbi asked Secretary of State Cordell Hull to convince the British to postpone implementation of the White Paper, Hull insisted that he had already done all he could. The United States had "gone beyond any boundaries in our effort to be of service in this matter." He even refused to issue a public statement of concern with British policy. He felt that such a declaration could be made only if America were willing to participate in a mandate over Palestine. Hull claimed that the U.S. Congress would throw him out of a window if he ever made such a proposal. Hull observed that there was "an awful state of nationalistic sentiment in this country since the League of Nations fight and we are surrounded by groups of isolationists." Hull advised Rabbi Wise that it had been one of his "deepest disappointments that after marshaling every influence we possessed the British government should have issued the White Paper."[26]

But Rabbi Wise reiterated the great disappointment Jewish people felt with British and American policies. "It was said years ago that it was a good thing that the Balfour Declaration had been written in English rather than in German; but the way the Chamberlain government was now acting the Balfour Declaration might well have been written in German rather than in English."[27] As Wise said to Hull, "moral right" had given way to "political expediency."[28] International politicians or diplomats had condemned the Jews to permanent exile, and the gas chambers. The German Nazis operated the murder camps, but it was Britain and its friends that had furnished the inmates by preventing them to escape to such places of refuge as the Land of Israel.

The Zionist answer to the British White Paper was illegal immigration or Aliyah Bet, and the formation of a Jewish army. Zionists like Ben-Gurion proposed that at least a million Jewish immigrants come to Israel and present the British with a *fait accompli* in the form of a strong and powerful Jewish army as a major factor in the Middle East. Writing to Justice Brandeis he said that we can "depend . . . only on ourselves."[29] When the war erupted in Europe, Ben-Gurion advised his fellow Zionists not to expect a reversal in British policy, but to concentrate on bringing young Jews to Palestine, acquire more land, and build a great united Jewish army as a new and major factor in the Middle East. He believed that if the Yishuv (the Jews of the Land of Israel) helped the British fight the Germans, the Jews could then gain self-respect and eventually establish their own independent state. Unless that help was given, it would not be possible to "absolve the Jewish people in the judgment of history from their failure to contribute to the destruction of the greatest enemy that ever arose against the very existence of the Jewish people."[30]

Once again American Jews were most apprehensive. They could not muster enough courage to help the Jews of the Land of Israel to form a strong Jewish army. When Zionist Revisionist leader Vladimir Jabotinsky came to New York in March 1940 to help promote the Jewish army, he found a timid and fearful group of Jewish leaders. He had "never seen American Jewry so scared of local anti-Semitism as they are now, that the danger seems really tangible and widespread."[31]

The Yishuv wanted to arm itself and fight. Rabbi Wise urged Roosevelt to help. But Roosevelt said that it was the business of the British. He advised Wise on June 9, 1941, that the "first lines of defense for Palestine are in the outlying areas, and it is my distinct impression that the British are using all their available arms and other equipment in the various active zones."[32] The president insisted that the British had to have the support of both the Arabs and the Jews.[33]

Some 125,000 Jews of the Land of Israel volunteered to serve in the British army. There was no such volunteering from amidst the Arabs. Haj Amin el-Husseini, the Iraqis, and the Syrians collaborated with the Germans as did many Egyptian nationalists like Anwar al-Sadat. Only after four years of pleading and insisting were the Jews of Israel able to achieve at least part of their goal—Jewish armed forces with Hebrew as the official language. By September 1944, the British finally announced the creation of a Jewish Brigade. Within one month, the Brigade fought in Italy against the German Nazis. Once the fighting stopped in Europe, the Jewish Brigade and various other Jews worked to liberate their fellow Jews from Europe and helped bring them to Palestine.

In June 1943, Weizmann spoke with Roosevelt and presented him with a plan of settlement as suggested by Harry St. John Bridger Philby, special advisor to Ibn Sa'ūd of Saudi Arabia, whereby Jews and Arabs would resolve their differences peacefully. Accordingly, a joint Anglo-American guarantee would ensure Jewish settlement in Palestine. Those Arabs who might be displaced would be resettled and the Jews would pay the Arabs some twenty million British Pounds Sterling, and all the Arab states would achieve independence.[34]

President Roosevelt seemed agreeable. He felt that perhaps a little "bakshish" might encourage a settlement with the Arabs, but before approaching King Sa'ūd he consulted with the British. The British approved, providing that no suggestions were made that might prejudice the interests of Arab states and that the conversations were purely exploratory.[35] Roosevelt sent the pro-Arab and pro-British Halford L. Hoskins on a mission to Saudi Arabia.

When Hoskins returned, he reported that King Sa'ūd warned that unless a federation were created that would include Lebanon, Syria, Transjordan, and a binational Palestinian state, there would be war between Arabs and Jews. Moreover, Hoskins claimed that Sa'ūd would not talk with Weizmann because he was insulted by the suggestion that he might take a bribe. He felt "impugned" by an attempt to bribe him with twenty million Pounds Sterling, guaranteed by President Roosevelt.[36]

But Roosevelt disclaimed any knowledge of such a suggestion.[37] In a memo written by David K. Niles to President Truman a number of years later, Niles recalled that Roosevelt had told him privately that "he could do anything that was needed to be done with Saud [sic] with a few million dollars." According to Weizmann, Philby had maintained that Sa'ūd would have accepted the proposal if Hoskins had not bungled it. Sa'ūd's angry outbursts against Weizmann were really directed against Hoskins's bungling.[38] The approach of the Roosevelt team and the British was entirely too pessimistic and could not have succeeded in reconciling differences between Arabs and Jews. Their interventionism only worked to prevent an understanding between Jews and Arabs.

The suggested approach to Sa'ūd had failed. According to Nahum Goldmann, of the World Jewish Congress, Winston Churchill had promised Weizmann that he would soon abandon the White Paper policy in favor of fulfilling the Balfour Declaration. After crushing Hitler "the Allies will have to establish the Jews in the position where they belong." Churchill recalled how much trouble the Arabs had caused the Allies during the war and he reassured Weizmann that the Jews would get his support, and that he "would bite deep into the problem, that it is going to be the biggest plum of the war."[39] By January–February 1944, Zionists had British reassurances of support.[40] In February that same British government helped persuade Roosevelt to kill a congressional resolution that favored the establishment of a Jewish commonwealth in Palestine.[41]

By December 1940, Ben-Gurion and Weizmann called for an end to using delicate diplomacy with British and American officials. In a meeting with American Zionist leaders in December 1940, Ben-Gurion called for the creation of a united Zionist policy. "We cannot live from hand to mouth." We must have "clear objectives in the immediate future, during the war and at the end of the war."[42] On July 17, 1941, Weizmann insisted that the Zionist movement openly declare its goals, "whatever the Arabs will have will be due to the efforts of England and America." We must make it "clear to England and America what they have to do in order to bring about what I call a decent solution to the Jewish problem." The Land of Israel should absorb "within 20 years about three million Jews, particularly the younger generation."[43] Weizmann proposed a confederation with the Arabs and he called for an open declaration of Zionist goals. Goldmann joined those who opposed Weizmann's proposition.

Goldmann argued that Weizmann's suggestions would give the Arabs much more of a "nuisance value than they have had."[44] He suggested that they wait until after an Allied victory would be at hand. But Weizmann found Goldmann merely echoing the British line of thought and that thanks to people like him "the British have got us where they want us." According to the British view of things, nothing could be done to embarrass them since they were at war: "You Jews are interested that we should win the war and therefore sit tight." By July 1941 Weizmann was no longer willing to sit tight. Nor was he willing to accept the argument that only the Arabs had a nuisance value. Weizmann wanted to create a "Jewish nuisance value." It was about time that the British stopped playing with the White Paper and the Arab question. "For two years we sat tight and swallowed every possible ignominy. We did not want to embarrass them. But we believe that we have a contribution to make toward victory and this contribution is that they should know the truth and that they should know what we want to do for the Jews in Palestine."[45]

By 1942 a conference was held. It was at the Hotel Biltmore in New York City and it was called the Biltmore Conference. There the Zionist goal of reestablishing the Jewish homeland was openly declared for all to know. But the Roosevelt administration—supporting the British position in the Middle East—fought against even having a congressional resolution in support of a Jewish homeland in the Land of Israel.

Secretary of War Henry L. Stimson advised Congress that a congressional resolution might prejudice the American war effort. Army Chief of Staff George C. Marshall refused to be responsible for the military complications in the Moslem world if the pro-Zionist resolutions were passed by Congress. Secretary of State Hull warned that the resolutions would inhibit negotiations with King Sa'ūd.[46] Congress yielded.

Members of Congress accepted the view that congressional resolutions in favor of a Jewish state might be used as propaganda by the Nazis to injure the Allied military position, and that the United Nations would have to devote its energies at keeping Arabs and Jews from killing one another. Breckinridge Long had persuaded members of Congress that while Roosevelt was trying to convince the British to change their White Paper policy, the president hoped that discussion could be postponed until after the war so that the United Nations could deal with the problem, and the United States would not have to shoulder the responsibility alone. Or as John J. McCloy, assistant secretary of defense, the same individual who had opposed the bombing of the death camps, would say, "from a military point of view, we would much prefer to let such sleeping dogs lie."[47]

Roosevelt's official policy was not at all satisfactory to the Jewish community, a community that was bordering on hysteria because of the murder of millions of their brethren in Europe. Roosevelt's expressions of good will would no longer suffice. The leadership provided by such individuals as Rabbi Abba Hillel Silver challenged Rabbi Wise and his group. In conversations with State Department officials, Rabbi Silver wanted to know what he should tell his people. How much longer must the Jews defer? Silver proposed that Roosevelt, at least, issue a statement saying that the cause was just.[48] State Department officials rejected Silver's suggestion. But on March 2, 1944, Roosevelt congratulated Henrietta Szold for her work with Youth Aliyah (Young People's Immigration to Palestine).[49]

On March 9, 1944, Rabbis Silver and Wise met with Roosevelt. The president "was most pleasant." At no time did the president indicate that he disapproved of the resolution before Congress.[50] He told the rabbis about a rumor that had come to his attention that Silver had blamed him for the War Department intervention. Roosevelt said that it was not he, but the State Department that was responsible. Silver noted that the resolution had been shown to the secretary of state and other government leaders and "then out of a clear sky came the War Department intervention and we were bewildered." It left the "Jews of Palestine very much disturbed and the Arabs jubilant and triumphant." They asked the president to issue a statement in support of the Jewish National Homeland. The president reviewed their statement and then said: "The first thing I would like to say is that the American people seem to forget that the American government approved the Balfour Declaration and the Mandate." Then he added that "something should be said to the effect that we are interested in the plight of all refugees." But he said that he would have to check that out with Prime Minister Churchill. At the conclusion of this meeting Roosevelt said that whenever the Near East was discussed he heard that there would be bloodshed there, but he concluded that with the help of his friends the Shah of Persia and Ibn Sa'ūd of Saudia Arabia he would be able to work out a solution.[51]

Despite strong State Department objections, the president complied with Rabbi Silver's request for a statement of support. Roosevelt authorized Wise and Silver, on March 16, 1944, to issue the following declaration on his behalf:

> The President has authorized us to say that the American government has never given its approval to the White Paper of 1939. The President expressed his conviction that when future decisions are reached, full justice will be done to those who seek a Jewish National Home, for which our government and the American people have always had the deepest sympathy, today more than ever in view of the tragic plight of hundreds of thousands of homeless Jewish refugees.[52]

Shortly thereafter, the Roosevelt administration would reassure the Arabs that no decision would be made without full consultation with Arabs and Jews.

Rabbi Silver would observe during the Zionist Executive Committee meeting of March 9, 1944, that "one of the main weaknesses of our Zionist work in this country was that the Administration was led to believe that it had the Zionist movement in its vest pocket." Especially during the last months it was "made clear that there was a growing resentment against the administration not doing anything."[53] Yes, observed Emanuel Neumann, "irrespective of Mr. Roosevelt's statements" his administration, insofar as it operated as a political machine, "worked against us for the past three years. We have a right to fight anti-Zionist policies."

The Zionist community was split. Goldmann advised the American Zionist Emergency Council on December 11, 1944, to be most cautious. He said that he agreed with Rabbi Silver "that we have to go on fighting because the President and the State Department will not do anything unless they are pressed." But the question remained as to "how far you can go." The "President and not the Senate will be the negotiator." Goldmann was afraid to "antagonize the President" because he would negotiate with Churchill and Joseph Stalin and might be "so resentful against us that we have much less chance that he will press on Churchill."[54]

ROOSEVELT'S LAST DAYS

Roosevelt confided to Rabbi Wise in January–March 16, 1945, that he had given too much consideration to King Ibn Sa'ūd's power and to the poor advice from the State Department and the British Colonial Office. He said that he wanted to see a Jewish state created in Palestine. "If necessary, we will build a fence around Palestine to keep the Arabs out and to keep the Jews in."[55]

During his January 23, 1945, conversation with the president, Rabbi Wise proposed that the "immediate need of the hour was large immigration, and ships, goods, medicine. . . . What was needed was mass transportation of Jews to Palestine." The president responded by saying that the Arabs were "afraid of the Jews" and he spoke of the Jews as infiltrating into Transjordan. Wise tried to reassure him that the Jews were not interested in Jordan and concluded: "We stand behind you, Mr. President. We expect you to support us. You have expressed your sympathy with us and we believe you mean it. All Zionists are with you." Roosevelt puffed on his cigarette and asked smilingly: "Did you say all? Would you be willing to put a fence around Palestine?"

"Yes," answered Rabbi Wise. "You keep the Arabs out and we will keep the Jews in."[56]

That was the way it was on January 23, 1945. Wise and Roosevelt met again on March 16, 1945, at which time the president would again reassure him of his good will.

But on February 14, 1945, Roosevelt met with King Ibn Sa'ūd, and he asked him for advice regarding the Jews. Sa'ūd said that the Jews should be granted "living space" in the Axis countries that had oppressed them. Roosevelt concurred, "The Germans appear to have killed three million Polish Jews, by which count there should be space in Poland for the resettlement of many homeless Jews."[57]

Roosevelt reassured the Arabian king that "he would do nothing to assist the Jews against the Arabs and would make no move hostile to the Arab people." When Sa'ūd proposed sending an Arab mission to America in order to present the case of the Arabs and Palestine, Roosevelt concurred that it would be "a very good idea because he thought many people in America and England are misinformed."[58]

In early March, Colonel Hoskins met with Roosevelt and the First Lady. Among other matters discussed were the Land of Israel and the

Jews. According to Hoskins's notes of the meeting, Roosevelt was very pessimistic about Jewish chances in Palestine, but Mrs. Roosevelt was pro-Zionist. She spoke of the "wonderful work that had been done by the Zionists in certain parts of Palestine." The president noted that on his flight over Palestine he found the area to be "extremely rocky and barren" except along the coastal plain. When Mrs. Roosevelt noted that the Zionists now felt much stronger and were ready to risk a fight for their homeland, the president reminded her that there were some twenty million Arabs in and around Palestine and he thought that "in the long run these numbers would win out."[59]

But on March 16, during his conversations with Wise, the president once again said that he favored unrestricted Jewish immigration and a Jewish state in Palestine. Wise reported that the "most important thing of all" was that Roosevelt was "resolved to help us." While Roosevelt was aware of Sa'ūd's limitations, "somebody in the State Department or in London" had given him the impression that Sa'ūd was an "important figure" and he had "overestimated" him. "I'm sorry to say I utterly failed with regard to Ibn Sa'ūd," said Roosevelt. Wise believed that Roosevelt was "absolutely resolved to appeal from an Ibn Sa'ūd drunk to a greater Ibn Sa'ūd sober—to some court of high appeal, to bring our care there."[60]

At conversation's end, Rabbi Wise asked the president if he would sign a statement on Palestine. "Certainly I will sign it," said Roosevelt.[61] Thus the March 16 statement pointing to the president's support was made public. That statement was to assuage Zionist apprehension concerning Roosevelt's intentions, but it almost brought the State Department house down. Murray warned that the president's statement would have "serious repercussions in the Near East" and "a most far-reaching effect upon American interests throughout the area."[62]

On April 5, President Roosevelt reassured Ibn Sa'ūd that "no decision would be taken without full consultation with both Arabs and Jews." Roosevelt promised once again that he "would take no action, in my capacity as Chief of the Executive Branch of this Government, which prove hostile to the Arab people."[63]

Thus was the diplomacy of Roosevelt towards the Jews, the Arabs, and the issue of the Jewish homeland in the Land of Israel. It was part of the game of international politics that the leaders of the world played, with little, if any, regard for the people involved. Roosevelt and the British acted in such a manner so as to prevent the rescue of European Jewry. Their policies enabled the Germans and their European collaborators to slaughter six million Jewish men, women, and children.

NOTES

1. James MacDonald Speech, May 4, 1933, Town Hall, Judge Julian Mack Papers, Box 14/File 84, Zionist Archives, New York. When I researched the Zi-

onist Archives, they were at the Jewish Agency Building, 515 Park Avenue, New York. They were later sent to the Zionist Central Archives in Jerusalem.

2. Memo of conversation between Stephen S. Wise and Bernard S. Deutsch, May 4, 1933, Julian W. Mack Papers, Box 14/File 84, Zionist Archives, New York.

3. Chaim Weizmann, *Trial and Error* (New York, 1949), p. 208.

4. Memo of conference with President Roosevelt and State Department, April 13, 1938, Robert Szold Papers, Box 25/File 16, Zionist Archives, New York.

5. Ibid.

6. Ibid.

7. Memo of telephone conversation between David Ben-Gurion and Rabbi Stephen S. Wise, May 12, 1937, Stephen S. Wise Papers, Brandeis University Archives; U.S. Department of State, *Foreign Relations of the United States, 1937*, Volume II (Washington, D.C., 1954), July 7, 1937, pp. 889–890.

8. *Foreign Relations, 1937*, Volume II, November 10, December 2, 1937, pp. 921–922.

9. Ibid., September 17, 1937, pp. 909–922.

10. Morris D. Waldman to Wallace Murray, Letter dated September 25, 1943, State Department File No. 867N.01/1993, National Archives, Washington, D.C. In his autobiography entitled *Nor by Power* (New York, 1953), Waldman made no mention of his anti-Zionist intervention with Murray.

11. Memo from Division of Near Eastern Affairs on conversation between Wallace Murray and Morris D. Waldman, September 29, 1943, State Department File No. 967N.01/19991/2, National Archives, Washington, D.C.

12. Ibid.

13. Near East Division Memo, January 10, 1944, Breckinridge Long Papers, Library of Congress, Washington, D.C.

14. Ibid.

15. Summary of the American Jewish Committee Position of Palestine, November 8, 1943, Palestine Files, American Jewish Committee Archives, New York.

16. Richard E. Gutstadt to Justice Louis D. Brandeis, August 16, 1940, Robert Szold Papers, Zionist Archives, New York.

17. Louis D. Brandeis, *The Jewish Problem and How to Solve It* (New York, 1915), p. 12.

18. Stephen S. Wise Memo on conversations with FDR, January 22, 1938, Stephen S. Wise Papers, Brandeis University Archives, Waltham, Massachusetts.

19. Justice Louis D. Brandeis to Stephen S. Wise, November 16, 1938; Stephen S. Wise to Robert Szold, December 27, 1938, Robert Szold Papers, Zionist Archives, New York.

20. Chaim Weizmann to Nahum Goldmann, Louis Lipsky, Stephen S. Wise, October 6, 1938; Franklin D. Roosevelt to William Green, May 3, 1939, Robert Szold Papers, Zionist Archives, New York. While he may not have been a Zionist, Bernard Baruch supported the proposition that the Jews should be given the opportunity to settle in Palestine and he presented Roosevelt with a water irrigation plan according to which a series of wells would be dug above the Jordan and the water would be used to irrigate the surrounding area for the settlement of some 120,000 Jews. Apparently the Arabs of the area concerned had approved the project for which Baruch could raise some $150,000. Nothing came of the

proposition. See memo signed by Aranow, November 1, 1938, Robert Szold Papers, Zionist Archives, New York.

21. David Ben-Gurion to Members of the Jewish Agency, Jerusalem, October 20, 1938, Zionist Organization Papers, Box 1940, Zionist Archives, New York.

22. U.S. Department of State, *Foreign Relations of the United States, 1939*, Volume IV (Washington, D.C., 1955), March 10, 1939, p. 731.

23. Chaim Weizmann to Justice Louis D. Brandeis, April 19, 1939, Robert Szold Papers, Zionist Archives, New York.

24. *Foreign Relations, 1939*, Volume IV, May 17, 1939.

25. Stephen S. Wise Memorandum of meeting with Cordell Hull, dated May 22, 1939, Robert Szold Papers, RG 1 x/22a, Zionist Archives, New York.

26. Ibid.

27. Ibid.

28. U.S. Department of State, *Foreign Relations of the United States, 1939*, Volume II (Washington, D.C., 1956), July 21, 1939, pp. 791–793.

29. David Ben-Gurion to Justice Louis D. Brandeis, June 6, 1939, Robert Szold Papers, Zionist Archives, New York.

30. David Ben-Gurion Memo, November 14, 1940, Robert Szold Papers, Zionist Archives, New York.

31. American Emergency Committee for Zionist Affairs, Manual for their Organization and Function (New York, 1943), pp. 7–8, Zionist Archives, New York.

32. Franklin D. Roosevelt to Stephen S. Wise, June 9, 1941, Robert Szold Papers, Zionist Archives, New York.

33. Ibid.

34. U.S. Department of State, *Foreign Relations of the United States, 1943*, Volume IV (Washington, D.C., 1964), June 12, 1943, p. 795.

35. Ibid.

36. Ibid., August 31, 1943, pp. 807–810.

37. Ibid., September 27, 1943, pp. 811–814.

38. Weizmann, *Trial and Error*, pp. 427–433.

39. Nahum Goldmann to Stephen S. Wise, January 17, 1944, Robert Szold Papers, Zionist Archives, New York.

40. U.S. Department of State, *Foreign Relations of the United States, 1944*, Volume V (Washington, D.C., 1965), February 3, 1944, pp. 562–563.

41. Ibid.

42. David Ben-Gurion meeting with U.S. Zionist leaders Louis Lipsky, Robert Szold, Nahum Goldmann, and Stephen S. Wise, December 5, 1940, Individuals Files, Zionist Archives, New York.

43. Minutes of meeting with Chaim Weizmann, July 17, 1941, Benjamin Akzin Folders of the American Zionist Emergency Council Papers, Zionist Archives, New York.

44. Ibid.

45. Ibid.

46. *Foreign Relations, 1944*, Volume V, February 3, 1944, pp. 562–563.

47. Ibid., February 22, 1944, pp. 574–576.

48. Breckinridge Long Memo, February 24, 1944, Breckinridge Long Papers, Library of Congress, Washington, D.C.

49. Individuals Files, Robert Szold Papers, Zionist Archives, New York.

50. Executive Committee Minutes of the American Zionist Emergency Council, March 13, 1944, Zionist Archives, New York.

51. Ibid.

52. *New York Times*, March 17, 1944.

53. Executive Committee Minutes of the American Zionist Emergency Council, March 13, 1944, Zionist Archives, New York.

54. Ibid., December 11, 1944, Zionist Archives, New York.

55. Stephen S. Wise to Felix Frankfurter, January 28, 1945, Stephen S. Wise Papers, Brandeis University Archives, Waltham, Massachusetts.

56. Stephen S. Wise conference with Franklin D. Roosevelt, January 23, 1945, President's File, 1943–1945, American Zionist Emergency Council Papers, Zionist Archives, New York.

57. U.S. Department of State, *Foreign Relations of the United States, 1945*, Volume VIII (Washington, D.C., 1969), February 14, 1945, pp. 1–2; William Eddy, *F.D.R. Meets Ibn Saud* (New York, 1954), pp. 311–316.

58. Halford Hoskins to Alling, *Foreign Relations, 1945*, Volume VIII, March 5, 1945, pp. 690–691.

59. Ibid.

60. Stephen S. Wise Memo on conference held with FDR, March 16, 1945, President's Files, 1943–1945, American Zionist Emergency Committee Papers, Zionist Archives, New York.

61. Ibid.

62. U.S. Department of State, *Foreign Relations of the United States, 1945*, Volume V (Washington, D.C., 1967), March 20, 1945, p. 698.

63. Franklin D. Roosevelt to King of Saudi Arabia, *Foreign Relations, 1945*, Volume V, April 5, 1945, p. 698.

2

The 1936–1937 Partition Plan

In 1917, American Zionists succeeded in winning President Woodrow Wilson's support for the Balfour Declaration. As Wilson backed the idea, Lord Arthur Balfour overcame his reservations about sending his historic letter to Lord Walter Rothschild. European and American Zionists cooperated in this endeavor and it was a great victory for the Jewish people. For American Zionists it was their first victory. But this was to be just the start of their long and difficult journey in search of support.

The 1920s and the 1930s were an especially combative and combustible time in the struggle for the Jewish homeland in the Land of Israel. Because Zionists were unable to come to terms on goals, ideology, and leadership, they failed to pick up on British proposals for the partition of Palestine in 1936–1937. Recent studies of Zionism such as those by Martin Gilbert,[1] Melvin Urofsky,[2] and Howard Sachar[3] did not consider the implications of the 1936 Peel report and the consequent struggle between American and European Zionists on this matter. The dispute on the partition within Zionist circles represents one of the most important crossroads in the history of Zionism. American Zionists wanted a greater Israel and they refused to accept a truncated Israel. European and Palestinian Zionists were prepared to accept a limited Israel so as to provide refuge for the Jews of Europe. This chapter is an account of that 1936–1937 history.

By 1936, it had become evident that Great Britain had failed to make good its Balfour Declaration and the Mandate commitments to establish a Jewish National Homeland in the Land of Israel. At every opportunity Britain sought to appease the Arabs, and the Arabs learned that the more trouble they would cause the more concessions they would get from the British rulers. In 1920–1923, Britain had severed the Transjordanian region from the Palestine Mandate, and in the late 1930s, because of

Fascist-Nazi-inspired Arab terrorist activities, they abandoned the idea of a Jewish National Homeland. And by May 1939, they closed the Land of Israel almost entirely to future Jewish immigration.

The reaction of the Zionist community to these betrayals was indecisive and divided. Available documentation indicates that while Britain may not have intended to carry out partition and the creation of a Jewish state in 1936–1937, the divisiveness among Zionist leaders contributed to its readiness to abandon partition and the idea of a Jewish National Homeland in the Land of Israel.

When the Arabs rioted in such cities as Jerusalem, Jaffa, Haifa, and Nablus in October 1933, Sir Arthur Wauchope, the British high commissioner, proposed the establishment of local self-governing councils. A Municipal Corporations Ordinance was enacted in January 1934, which provided for councils of Jews and Arabs, and in December 1935, the British went a step further by calling for the establishment of a legislative council of twenty-eight members, for the entire country. There would be eleven Moslems, three Christians, seven Jews, five government officials, and two representatives of foreign commercial interests. The three Christians were also to be Arabs, and the high commissioner would maintain a veto power over the legislative council as well as control over immigration.

The Zionists rejected the council idea during their September 1935 Congress, which was held in Lucerne, Switzerland, because they felt that such a council would transform the Yishuv into a permanent minority, and the Jewish National Homeland would be endangered while the Arabs would obtain constitutional and permanent platforms for agitation against the Jews and the Mandate. The British Parliament likewise rejected the council idea as it observed that such an arrangement would only increase tensions. The Arabs called for an end to Jewish immigration and the establishment of a representative government.

In a meeting with the high commissioner, the colonial secretary and the undersecretary of state on October 15, 1935, Chaim Weizmann and David Ben-Gurion stated their opposition to the legislative council idea, and they likewise called for large-scale Jewish immigration to the Land of Israel as well as extensive economic development of that land. Weizmann insisted that the time had come for greater Jewish control there. It was not enough to have a Jewish Agency. The Yishuv was tired of being considered as an unwanted stepchild of the British authorities. Writing to Stephen S. Wise in February 1936, Weizmann insisted that it was "time to reopen the whole of our problem with much more force, because of our achievements in Palestine and because of the critical situation of our people, than we did in 1916." Weizmann observed that the League of Nations had "solved the Greek and Turkish problem . . . through an exchange of populations" and a similar solution had to be found for the Land of Israel. He observed that it was essential to open up Transjordan to Jewish settlement and to establish "some sort of organization which may be less than a state, but certainly more than what the Jewish Agency is now." "The time for action is now."[4]

Morris Margulies, secretary of the Zionist Organization of America, advised Leo Herman of the United Jewish Appeal that some nineteen thousand dunams of land were available for purchase in Transjordan. It was some twenty minutes from Amman and he wanted to know if the American Zionist community was prepared to purchase it. Herman thought that they were interested, but that the attitude of the Transjordan government was such that he did not believe that a deal could be arranged.[5]

Fascist and Nazi regimes gave aid and comfort to Arab extremists in the Land of Israel as they did to Francisco Franco in Spain. But France, Britain, and the United States pursued a policy of appeasement throughout the world in the hope that they would not have to fight another war. Appeasement did no one any good whatsoever. When Britain and France gave Italy the green light to invade Ethiopia in 1935, their own position and influence in Africa and the Middle East declined. The Ethiopian conflict inspired Arab leaders to use whatever influence and pressure they could muster in order to achieve their own ends. In the Land of Israel, Arab extremists led by the Mufti rioted in order to intimidate the British and to destroy the Jewish homeland. One such eruption occurred on April 19, 1936. Arab mobs attacked Jews in Jaffa and the trouble spread throughout the Land of Israel. Arab murder gangs, armed with guns and assisted by neighboring Arab states as well as Nazi agents, sought to destroy Jewish life and property. When they saw that the British were either unwilling or unable to quell the rioting, the Arabs declared a general strike. They demanded that all stores and transportation shut down until their demands for an elected government would be established and that Jewish immigration as well as the sale of land to the Jewish people of the Land of Israel be stopped. If those Arab demands had been granted then the country would have been transformed into just one more Arab state.

From the start of the Arab riots the Jewish Agency worked twenty-four hours a day to keep the Yishuv alive. Ben-Gurion reported that there was telephone communication with all the urban and rural Jewish settlements to help secure their safety.

As he saw it, the Arab leaders had been "awakened" by the Italo-Ethiopian conflict with "the hope that the event of a world war would give them the opportunity of achieving fundamental changes in the political status of Arab countries, particularly Syria, Egypt and Palestine." The Italo-Ethiopian War had "conjured up grave political complications" for the British in the Middle East. Treaties of peace and friendship were concluded between Britain and Yemen, and Saudia Arabia and Iraq; and Egyptian independence had been set in motion so as to "secure a Pax Britannica" in the Arab world. Ben-Gurion foresaw the next step as a British effort to further appease and conciliate the Arabs.[6]

Ben-Gurion was not so much concerned with the troubles caused by the riots and strikes as he was with the ensuing political struggles with Britain that might result in Britain's closing the doors of Palestine to the Jewish people. This, above all times, required that Palestine would be a place of refuge for the Jewish people. The horrid conditions for the Jews of Europe made it essential to keep Palestine open, and "the most rapid solution to our political difficulties within Palestine lies in increased immigration and accelerated upbuilding of the National Home." He advised Justice Louis D. Brandeis that only when the Jews of the Yishuv would become "a great force . . . utterly impossible to repress, will the Arab leaders understand that they must make their peace with the presence of the Jewish people in the country."[7]

Since the Arab strike closed the port of Jaffa, the Jewish Agency demanded that the high commissioner open up that port and permit the Yishuv to open port facilities in Tel Aviv.

The British continued their appeasement policies. In August 1936 they encouraged outside Arab intervention by inviting the foreign minister of Iraq to negotiate with the Arab Higher Committee. Britain thereby gave official recognition to those who employed Fawzi Kawakji, a friend of the Mufti, the terrorist who had moved into the Land of Israel, to organize Arab bandits. As Weizmann observed, this was "all in the true spirit of appeasement."[8]

The abortive Arab attempts to destroy the Yishuv only served to bolster Jewish self-defense forces. Several thousand Jews were admitted to police service; the Haganah, a Jewish self-defense force, had some twenty-five thousand members who served to protect the Yishuv and its communities. While the policy pursued by the Haganah was one of *Havlagah* (self-restraint), they developed skills in night as well as day combat. Trained by Yitzhak Sadeh and by the British "friend" Captain Orde Wingate, they learned how to search for the enemy in the hill country as well as in the other regions. He taught them how to ambush, to carry out raids, to outflank the enemy, and to disengage whenever necessary for either military or political reasons.[9]

Some were not satisfied with *Havlagah* policies and they joined such underground units as Etzel (the Irgun) and Lehi (the Stern gang).

British reaction to the Arab riots and terrorism was, at times, supportive of the terrorists. Only when the British were hit directly by the Arab terrorists did they undertake countermeasures, as in September 1937, when the British district commissioner for the Galilee and his police escort were assassinated. The British then rounded up some of the Arab leaders and deported them. They also made an effort to drive Arab gangs from the hill country. But the Mufti fled to Lebanon from where he directed his murder gangs while Kaukji led them.

THE PEEL COMMISSION

On May 18, 1936, the British government announced that it would appoint a Royal Commission to "investigate the cause of unrest and alleged grievances of Arabs and Jews." This was to be the Peel Commission named after William R. Wellesley, the first Earl Peel, who was chairman of that investigatory group. Among those in the commission were a former administrator of an Indian province; a professor of colonial history at Oxford; a former British ambassador; a judge of the High Court; and a prominent British lawyer. The commission arrived in Palestine and investigated until November 1936. Weizmann believed that it might bring "a new and possibly decisive phase in our movement."[10]

Back in July 1936, an agreement was reached between King Emir Abdullah and representatives of the Zionist executive "for Jewish colonization of Trans-Jordan." According to Pincus Rutenberg, this agreement was reached while the Arab riots of 1936 were in full swing. Rutenberg felt that "Jews can reach an agreement with the Arabs."[11]

In his testimony before the Peel Commission on November 25, 1936, Weizmann spoke of the "permanent principles of the Zionist movement and the immediate urgency of the Jewish problem." During his testimony he spoke of six million Jews "pent up in places where they are not wanted, and for whom the world is divided into places where they cannot live and places which they may not enter." He informed the commissioners of how Jews had successfully developed the Land of Israel and he advised them that Jewry needed that land desperately.[12]

Restrictions had been placed on Jewish immigration, but none were imposed on the Arabs. As Eliahu Epstein (Elath) and Moshe Shertok (Sharett),[13] both of the Jewish Agency, had testified, "Arab immigration from neighboring countries to Palestine was neither temporary nor modest." The Arab immigrants came to the Land of Israel mainly from Syria and Transjordan. Those from southern Syria did "not apply to the British authorities for permission to enter." They crossed the frontier "with ease, especially when the Jordan and the Yarmuk rivers were at low ebb." Thousands of Arabs were involved and they were employed by the British authorities "with the knowledge of their illegal entry." According to Epstein, many of those that came from Syria "played prominent parts in the riots of 1933, especially in Haifa, and the same thing happened to a larger degree" during the riots of April 1936.[14]

But Arab immigration from the Transjordan was even "more complicated," according to Shertok, since the inhabitants of Transjordan did not need permits to cross the Jordan River. Shertok urged that Transjordanians be required to have special permits that would specify that they could not accept any work without additional special permission.[15]

Shertok found that the lack of supervision of the borders of the Land of Israel presented an "intolerable" situation for it not only involved Arabs seeking work, but also "many undesirable elements"[16]—such as people and military arms—that were smuggled into the country.

Lord Peel then asked Shertok, "You spoke of illegal immigration and I was given to understand that you did not hold the same objections against legal immigration. Let us for arguments sake put the country's absorptive capacity at 30,000 immigrants. . . ."[17]

Shertok asked, "Laborers?"

Peel replied, "Yes, we are discussing labor immigration. You would not raise any objection . . . if the government allowed a definite percentage of Arab immigrants? Would you say: We Jews demand the complete 30,000?"[18]

Shertok answered, "Certainly we insist that the Jews demand the complete 30,000 except in special cases. We have no objection to admitting a non-Jew who is a specialist in his field and is needed in Eretz Israel." But it was not part of Britain's obligation to "facilitate the immigration of other nations to the Land of Israel."[19]

After months of testimony the Peel Commission recommended in July 1937, that Palestine should be partitioned into separate Jewish and Arab states. Weizmann recalled that when he first received indication of the commission's recommendation on January 8, 1937, he felt that the idea had "great possibilities" but that he would have to consult with his "colleagues" before making any firm commitments. The idea of a "Jewish State" was something special and it could not be treated lightly. He told his colleagues that "our business as poor humans, who live in a different age, is to save as much as we can of the remnants of Israel." If the partition idea would be adopted he predicted we could "save more of them than by continuing the Mandatory policy."[20]

The Peel Commission report and the subsequent White Paper of 1937 was filled with contradictions. On the one hand the British observed that the Arabs had benefited from Jewish enterprise and that there had been no valid grounds for complaint. The report also contended that the primary purpose of the Mandate had been to establish a Jewish National Homeland and the commission "deprecated" the way "the policy of conciliation" had been pursued by the British government. The commission recognized that in due time a Jewish state would come into being and it quoted Wilson's statement of March 3, 1919, "that the allies, in complete agreement with our government and people, have decided on the establishment of a Jewish Commonwealth in Palestine." But at the same time it recommended a severe curtailment of Jewish immigration and declared that Jewish immigration was to be based on "political and psychological factors." The Peel Commission disregarded the original Mandate stipulations that Jews were in Palestine "as of right," and that Jewish immigration was to be based on the absorptive capacity of the country.

The commission concluded that since the Mandate had been "unworkable" and Arab-Jewish interests were "irreconcilable," the area should be divided into three parts. One-tenth, including Jerusalem, was to be under a British Mandate; two-tenths was to be Jewish and was to include much of the Galilee and the maritime plains. The rest of western Palestine, including most of the mountainous regime, was to constitute an Arab state joined with Transjordan. Britain's part was to be connected to the Mediterranean by a "corridor" ending in Jaffa, thereby dividing the proposed Jewish state in two. Haifa, Tiberias, Safad, and Acre were to be administered by the British and they would be the collectors of customs duties. The revenues collected would be divided proportionately.

Population-wise, the Jewish state was to include some 650,000 people of whom 300,000 were Arabs. While the area that encompassed the Arab state was to have some 550,000 people of whom 5,000 were Jewish. The British mandated area was to have some 180,000 people of whom 75,000 were Jews and 85,000 were Arabs.

The British government accepted the Peel report as being "the best and most hopeful solution" and it announced new measures curtailing Jewish immigration and land purchases in the areas allocated to the future Arab entity. Both houses of Parliament criticized the report for not providing more territory to the Jews and for failing to include the Negev and Jerusalem in the future Jewish state.

THE ZIONIST REACTION

The American Zionist reaction was reflected in Justice Brandeis's instantaneous response: "I am against."[21] Ben-Gurion and Weizmann favored the Peel recommendations, but as Emanuel Newmann recalled, he and many within the Zionist community were against. Among those against were Berl Katznelson, editor-in-chief of the newspaper *Davar*, Rabbi Wise, and Robert Szold. They were against it because it did not offer enough territory or sovereignty to the Jewish people.[22]

Brandeis and many other American Zionists opposed the Peel plan. By February 1937, they were fully aware of British intentions to restrict Jewish immigration. The high commissioner had advised Shertok of the Jewish Agency that he "would prefer a reduction for ten years." The quota of Jewish immigration was to be no more than thirty-five thousand to forty thousand per year, which would keep the Jewish population of the Palestine area between 31 and 35 percent of the total population. They were also aware of British plans to make Haifa and Jerusalem into international cities and to divide the country as France had separated Lebanon from Syria. Shertok had serious reservations about such a plan and he did not believe that it could be achieved "without bloodshed." He felt that such sacrifice would not be worth it over such a "truncated portion of Palestine."[23]

American Zionists refused to accept the British plan of keeping the Jewish population of Palestine between 31 and 35 percent of the total. The American Zionist reaction was reflected in Justice Brandeis's instantaneous response: "I am against."[24] They refused to accept the internationalization of Jerusalem and Haifa. Brandeis and other American Zionist leaders like Wise felt that Britain was determined to prevent the Yishuv from becoming a power. As they saw it, the Peel plan was not aimed at resolving possible Arab-Jewish differences, but at preventing Jewish development. Britain might have the power "to do this," but as Justice Brandeis put it, "we must not make it easy for them." The Mandate had granted the Jewish people their rights to Palestine and he would "consent to no change." Furthermore, "if we withhold our assent, we will always be free to open the case again. Let us have another 500,000 Jews in Palestine, and we will be able to solve the problem."[25]

Writing from the Land of Israel in February 1937, Rose Jacobs of Hadassah was annoyed that Weizmann was "moving heaven and earth" to pump the Yishuv full of enthusiasm for "partition," and creating the impression that the Yishuv was for it so that the delegates of the forthcoming Zionist Congress would feel obliged to follow the Yishuv's example. The structure and funding of the Zionist organization, according to Jacobs, was used to obtain support for partition while the opponents of partition were "unorganized and without funds or press" and they were dependent primarily upon "miracles."[26]

The main problem, as Jacobs saw it, was not that the British were preparing to halt Jewish immigration or that capital investment might be curtailed, but that the Zionists were poorly organized. She proposed that the "Tammany machine" should be replaced if there was "still time for it."[27]

She was alarmed that Weizmann was winning the Yishuv's support for partition. Weizmann was "so clever and really so gifted—if only he had character I venture to say that he would be one of the greatest men of our time, not alone in the Jewish world but altogether."[28] She could not understand or appreciate the reasoning of the propartitionists who felt that:

1. There will surely be a war
2. The war will be concentrated in the Mediterranean

3. Great Britain has vested interests here as a result
4. Great Britain cannot rely on Arab support or military, since the Arabs lack organization
5. Under the Mandate, Jews cannot receive military training as independent units
6. Under the Mandate, Jews cannot be brought in to make for a large military force
7. Hence, by partition, Jews will immigrate and a large soldiery will be raised for the war[29]

Jacobs could not understand the partitionist viewpoint.[30] Was "this why we came to Palestine?"[31] But who was the "we"? Had Jacobs and her husband moved to the Land of Israel, to Palestine? Did she face the continued attacks from Arab terrorists and harassment from British officials?

She asked her husband to send her an autographed photograph of Justice Brandeis so that she could be "surrounded" by her "Zionist heroes from America as well as the others."[32] However well intentioned Jacobs and other American Zionists may have been, they were "surrounded" by their own limited experiences. They could not begin to fathom the experiences of the Jews of Europe or the Jews of the Land of Israel. They could not begin to comprehend the tensions brought on by Arab terrorism compounded by British refusals to permit Jews to defend themselves and to live. Nor did they begin to comprehend the dangers that European Jewry faced from the Nazis. She and many others could see that the Zionist organization was not well organized, and she wanted more of a say in Zionist affairs since American supporters were helping to provide monies. However, she was prepared to cut off those monies unless things went her way.

Rutenberg, in a letter to Sir John Maffey, opposed partition because of the "relatively small number of Jews" in Palestine and the "anti-British foreign factors already assisting the Arabs." He felt that if the partition plan were adopted, the Jews would deal with "scrupulous fairness" towards the Arabs. But he thought provision should be made for the voluntary transference of Arabs to the Arab territories, and that the Jewish state should include the Galilee, the Negev, the Dead Sea Works, Jerusalem, and Haifa. Finally, he called for mass immigration of "physically and morally" fit Jews to an independent and sovereign state.[33]

Rutenberg's antipartitionist stand angered Ben-Gurion. For Ben-Gurion, the partition proposal meant that some ten million dunam of land would be made available to Jews in a Jewish state that would have access to world trade throughout the Mediterranean. He believed that the Jewish people were facing "the most momentous problem" in Jewish history "since the destruction of our independence."[34] He asked Wise and Felix Frankfurter to join him in London for the discussions and negotiations that were going on there with the British: "It is necessary for you and Felix to come here, so that we may talk things over, take your advice and act together."[35]

American Zionists turned to President Roosevelt. They asked him to intervene with the British and to stop the partition. They petitioned Samuel Rosenman, one of Roosevelt's advisors, to approach the president on this matter. Rosenman spoke to the president. He presented the views of his American Zionist friends and he told him that Palestine was "a place of refuge which our people sorely need." Roosevelt asked to see maps of the area in question and spoke of the possibility of buying "great areas of land in Trans-Jordan provided they could be brought under the immediate Mandate or trusteeship" for the Jews. Wise found the president's proposal to be "startling" in view of what the British were now doing.[36]

Weizmann felt that the British had never given the Mandate a chance to succeed. The British had regarded the Palestine question "as a festering sore" and "an additional trouble on top of all the terrible worries with which governments in Europe are now faced." Palestine was taking up time and troops and it was "a danger point in the Mediterranean, where Italy was constantly intriguing, making capital out of the latest mischance, bribing, corrupting wherever she could; where Arab nationalism was being artificially fomented and brought up to white heat."[37]

Weizmann advised Wise, that while partition was never his project he, nevertheless, viewed it as "an audacious proposal" and that it contained "the germs of a great future, but also grave dangers." If partition were to come about, Weizmann believed that the best possible solution should be sought and that the Jewish people should try to make the best of it. "If it is inevitable that it should come about, we must try to influence this new proposal in such a way as to make possible the realization of the aspirations embodied in the Mandate through this new medium." He did not feel that partition should be rejected outright:

> It would be wrong to let the thing go by default by simply saying "No" because the result of that would merely have been that the Mandate would have been discredited anyhow . . . and no other policy would have been available in its place; we would have fallen between two stools, and taken the responsibility for almost certain failure within the next twenty-five years.[38]

Weizmann believed it to be Jewish "destiny to get Palestine" and that destiny would be "fulfilled someday, somehow." Within the partition area allotted, some sixty thousand Jews could be brought to the Land of Israel per year. He saw it as the job of Zionists "to make the best of such an opportunity in our own house, with our own forces, as a small sovereign state, leaving the problems of expansion to future generations. There is no absolute in this world; everything is a flux." While the proposal for partition was not his "child," it might be "either a Solomon's judgment or a Caesarean operation; it depends on how it is carried out."[39]

Weizmann had found it all very difficult. It had been especially difficult to talk to the Royal Commission because in front sat the British, "at your back" the Jews and Arabs, and "above you the stern Jewish God, who seemed very near." It seemed like some sort of "Day of Judgment."[40]

On June 30, 1937, Weizmann called from London and informed Wise, Louis Lipsky, and Frankfurter that the Peel Commission would recommend partition. He asked them to come to London and negotiate with the British. He once again said that partition would be better than the "existing" conditions and that it would usher in a "new era." But the American Zionists had their own idea as to what was best for the Jewish people and the Zionist cause. At their fortieth annual convention, American Zionists had taken a firm stand against partition. As Rabbi Wise got the final word from Weizmann that the British would go ahead with their partition proposal, he asked the secretary of state and President Roosevelt once again to intervene with the British. This time Wise stressed that both Zionists and non-Zionists in America were opposed to this partition. As far as Wise was concerned, there could be no "solution of any Palestine problem without ending the divorce between Palestine and Transjordan." Instead of giving in more, said Wise, "we must demand more, to which we are entitled."[41]

But while Weizmann tried to persuade his colleagues to support partition he warned British officials that the Jews would not accept a minority status and the deprivation of their homeland. He was perturbed by the failure of the British to provide him with an advance copy of the Peel report or the accompanying White Paper. Writing to William Ormsby-Gore on July 4, 1937, he said that Ormsby-Gore's refusal to let him have a copy a few days in advance of publication "rendered more difficult" for him what was already a "very difficult situation." Moreover, the British had failed to maintain law and order and now they suggested that the Jews were guilty of provoking riots. This was blaming the victims for the crimes of the aggressors. It was a practice with which Weizmann was "painfully acquainted after the pogroms of czarist Russia."[42]

When Zionist leaders like Wise read the published report of the Royal Commission and the White Paper, they observed that it was "about as bad as it could be." Wise was greatly disappointed with Britain's action. If there was an excuse for British action it would be that it stood "with

German and Italian guns leveled at its head," and that the British did not "understand that a decently treated and loyal Jewish Palestine could be of immense help to them." Non-Zionists like Felix Warburg expressed the fear that if partition would take place the Jews would be accused of conflicting loyalties. They were concerned that their position in America would be damaged.[43]

The Zionist Congress met from August 3 to August 16, 1937, in Switzerland. Weizmann addressed the meeting by advising the membership that if the actual partition plan were rejected, another plan of partition should be accepted provided it included a basis for an independent national life and room enough for at least two million Jews. From the very start of the congress, there was a split between those who favored partition and those who were against it. The naysayers included the Jewish State Party, the Hashomer Hatzair, Mizrachi, Stephen Wise, Abba Hillel Silver, and Hadassah as well as some seventy members of the Labor Party. But "from the first" it was clear to observers like Szold that while the congress would not accept the Peel Commission report, "the completely thorough-going anti-partitionists were in a minority." Among the "fighting conscientious Labor Party" naysayers were Katznelson, Chaim Greenberg, and Goldie Meyerson.

The Mizrachi view was a religious standpoint. No part of the Land of Israel was less important than any other and the Jewish people had no right to give away any part of it. The Hashomer Hatzair (a leftist Zionist organization) opposed partition on the ground that it involved permanent acceptance of the proposition that Arabs and Jews could not live in peace together.

Weizmann's followers maintained that since Great Britain had no intention of carrying out the Mandate it was a dead issue and partition could be a way out.

Ben-Gurion was sure that partition was far better than the Mandate. Palestine was never entirely Jewish and the sea front to be included was of great value. The Yishuv could raise a good army and this would help them survive. There could be no peace with the Arabs unless the Jews were a strong people. When Wise challenged Ben-Gurion and asked if he would have accepted the plan before the 1936 disturbances, Ben-Gurion shouted back, "Yes, with enthusiasm."[44]

Whether they were for or against partition, most delegates were dismayed by some of the general observations that appeared in the Peel report. They objected to the false claim that Jews and Arabs had been unable to live side by side in peace. This statement was altogether untrue since Jews and Arabs had lived in peace in the Land of Israel, Spain, Morocco, Algiers, and elsewhere for centuries. Such a proposition only served as ammunition for the anti-Semitic claim that Jews could not live in peace with other people. They likewise rejected the Royal Commission's claim that the Balfour Declaration had been issued by Great Britain in order to gain Jewish support for the Allied cause during World War I. Those Jews who lived and fought for the Allies were loyal to the Allies and those who lived and fought for the Central Powers remained loyal to those countries. The Balfour Declaration did not change a thing in that respect.

Those who favored partition felt that it would help bring peace to the area. Since the Arabs were increasing in strength and were in continuous revolt, the partitionists believed that the Jews would be better off in a state of their own, protected by their own people and their own weapons. They believed that partition would be the only opportunity for the Jews to achieve a Jewish state. "Better a small state than none at all." The deteriorating conditions in Nazi and communist sections of Europe pointed to the need of a Jewish state. Within the area granted by the British, the Yishuv could make a go of it, even without displacing the Arabs. Once the Jewish state would be established it would be in a position to make peace with the neighboring Arabs and "peaceful penetration into the neighboring Arab kingdom could be arranged with mutual satisfaction."[45]

Those opposed to partition as proposed by the Peel Commission did not seem to feel that the plan would solve anything. It failed to bring peace, but it helped make Arabs and Jews into permanent antagonists. The Yishuv would have to face customs, railway, and transportation difficulties as well as never ending border raids and perhaps some 225,000 Arabs within their own state. British interferences would not stop once partition would be enacted. It would bring more British officials into the area, and those British officials would interfere more than ever before. Economically, the Jewish state would not be viable since most of the revenue would go to the British and there was not enough hinterland in the truncated state to support a sound economy.

The antipartitionists argued that within the area allotted there was no room for mass immigration. They estimated that the area could not absorb more than eight hundred thousand newcomers, and in view of the perilous European situation millions of European Jews would need the refuge that the Land of Israel could offer them. Moreover, if a Jewish state were established, the Jews living in Syria, Iraq, Yemen, Morocco, and in other Arab-dominated entities might then be forced to seek safety in the Land of Israel. As Szold viewed it: "We must have in mind not only the needs of the Poles during the years 1937 and 1938, but also the needs of the Poles in more distant years." The proposed frontiers had no national boundaries, followed no river or mountain system, and would be almost impossible to defend. In view of this lack of natural frontiers the military costs of keeping the Jewish state from destruction would be prohibitive. At some points the width of the proposed Jewish state was less than ten miles, while potential Arab marauders would be situated in the adjoining hills. On top of the untenable geographical situation, such Jewish enterprises as the hydroelectric development of the Palestine Electric Corporation and the Palestine Potash Works had been excluded from the area allocated to the Yishuv. Some of the oldest Jewish settlements south of the Sea of Galilee were excluded from the "Jewish State" as were the one hundred thousand Jews of Haifa and Jerusalem. American Zionists would not accept the British concept of a Jewish state that had only twenty-three hundred square miles, while the Arab state, including Transjordan, was to have over forty-two thousand square miles.

Those against partition felt that the lesson of Transjordan and the 1920s had to be kept in mind. When Transjordan was separated from Palestine, the British won Zionist acquiescence by promising greater support for future Jewish development in the remaining areas of the Land of Israel. They also contended that Arab nationalistic ambitions would be satisfied and Jews would be permitted to settle in Transjordan. Quite the contrary occurred. As it turned out, the British did not give Jews greater support for settlement projects in the Land of Israel. Jews were not permitted to settle in Transjordan. Through their quotas and schedules, the British limited Jewish immigration and made it more difficult for them to purchase land in Palestine. It was believed by the antipartitionists that once the western part of the Land of Israel would be carved up, Jews would no more be able "to enter the part cut off in the future than we have been enabled to enter Transjordan in the last 15 years." The antipartitionist Zionists felt that they had no right to give up their legal position under the Mandate even if the British chose to do so.

As Szold saw it, if the British partition were accepted, Zionism and the Jewish state idea would collapse. He found it very strange that people like Weizmann and Ben-Gurion were so insistent on partition:

> They were too eager to say yes—influenced by panic from the genuine but temporary difficulties, and by the glitter of the illusory state. We cannot forgive them. Even now despite the majority resolution, they are satisfied and go right ahead. A year or two ago Ben Gurion was enthusiastic over the prospects of Akaba. Now the south is said to be worthless, and the glorious future will come, he says, from the sea.[46]

The partition question of 1936–1937 found the Zionists badly divided. As Weizmann observed, it was "one of the most violent controversies that . . . ever divided the Zionist movement." The naysayers would not be persuaded that the proposed Jewish state could absorb one hundred thousand Jewish immigrants a year and support a population of three million. But while the twentieth Zionist Congress turned down the Royal

Commission's partition proposals it did not reject partition altogether. On August 11, 1937, the Zionist Congress adopted the following resolution by a vote of 300 to 158:

> The Congress declared that the scheme of partition put forward by the Royal Commission is unacceptable.
>
> The Congress empowers the Executive to enter into negotiations with a view to ascertaining the precise terms of His Majesty's Government for the proposed establishment of a Jewish State.
>
> In such negotiations the Executive shall not commit either itself or the Zionist Organization, but in the event of the emergence of a definite scheme for the establishment of a Jewish State, such scheme shall be brought before a newly elected Congress for decision.[47]

The antipartitionists thought that it had been "a good fight." But while they had opposed any form of partition, the majority of naysayers had not rejected it altogether, and they had authorized an inquiry into the scheme, reserving the whole question to a future congress.

Szold thought that with the help of such leaders as Neumann, the antipartitionists had performed rather well. While Neumann had steered the naysayers through the debate and had drafted their resolutions, even Neumann had "come to Zurich ready to accept partition on the theory that there was no alternative." Many of the naysayers had voted to go along with the majority resolution so as not to reject "England out of hand" and in order to wait and see what the actual concrete proposals would turn out to be. Such was the case with individuals like Lipsky and Rabbi Israel Goldstein. The non-Zionists like Warburg were and remained altogether opposed to any form of partition and some of those who had been very strongly opposed to partition like Henrietta Szold, Wise, and Menachem Mendel Ussishkin wondered whether they should join the ranks of the Warburg group. But they did not.[48]

When the Zionist Congress adjourned, Robert Szold concluded that Weizmann had gotten his way, and as far as he was concerned Weizmann was "our great misfortune, together with the great misfortune that there is no candidate with whom to put Weizmann out." Szold observed as the Zionist Congress adjourned, the old executive was reelected and Weizmann would try to "go ahead to carry out his partition." "The Mandate is dead, Long live Weizmann."[49]

Partition had been defeated thanks to the Arabs and thanks to a good part of the Zionist community, and yet the American Zionists continued to fight against it. They continued to oppose the Jewish state idea since they believed the state that the British had in mind could not last and its collapse would be permanent. They called for adherence to "elementary principles of zionism." What were those elementary principles as Szold saw them in August 1937? That Jews and Arabs could live in peace with one another; that there was an historic connection to a large Palestine; and that there was a need for a real state and not a sham immitation that might prevent the real thing from coming into being. Szold insisted that he had "stood pat, clear one hundred percent against partition, directly or indirectly, in whole now or steps leading thereto."[50]

But while the fight against partition continued, it was half-hearted and disorganized. All the debating and infighting would be for naught because the British would not follow up their Royal Commission report with any serious steps for its implementation.

During an October 26, 1937, meeting, representatives of various Jewish organizations and parties expressed their readiness to fight against partition. Mizrachi leaders like Rabbi Kowalsky stood "definitely against partition." They planned to carry out a publicity campaign against partition. Miss Benjamin of Hadassah likewise "definitely opposed" partition. Hashomer Hatzair, American section, was "100 percent opposed to partition" and was "working at present to its full capacity against it." Poale Zion claimed that their "international leadership" was opposed to partition. Cohen of Avukah said that his party was "definitely committed against partition." Szold spoke for the General Zionists in opposition to partition. He said that they had published a book by Herman Wiseman outlining their position. All the representatives said that their organizations planned lectures, speeches, and publications against partition.

In October Justice Brandeis felt that Americans had to be made to see that "while we are absolutely opposed to partition we agree with Ben-Gurion that Jewish Palestine must be strengthened and developed—and to this end we must give not only as much but more than ever before." But there had to be one difference: Now they wanted to "select the purpose or subject of expenditure."

That same October Weizmann tried to reassure American Zionists that the British would come through and give the Jews a better deal. He believed that the British would agree to have the Negev included in the new Jewish state since Egypt and Ibn Sa'ūd of Saudi Arabia objected to the Negev going to the proposed Arab state as it might then become a base for Benito Mussolini. Weizmann advised that Zionists should concentrate their efforts at improving the project of the Royal Commission rather than in fighting one another. He believed that "something very substantial" could be achieved from such discussions.[51]

As Weizmann tried to persuade American Zionists not to fight against partition he was challenged by some Yishuv antipartitionists. One of those detractors was Ussishkin. Ussishkin claimed that there were many Palestinian Jews who were opposed to partition.[52] But while Ussishkin claimed that he and others were leading the fight against partition, another observer in the Land of Israel, Meir Grossman, found that there was no real opposition to partition within the Yishuv community and that even Ussishkin opposed partition only at Zionist meetings. Grossman did confirm Jacob's assertion that Weizmann and Ben-Gurion tried "to create the impression in Jewry that the partition of Palestine was a *fait accompli.*" In order to counteract Weizmann and Ben-Gurion, he suggested that there be a unity party of Revisionists, General Zionists, the Jewish State Party, and those Zionists outside Zionist politics.[53] Grossman called for the reorganization of Zionist institutions and funds, and that they should be made available to a wider circle of the Yishuv as well as Diaspora Jewry. He also envisioned an election system with the franchise going to all those who subscribed to the program of Zionism and who supported the establishment of a Jewish state and the reconstruction of the Jewish Agency along democratically elected lines.[54]

By December 1937, some antipartitionist Jews of Palestine like the expatriate American rabbi, Judah Magnes of the Hebrew University, conferred with Arab leaders on ways to prevent partition. Magnes apparently found that while some Arabs preferred to keep Jews as a permanent minority, others might go along with Jews having political and numerical equality in Palestine and Transjordan if they could be convinced that Jews would help establish an Arab federation with Palestine as part of that federation. Julius Simon reported that the Iraqi minister had informed the American consul in Jerusalem that Iraq, Egypt, Turkey, Yemen, and Syria would favor the creation of a state on both sides of the Jordan under the present ruler of Transjordan if the Jews would agree to remain only forty percent of the total population.[55]

CONCLUSION

The discussions over partition were complex in 1936–1937. By the end of 1937, Zionists witnessed Britain abandon the idea of a separate Jewish entity in Palestine.

Many of those who had participated in the 1936–1937 debate had wanted the best possible life for the Jews of a greater Land of Israel. Some so-called non-Zionists like the Warburg group were against the Jewish state idea. But the vast majority of American Zionists wanted a Jewish state. They did not want to see it become a tiny entity and they did not want to take a backseat to the Yishuv leadership.

Weizmann, Ben-Gurion, Shertok, and other supporters of partition were apparently more aware of the consequences of the Nazi totalitarian rule in Europe and they realized that Jews would not find refuge anywhere else except in the Land of Israel. They were willing to accept a smaller Israel in order to save European Jewry and to protect the Yishuv against Arab extremists and Anglo-Saxon heads of state. Independence was life itself to them.

Gerhard Riegner of the World Jewish Congress, in an interview, lamented: "If Jewry had been united and accepted the Peel plan of 1936–1937 we could have had something . . . we could have had a place for the Jews of Europe."[56]

NOTES

1. Martin Gilbert, *Israel: A History* (New York, 1998).
2. Melvin Urofsky, *American Zionism from Herzl to the Holocaust* (New York, 1975).
3. Howard M. Sachar, *A History of Israel: From the Rise of Zionism to Our Time* (New York, 1996).
4. Chaim Weizmann to Stephen S. Wise, February 27, 1936, Justice Louis D. Brandeis Papers, Reel 25/222-223, Zionist Archives, New York.
5. Morris Margulies to Leo Herman, March 22, 1935, Individuals Files, Zionist Archives, New York.
6. David Ben-Gurion to Justice Louis D. Brandeis, May 7, 1936, Brandeis Papers Reel 25/82-90, Zionist Archives, New York.
7. Ibid.
8. Chaim Weizmann, *Trial and Error* (New York, 1949), p. 382.
9. Yigal Allon, *The Making of Israel's Army* (New York, 1971), pp. 12–13.
10. Weizmann, *Trial and Error*, p. 383.
11. Notes on Pincus Rutenberg's interview with Secretary of State for the Colonies October 5, 1938, Robert Szold Papers, Zionist Archives, New York.
12. Weizmann, *Trial and Error*, p. 384.
13. Eliahu Epstein, Moshe Shertok, and Goldie Meyerson among others would change their names to modern Hebrew names.
14. Testimony of Eliahu Epstein and Moshe Shertok before the Royal Commission, 1937, Zionist Organization of America. Papers, 1936–1938, Zionist Archives, New York.
15. Ibid.
16. Ibid.
17. Ibid.
18. Ibid.
19. Ibid.
20. Weizmann, *Trial and Error*, pp. 385–386.
21. Notes of a meeting among Justice Louis D. Brandeis, Eliezer Kaplan, and Stephen S. Wise, February 7, 1937, Julian W. Mack Papers, Box 5, File 24, Zionist Archives, New York.
22. Emanuel Neumann, *In the Arena: An Autobiographical Memoir* (New York, 1976) pp. 135–136.
23. Notes of a meeting among Justice Louis D. Brandeis, Eliezer Kaplan, and Stephen S. Wise, February 7, 1937, Julian W. Mack Papers, Box 5, File 24, Zionist Archives, New York.

24. Ibid.
25. Ibid.
26. Rose Jacobs to Edward Jacobs, February 10, February 15, February 18, February 20, 1937, Robert Szold Papers, Box 26, Folder 18, Zionist Archives, New York.
27. Ibid.
28. Ibid.
29. Ibid.
30. Ibid.
31. Ibid.
32. Ibid.
33. Pincus Rutenberg to Sir John Maffey, June 5, 1937, Julian Mack Papers, Box 5, File 24, Zionist Archives, New York.
34. Notes of meeting among Justice Louis D. Brandeis, Eliezer Kaplan, and Stephen S. Wise, February 7, 1937, Julian W. Mack Papers, Box 5, File 24, Zionist Archives, New York.
35. David Ben-Gurion to Stephen S. Wise, June 23, 1937, Julian W. Mack Papers, Box 5, File 24, Zionist Archives, New York.
36. Memo by Stephen S. Wise to Justice Louis D. Brandeis, Julian Mack, Felix Frankfurter, and Robert Szold, June 25, 1937; Chaim Weizmann to Stephen S. Wise, June 29, 1937; Julian W. Mack Papers, Box 5, File 24, Zionist Archives, New York.
37. Ibid.
38. Ibid.
39. Ibid.
40. Ibid.
41. Stephen S. Wise to Chaim Weizmann, October 26, 1936, Robert Szold Papers, Box 25, Folder 14, Zionist Archives, New York; Stephen S. Wise to Justice Louis D. Brandeis, July 5, 1937, Julian W. Mack Papers, Box 5, File 24, Zionist Archives, New York.
42. Ibid.; Weizmann, *Trial and Error*, p. 391; Stephen S. Wise to Justice Louis D. Brandeis, July 5, 1937, Julian W. Mack Papers, Box 5, File 24, Zionist Archives, New York.
43. Ibid.; Notes of a conference between Felix Warburg and Julian Mack, July 12, 1937, Julian W. Mack Papers, Box 5, File 24, Zionist Archives, New York.
44. Robert Szold to Julian W. Mack, August 16, 1937, Julian W. Mack Papers, Box 5, File 25, Zionist Archives, New York.
45. Ibid.
46. Robert Szold to Julian W. Mack, August 15, 1937, Julian W. Mack Papers, Box 5, File 25, Zionist Archives, New York.
47. Robert Szold to Mrs. Robert Szold, August 11, 15, 1937, Robert Szold Papers, Box 26, File 22, Zionist Archives, New York.
48. Ibid.
49. Ibid.
50. Robert Szold to Mrs. Robert Szold, August 7, 1937, Robert Szold Papers, Box 26, File 22, Zionist Archives, New York.
51. Chaim Weizmann to Stephen S. Wise, October 24, 1937, Robert Szold Papers, Box 26, File 18, Zionist Archives, New York.

52. Menachem Mendel Ussishkin to Stephen S. Wise, November 7, 1937, Robert Szold Papers, Box 26, Folder 18, Zionist Archives, New York.

53. Meir Grossman memo of November 21, 1937, Robert Szold Papers, Box 26, File 18, Zionist Archives, New York.

54. Ibid.

55. Julius Simon to Robert Szold, December 22, 1937, Robert Szold Papers, Box 26, File 18, Zionist Archives, New York.

56. Interview with Gerhard Riegner, April 20, 1973.

3

White Paper 1939

Late in 1937 and early 1938, Chaim Weizmann learned that the British were about to adopt a policy that would deny the Jews their right to exist as a free and independent people. He warned the British that the Jews would never accept "minority status" in an Arab-dominated state in Palestine.

> It is not for the purpose of subjecting the Jewish people, which still stands in the front rank of civilization, to the rule of a set of unscrupulous Levantine politicians that this supreme effort is being made in Palestine. All the labors and sacrifices here owe their inspiration to one thing alone—to the belief that this at least is going to mean freedom and the end of the ghetto.[1]

British diplomats and political leaders chose to ignore the Jews as a factor in the war against the Nazis. They were more concerned with the Arab factor. They seemed to shake with every Arab demonstration and "uprising." British Colonial Secretary Ramsay MacDonald felt that the Arabs had to be treated with great care and delicacy lest they cause disturbances in Palestine. He was afraid that the Zionist proposition that one hundred thousand Jews be admitted to the Land of Israel would only serve to irritate the Arabs and consequently make any agreement with them most difficult. By the fall of 1937, it was evident that the British planned to limit Jewish immigration to some ten thousand a year.

Pincus Rutenberg of the Zionist executive dismissed MacDonald's concerns as irrelevant and petty. He tried to help the British understand that a new set of circumstances had been created by the Fascists and Nazis as they rose to power. The Jewish people could become an effective force against this new terror. If one hundred thousand Jews were admitted to the Land of Israel within the next few months, they could help defend the Middle East against possible Fascist-Nazi encroachments. There was still time to build an effective Jewish fighting force, later it might be "too late and perhaps impossible."

MacDonald suggested that the matter be taken up with the high commissioner. When Rutenberg met with Colonial Secretary William Ormsby-Gore, he was told that the high commissioner for Palestine had rejected the idea that one hundred thousand Jews be admitted to Palestine. Rutenberg advised the British that they were making "a fatal mistake" not only from the Jewish point of view but from the British viewpoint as well. There would come a time when the British would wish that they had these Jewish men and women on their side.

During his conversations with Ormsby-Gore in February 1938, Weizmann discovered that the British Foreign Office had received memos from Sir Percy Loraine in Turkey and Sir Miles Lampson in Egypt expressing opposition to partition from various British embassies. Ormsby-Gore claimed that he had received letters from various members of the American Jewish community who opposed the establishment of a Jewish state. Weizmann tried to dispel the impression that American Jews were against partition. They were not opposed to the establishment of an independent state, but they were against the creation of a state that had no chance of survival. Weizmann said that he had read many of the reports to which Ormsby-Gore had made reference and he knew a great deal about what was passing between British and Arab leaders, but that his information regarding Arab feelings was far different from that which Ormsby-Gore had apparently received. Moreover, he found the correspondence between British and Arab politicos more than a little disturbing.

Weizmann had met with Sir Lampson as well as the Syrian nationalist leader Shahabandar and Prince Mohammed Ali. Weizmann observed that Sir Lampson was influenced by his secretary, Smart, whose wife was a sister-in-law of Antonius, and a daughter of the owner of *Mokattem,* the strongly pro-Palestinian Arab paper in Egypt. Sir Lampsom wanted an easy life and the best way for him to get that was by supporting a "five-year standstill." Nahas Pasha observed that the Egyptians were not Arabs and that they were not interested in Palestinian developments, but since they were Moslems they felt obliged to say something in support of their fellow Moslems.[2]

Weizmann challenged the attitude of certain British officials. The Arabs "were permitted to do whatever they thought fit," and the British were overly concerned with the notion that what neighboring Arab states might think or do was of any real consequence with respect to Palestine. The terrorists of Syria were of no great importance. According to intelligence information available to Weizmann, some seventy chauffeurs were engaged in the business of organizing terrorist gangs in Syria. With money, Weizmann said, he too could "organize bands in Syria if he wanted to do so."[3]

Weizmann observed that Ibn Sa'ūd's "military importance was nil" as far as Palestine was concerned. Weizmann believed that Sa'ūd was one of the most reasonable of the Arab leaders and he was surprised that the British had not made the way easier for him.[4]

Towards the end of the interview, Weizmann challenged Ormsby-Gore regarding the view he had expressed to Nuri Pasha that the Royal Commission had gone too far in regard to allocating territory to the Jewish state and that the Arabs should insist on getting the Galilee.

Ormsby-Gore claimed that the Foreign Office had foisted Pasha on him, and he denied ever having made such a statement. Weizmann insisted that his sources of information were "extremely good and reliable." Pasha had made his statement before a group of six people, one of whom had been Weizmann's agent. Weizmann insisted that he had "irrefutable proof of what had been said at that meeting." Moreover, Ormsby-Gore had urged that the area south of Jaffa should not be included in a future Jewish state and that special care should be taken for the Arab citrus growers. If such British policy were pursued, then the Jewish state would be left with a strip of land from Tel Aviv to Haifa—with no Galilee, no Jerusalem, no Haifa, no South, and no Negev.

Weizmann said that he knew the British were preparing a plan that would deny the Jews their right to exist as a free and independent people. He could not understand the purpose of such a plan since it would be rejected by the Jewish people without question. "To proceed in this way," said Weizmann, "would be an act of cruelty to the Jewish people and would embitter their relations with their only remaining friends."[5]

Ormsby-Gore suggested that Weizmann inform the Royal Commission that he thought the Galilee was essential for the security of the Jewish state.

Weizmann advised Ormsby-Gore in the strongest possible terms that the Jews would not take the new British view of things lying down. He wanted Ormsby-Gore and all the other British officials to know that the Jewish people had many friends in England. The Jews have friends in Parliament and those friends "would not allow us to be betrayed in this way, and in Palestine there are 450,000 Jews who would fight to the last ditch. Let the government, if it wished, face the task of shooting down the Jews."[6]

When Ormsby-Gore responded by saying that the trouble stemmed from the fact that "there are new Pharaohs who knew not Joseph," Weizmann warned him not to "wait for all the ten plagues." Ormsby-Gore also blamed the Foreign Office attitude on certain assimilationist Jews like Freddy Stern, Albert M. Hymanson, and Newcombe "who came to the Foreign Office." It was that same sort that had opposed the Balfour

Declaration and he advised Weizmann to stop off at the Foreign Office to talk with people like Alexander Montegu George Cadogan and Sir Robert Gilbert Vansiettart.[7]

Weizmann agreed, but said that he wanted to see P.M. Neville Chamberlain before the prime minister would meet with Benito Mussolini. Weizmann observed that "it was instructive that the anti-Semitic front coincided with the dictatorial front."

When Rabbi Stephen S. Wise received a copy of the Weizmann–Ormsby-Gore conversation he felt that his "worst fears" had been confirmed. This was the consequence "of bargaining with the British government over bits of the map." Wise reported that Weizmann believed that there was a "cabal against us, operating from the Foreign and not the Colonial Office." The new map that the British were about to propose was frightening:

> Excepting for the Huleh, everything above and including Haifa is to be British. [The New] Jerusalem is to be British; instead of the Jewish coastal strip going up to Gaza, as we had imagined, the Jewish division is to end at Jaffa, with the coast south of Jaffa Arab, up to the continuance of a line running from the sea across the country to the southern point of the Dead Sea; that line a little south of Beersheba. The Negev country or what will be left of it is to be British . . . with access to some parts of it granted to Jews.

The Jewish coastal strip, in the words of Weizmann, was to run south to north from Tel Aviv to Zichron. "Upon one term we were all agreed, namely, impossible."[8]

According to Rabbi Wise, when Weizmann had conferred with members of the British cabinet in November 1937, he was left with the impression that a provisional Jewish "set up, if not a State" would be established "almost immediately" and certainly not later than in one year's time. But in the meantime, the British cabinet had been divided on Palestine with such individuals as Anthony Eden "definitely against us." But the prime minister would not go along with the views of the Foreign Office that the Jews in Palestine had "become a liability to the Government" and that "Palestine had to be liquidated."[9]

At this point Weizmann called upon the Americans to intervene so as to break the British anti-Jewish cabal. But Wise observed that since the British had whittled down Jewish Palestine to less than what had been recommended by the Peel report and the subsequent White Paper of 1937, it was no wonder that Roosevelt suggested that the Jews look elsewhere because he believed that Palestine could not absorb more than seven-thousand Jews per year. Wise believed that Roosevelt had "an inkling of what was in the mind of the Foreign Office" and he took "it for granted that this was a finality."[10] The pieces of the puzzle were falling into place.

American Zionists of almost every persuasion opposed the Peel partition plan and its recommendation for the reduction of Jewish Palestine. This newest 1938 British turn indicated that they could not be trusted. To some observers it seemed that the British were playing games of power politics. British diplomats had appeased Italy and Germany in order to achieve their goals and now they further appeased Arab extremists and sold out the Jews.

Amid the depressing news from London, some American Zionists continued their debate for and against partition, but for the most part such individuals as Justice Louis D. Brandeis, Robert Szold, and Rose Jacobs were against partition. Jacobs, the Hadassah president, again declared herself against the political "machine" of Weizmann and called upon her colleagues not to surrender "by default" to the partitionists. She once again raised the specter of money contributed by Americans for Palestine and claimed that the American Zionists had a right to have an input into Jewish affairs in Palestine. "The money of the non-Zionists, now termed 'anti' for tactical purposes among Zionists was not considered unholy, nor is it now, but any assertion on fundamentals by them is so considered."[11]

Emanuel Neumann advocated a grassroots movement against partition "detached from the present Zionist parties and their leadership." Szold "did not see any organized Zionist bodies who are serious and determined about the business of anti-partition." The Hashomer Hatzair were too closely bound to the Histadrut. If they had seen the antipartitionists as a strong force, they might have joined.[12] Neumann believed that he could gather support from British, Belgian, South African, and French Zionists to oppose partition, but it would all depend upon the effectiveness of the American Zionists and "the only American antipartitionists whom I take seriously are you and your friends."[13]

David Ben-Gurion tried to impress such Americans as Benjamin V. Cohen that partition was the more desirable course for Palestine. Cohen observed that Ben-Gurion was "hopelessly, uncompromisingly and almost fanatically for partition." Ben-Gurion believed that Jews could make progress in Palestine only if they had their own administration and government. He envisioned Tel Aviv with a million Jews involved in productive activities, exporting their industrial products throughout the world. The Arabs would form an alliance with the Jews once they became aware of the "strong Jewish position in the Near East." It would then be easier for the Yishuv to defend itself.[14]

Cohen found Ben-Gurion "dreaming dreams and rather dangerous dreams." But Ben-Gurion insisted that he was "speaking realistically about hard facts."[15]

Weizmann confessed to Cohen that he had accepted partition because he wanted the Jews to have "some control over immigration." But prospects for a Jewish homeland seemed less and less hopeful. The situation had been "radically altered by Anthony Eden" who had transmitted a memo to the British cabinet insisting that the entire Jewish experiment had been a bad mistake and that Zionism had to be liquidated since it antagonized British interests in India, Egypt, Iraq, and even Turkey. Weizmann found Eden's report entirely "misleading as to the facts." For instance, said Weizmann, there was no basis for the assertion that Turkey was antagonistic to the Jews or especially sympathetic to the Arabs. Eden's report had a detrimental effect on the attitude of the British government towards the Jews, and Weizmann wanted to know what help might be expected from the United States.[16]

Cohen found Franklin D. Roosevelt sympathetic to the Palestine experiment but saw that the president did not feel that Palestine would be adequate "as an outlet for the European refugee for whom a home must be found" since the British were about to reduce the territory for the Jews.[17]

Because Weizmann and Ben-Gurion were convinced that the British were "contemplating a radical modification of the Balfour Declaration and the Mandate as we have understood it," they wanted to know what the Americans would do to help "avert a disastrous decision."[18]

British policies likewise concerned Cohen. He saw the British as taking advantage of the divisions over partition within the ranks of the Zionist community in order to further restrict Jewish immigration. He warned Szold that the Zionists had to be on "guard not to lose the substance in a quarrel over the form."[19]

THE WOODHEAD REPORT

Weizmann's worst fears would soon be realized. In March 1938, British High Commissioner Sir Arthur Wauchope was replaced by Sir Harold MacMichael. Sir John Woodhead was placed in charge of a new commission to investigate conditions in Palestine. That commission arrived in Palestine in April 1938, and for three months it conducted its investigation amidst a background of Arab riots and the coming of war in Europe. The Woodhead Commission issued its report in November 1938, a month after the Munich Pact and just about the time the Germans launched an all-out campaign against its Jews. The report rejected the Peel partition plan, but it provided no substitute boundaries for a Jewish state. The British followed up the report with another White Paper that declared the creation of a Jewish and an Arab state out of Palestine was impracticable. Regardless, the British said that they looked forward to another solution through an Arab-Jewish conference to be held in London. Moreover they suggested that if the Jews and Arabs could not come to some agreement at the forthcoming conference Britain would impose a solution of its own.

In a meeting with some of England's most prominent Jews, Rutenberg described the Woodhead report as not being "worth the paper it was printed on." It was nothing more than a total distortion and sought to destroy the prospects for partition. If the Jews of Europe were forced to remain there they would face the greatest danger ever. From March 1933 to the Evian Conference of 1938, the Jews saw that they could not find refuge anywhere. Palestine was "the only one address which they can claim as a right to go and where therefore they must go." There could be no negotiations without the issue of immigration as a starting point and there had to be an agreement between Arabs and Jews. No longer was it enough if the British and the Arabs arranged some sort of agreement. The way to satisfy the Arabs was to form a federation of Arab states together with a Jewish state.[20]

Rutenberg insisted that there was a large section of the Arab population with which Jews could find "a common language" and with whom they could come to an understanding, but the terrorists and certain British government agents stood in the way of agreement. He called upon the Jews outside the Land of Israel to help with a capital investment of ten million British Pound Sterling that would be used to help develop harbors, water supply systems, sewerage, shipping, building as well as land development. This investment would help the immigrants and it would give useful occupations to everybody concerned—Jew, Arab, and Christian. All this would be within the context of a federation with the Arab states.[21]

Rutenberg claimed that at the height of the Arab riots of July 1936, he had been able to reach an agreement with King Emir Abdullah of Jordan "for Jewish colonization within Jordan."[22] He had even sent a copy of the agreement to the Peel Commission. Herein was an indication of what could be achieved in the way of Jewish-Arab collaboration.[23] MacDonald insisted that the Arabs should be treated with a great deal of care and that they should not be irritated with a Zionist proposal of "bringing in large numbers of young Jews to Palestine." Such a proposition, said MacDonald, would only serve to irritate the Arabs and make any agreement with them very difficult.[24]

Abdullah was not as cooperative as Rutenberg may have liked to believe. When Rutenberg talked with Abdullah in late December 1938, he heard Abdullah speak of how he distrusted the British and that he did not wish to see any further Jewish immigration into Palestine. Six hundred thousand Jews in Palestine was more than enough for him:

> You are now 600,000 souls, and some agreement between us is necessary. Fighting will bring to nothing. We must find a solution which would ease your bur-

dens and will not hurt our honor in the eyes of our people. What is happening in Germany is the most cruel thing that could happen in the world. He who believed that in Germany there is conscience is a fool. What happened is a catastrophe. The sorrow is great and we Arabs are bound to take this into consideration. . . . The matter must be settled between the Jews and the Arabs in Palestine and Trans-Jordan. For the time being I would advise you as a devoted friend to satisfy yourselves with the number of people that have already entered Palestine. When things will quiet down it will be possible to continue a moderate immigration to Palestine and also to Trans-Jordan. Now the Conference is coming and nobody knows on what rails the carriage will travel. I repeat—Do not stress the question of immigration. The rope is already strained till its end. Any further pulling of it may break it.[25]

Abdullah knew that the Jews were suffering at the hands of the Germans, but he did not want them in Palestine.

During Rutenberg's conversations with MacDonald, he advised British officials that the situation was worsening for the Jews and that they needed Palestine as a place of refuge:

To Germany has been added Austria, Poland, Romania, Hungary, Italy, and now Czechoslovakia. Millions of Jews have to be taken from there. The Evian conference has shown that there is no other place for the Jews but Palestine. We may have to sacrifice the old generation, but there are still remaining two to three million of young who must be saved. And they can be brought only to Palestine.[26]

Rutenberg asked for negotiations among Jews, Arabs, and British officials. It was no longer a matter of the creation of a Jewish state or the percentage of Jews versus Arabs in Palestine. "The essence was that large numbers of Jews must be brought to Palestine." This was the only way for the Jews of Europe to be saved and the "Arabs should be asked what and how much they want for it." Even if the "price may be high, we have no other way."[27] Rutenberg dismissed MacDonald's argument concerning Arab irritations as being only a minor factor. More important was the threat of world war and that threat created a new set of circumstances. Moreover, it would be to Britain's military and strategic advantage if more Jews were admitted to the Land of Israel. Every Jew brought to Palestine would mean "one less fighting against England and one more fighting for it. That is two men." If one hundred thousand Jews were brought to Palestine in the next few months, they and some ten thousand British soldiers could effectively "defend that part of the world for England." There was still time, later it might be "too late and perhaps impossible."[28] MacDonald suggested that Rutenberg should discuss the matter with Lord Walter Edward Guiness Moyne (Secretary of State for

Colonies, 1941–1942; British Resident Minister for the Middle East, 1942–1944).

The British would not be persuaded that the Jews had any rights. Their concern was the empire, not Jews. On October 19, 1938, MacDonald advised Rutenberg that the British government was opposed to any "large numbers of young Jews" entering Palestine. "You are making a fatal mistake," said Rutenberg, "not only from the Jewish point of view, but from the point of view of English interests." The time would come, he cautioned, when England would wish "to have the men there but you will not be able to."[29]

RUTENBERG'S PLAN

There was a desperate need for an Arab-Jewish understanding that would enable large-scale Jewish immigration to the Land of Israel, and Rutenberg had a plan. Since the British had failed to protect the Jews they also failed to protect the vast majority of Arabs from the Mufti extremists. Arabs were being "murdered by the Mufti's agents" and many had "to escape from Palestine" in order to save their lives. There was a large section of the Arab population with whom Jews could find "a common language and come to an understanding," but the terrorists and British government agents worked to prevent such an understanding. Rutenberg believed that an Arab-Jewish understanding could be achieved through a federation of Syria, Lebanon, Transjordan, and Iraq. He was prepared to form a corporation with a capital of ten million British Pound Sterling. Some four to five million would be used for public works construction of Tel Aviv harbor; water supplies and sewage disposal systems for Haifa and Tel Aviv; and irrigation and shipping. Another two to three million would be used to acquire and irrigate land and three million more would be used for economic development of the federation. This, in turn, would help facilitate Jewish immigration and promote the work for Arab populations. Weizmann was in full agreement with his plan and he presented it to MacDonald. The British refused to listen. They also refused to agree that some one hundred thousand Jewish people should enter Palestine.[30]

Rutenberg once again advised British officials that they were wrong and that temerity would not help matters.[31]

Zionists wanted to know why the British refused to listen. Apparently a Jewish Palestine did not fit into British plans and appeasement policies, but Rutenberg found that at least part of the blame could be placed on the Jewish leadership that failed to back up his scheme. The British saw the Zionist community as split and they did not take Weizmann and Rutenberg seriously. Rutenberg complained to Justice Brandeis that only Lord Hugo Hirst had "full-heartedly" agreed to participate both on the board and financially. Lord Walter Horace Samuel Bearstead and Lord Julius Salter Elias Southwood had declined to participate on the board, "being too busy with their own work." He found that "charity was the only way in which London Jews are able to think." He observed that this condition would continue "till—God help I should be wrong—they will find themselves in the same position as the German Jews."[32]

Since he could not get the help of the Rothschild, Mark, and Spencer families that were "big enough to be entrusted with the responsibility of an undertaking of such magnitude," Rutenberg asked Brandeis if there were some American Jews that could head such a program. He was prepared to handle the Palestine end of such an organization.[33] By January 1939, he wrote Brandeis that he was making some better progress with the British Jews. Baron James de Rothschild had promised two hundred thousand British Pounds Sterling and he believed that if "American Jewry will fully support me in my endeavors," the prime minister and the colonial secretary would change their policy.[34]

Rutenberg continued the fight. Others like Wise apparently gave up because they believed that the fight could not be won in view of British government attitudes. As Wise saw it the British officials had made up their minds. They would "yield as much as necessary to the Arabs and deny as much as necessary to the Jews."[35]

At this time, there were some influential British Jews who worked actively against Zionism and in effect the survival of the Jewish people. One such individual was Sir Herbert Samuel. Speaking in the House of Lords in early 1939, Sir Samuel, former high commissioner for Palestine, proposed that Britain impose a limitation on Jewish immigration to Palestine. He called for the liquidation of the Mandate and the Balfour Declaration and he justified his appointment of the Haj Amin el-Husseini as Mufti of Jerusalem: "May I say a word or two in regard to the Mufti, Haj Amin el-Husseini, whose personality has aroused great interest? I was responsible for his appointment, and, looking back over the circumstances of the case, I have no doubt that the appointment was a right one."[36]

The *New Palestine* reported that Samuel was an intruder:

> He intrudes by these utterances upon the negotiations. In effect, he deliberately weakens the position of the Jewish people by continuing to offer peace proposals, without taking into account the opinion of either Jews or Arabs. But this was not the first time that Samuel had done a disservice to the Jewish people. Besides playing an instrumental role in the separation of Trans-Jordan from the Land of Israel in the early 1920's, Lord Samuel on every occasion of crisis, regardless of prevailing Jewish opinion . . . prejudiced the Jewish cause.[37]

The Jews were divided. Some, like Weizmann, Ben-Gurion, Moshe Shertok, and Rutenberg believed that partition could save millions of

Jewish lives from the jaws of the totalitarians and their killers. Others like Szold, Neumann, Jacobs, Brandeis, and Cohen rejected any notion of compromising with the British on a partition plan. They wanted the Jews to have the greater part of the Land of Israel, and they became embroiled in struggles with Weizmann and Ben-Gurion as to who should have control in the Zionist movement. This continued division within the Jewish communities made it easier for the British to reject the Zionist requests and to pursue their appeasement of the Arabs.

When the British sponsored still another Arab-Jewish conference, they invited representatives of Egypt, Saudi Arabia, Yemen, Transjordan, and Iraq. While most of those Arab representatives came from areas that had not achieved independence or sovereignty, the British still permitted them to have a say in the affairs of the Land of Israel. The conference failed and the British issued their White Paper of 1939, which ended British pretexts of establishing a Jewish National Homeland in the Land of Israel.

During the London discussions, the Jewish representatives made it clear that under no circumstances would the Jewish people accept any plan, "no matter how sugar-coated," that was aimed at imposing a minority status on the Jews of the Land of Israel. As Ben-Gurion put it, "The controversy was not between us and the Arabs, but between the Jewish people and the civilized world." The Jewish connection with Israel did not originate in 1917. Jews may have been dispersed but "at no time was Palestine devoid of a Jewish community."[38]

With their policy declaration or White Paper of May 15, 1939, the British closed Palestine to the Jews. Only one hundred thousand Jews were to be admitted to Palestine from 1939 to 1944. After this time period the people of Palestine were to determine their future by means of a plebiscite. The British set no limit on Arab immigration to this land.

Did the closing of Palestine to further Jewish immigration help the British Empire cause? Iraqi leaders, Anwar al-Sadat of Egypt, Haj Amin el-Husseini of Syria, among other Arab extremists, favored the Nazi German cause.

Weizmann regarded the British and American claim that Jewish immigration would arouse the Arabs to exterminate the Jews of Palestine as an excuse to exclude Jews from entering Palestine. The British seemed more fearful of helping the Jews than of losing Arab cooperation. Or, as he wrote to Marshall Jan Smuts, the Allies were afraid that the next war would be called a Jewish war: "Developments in the Middle East have been utilized by the Arab leaders to achieve a very advantageous position: when loyal they have to be rewarded; when rebellious they have to be placated, and it would be tactless to mention the case or the rights of the Jews. This is a situation in which the Jewish people and their leaders cannot acquiesce." Weizmann thought that after the war some four million uprooted Jews would try to make their home in Palestine and they would not seek the "impractical, non-operative dream of neo-territorialist projects." Only the Land of Israel would do. The Jews would never permit that land to become an Arab country nor would they let the United States disclaim its responsibilities there. As Weizmann saw it, pressure would be brought to bear to make the United States help create a Jewish Land of Israel.[39]

American Zionist leaders had tried to get some sort of U.S. intervention to stop the British from issuing their White Paper restrictions. But those efforts brought no concrete results. Roosevelt did ask the British not to issue their White Paper restrictions, but the British responded with a request that the United States join them in the Mandate over Palestine. The United States would not do so and it ceased its criticism of British policy. The leaders of the Zionist movement and, in particular, the American end of it, realized that their influence was severely limited.

On May 22, 1939, Rabbi Wise met with Secretary of State Cordell Hull and recalled that years ago American Zionists had thought that it had "been a good thing that the Balfour Declaration had been written in English rather than in German, but the way the Chamberlain Government was now acting the Balfour Declaration might well have been written in German." He advised Secretary Hull that Jews would not accept "a minority status in their own Homeland."[40]

The secretary of state reassured Wise that the United States had made every effort to be helpful: "You know, Rabbi Wise, that from the beginning we exerted every possible influence on the British officials. This influence was brought up until the very day of the issuance of the White Paper. We have gone beyond any boundaries in our effort to be of service in this matter. We have hammered away on American interest in the problem up until the last moment." But all of this could not be made public, said Hull, because of "an awful state of nationalistic sentiment in this country since the League of Nations fight." Hull complained that he was surrounded by groups of isolationists. Wise chose to disregard Hull's excuses. Once again he repeated the deep concern that Jews had over the future of the Land of Israel. More than one million American Jews had repeated the oath: "If I forget thee O Jerusalem, may my right hand wither."[41]

Some American Zionists were impressed by their accomplishments. Solomon Goldman felt that American Zionists had accomplished a great deal in the spring and summer of 1939. He believed that American Zionists had been "awakened from their lethargy" by the White Paper. There were twenty thousand new members in the Zionist organization and a Washington bureau had been established.[42] There had been visits to the White House, including two such visits by Justice Brandeis. "Felix Frankfurter and Benjamin V. Cohen have frequently discussed Palestine with the President. Dr. Wise and I have also been at the White House." And from all of those visits Goldman concluded that President Roosevelt had "the finest understanding" and "deepest sympathy with our movement." Roosevelt reportedly believed that some two to three hundred thousand Arabs could and "must be moved from Palestine to Iraq." This move would cost some $300 million. The Jewish people would provide $100 million, Britain and France would furnish $100 million, and the United States would likewise provide $100 million. Roosevelt noted that some three hundred thousand Arabs had entered Palestine since 1917. Goldman had confidence in the goodwill of Roosevelt, but he was suspicious of the State Department where there "are secretaries and under-secretaries and under-under secretaries and some of them have not escaped the virus anti-Semiticus."[43] Among those responsible for this were the British diplomats who poured "into their ears praise of the Arabs and condemnation of the Jews."[44]

Days after the British issued their White Paper, a Zionist conference was held in Washington, D.C., at which time various members of the U.S. Congress were interviewed on the Land of Israel question. Of the twenty-five members of the Foreign Affairs Committee interviewed, fifteen left protests against the British White Paper at the State Department.[45]

While American Zionists tried to win some political support for the Zionist cause, people in the Land of Israel, responded to the British White Paper with "illegal" immigration, which they called Aliyah Bet. The way to defeat the British White Paper, suggested Ben-Gurion, was to bring in thousands of Jews to the Land of Israel every week. This could be done with a minimum of cost and if it were done the British could do little to prevent immigration and the defeat of the White Paper.

Did the Jews of Europe want to go to the Land of Israel? Did establishment Zionists want to see all of Europe's Jews in Palestine? Available documentation provides no definitive answer to those questions. Some documents seem to indicate that at least some of the Zionists like Ben-Gurion, Weizmann, Richard Lichtheim, and Leo Herman seemed to have favored selective immigration. Ben-Gurion's letter of June 6, 1939, to Justice Brandeis reflected that viewpoint:

> We have in the minimum of time to bring the maximum of immigrants, but immigrants of the right type, well trained, devoted and ready to make sacrifices in order to ensure the defeat of the policy now adopted by the Government.
>
> . . . we can depend only on ourselves. The establishment of a force strong enough to decide the issue when the time comes.[46]

On November 14, 1940, Ben-Gurion addressed the Emergency Committee for Zionist Affairs on the need for greater militant action. While Zionists should continue to help the British in their efforts to destroy Adolf Hilter, they should take every possible measure to "reverse" the White Paper policy "so as to absorb a maximum number of Jews from Europe in the shortest possible time." It was folly to "suppose that the British Government would of its own accord risk a quarrel with the Arabs" or that the United States would side with the Jews against the will of Great Britain. The only way to save the future would be to build up Jewish strength during the war so that at the end it would be "impossible, or at least very difficult" for the British to implement the White Paper. Ben-Gurion advised that in order to do so it was necessary to establish new settlements, to build up defenses, and to "bring in as many young people to Palestine as possible and to acquire new land." It was absolutely necessary to have a Jewish army. It was "a political and moral necessity from a purely Zionist as well as from a general Jewish point of view." With a Jewish army the Jewish people would help defeat Hitler, and a Jewish army could play a major role in the Middle East theater of operations during the war.[47]

In November 1940, Rabbi Abba Hillel Silver thought it paramount to do everything to save the Jews of Europe and the Jews of the Land of Israel. "Relief for the suffering thousands on European soil is essential. Maximum help must be given [to] those unfortunate men and women who have been caught in the maelstrom of war and who have been overtaken by persecution and disaster." But even more "statesmanship would recognize the fact that we have a paramount duty to save the one community which, allied with Great Britain, is engaged in a task the ultimate goal of which is the liberation of the Jews of Europe, as well as of Palestine." Rabbi Silver underlined the last line of his message to Szold which read: "Any act tending to weaken the Yishuv, jeopardizing its ability to maintain its structure, would be construed as a desertion of the Jewish National Home, as a desertion of Palestinian Jewry in the most difficult hour in its history."[48]

But, at times, there seemed to have been an antipathy toward illegal immigration among the ranks of some of the so-called Zionist leadership. On November 27, 1934, Herman, an executive in the American Zionist movement, favored legal immigrants who had prepared for the life in Palestine and waited "for years and years for a visa." He warned the Zionist Executive "not to be involved in the illegal smuggling otherwise the Zionist Organization would be unable to negotiate with the Palestine Government on the question of legal immigration."[49]

Lichtheim, a Jewish Agency representative based in Geneva, Switzerland, in 1940, favored "5,000 carefully chosen legal immigrants to 7,000 or 8,000 illegals."[50]

Others like Rabbi Silver urged that every possible assistance be given to European Jewry, but he was not willing to sacrifice the Jewish community of Palestine for the sake of the Jews of Europe. As Rabbi Silver put it, relief had to be provided for the "thousands on European soil," yet, said Silver, "the paramount duty was to save the one community which, allied with Great Britain is engaged in a task the ultimate goal of which [was] the liberation of the Jews of Europe, as well as of Palestine." He stressed that anything which tended to "weaken the Yishuv" and thereby jeopardized "its ability to maintain its structure, would be construed as a desertion of the Jewish National Home" and a desertion at "the most difficult hour in its history."[51]

The British government did everything possible to prevent and stop Jewish immigration to Palestine. They even went so far as to claim that some of the immigrants were Nazi agents and that the Nazis had promised the Arabs independence if they helped the Axis powers win the war. British officials claimed that by sending Jews to Palestine, the Germans were systematically inflaming the Arabs against Britain and the Allied military position was thereby endangered. Neville Butler of the British embassy in Washington tried to advise Rabbi Wise on November 25, 1940, that the

> Axis powers are encouraging an influx of Jews to Palestine (giving them the choice of embarking on a ship for Palestine or of remaining in a concentration camp) their object being not only to embarrass His Majesty's Government by inflaming Arab sentiment, but to introduce enemy agents into Palestine and the Middle East. His Majesty's Government are persuaded that to admit into Palestine any further shiploads of illegal immigrants and to allow the law of Palestine to be openly flouted would undoubtedly involve risk of serious trouble with the Arabs and jeopardize the whole British military position in the Middle East. It is hoped that when it has been widely known that immigrants without permits will not be able to gain admission into Palestine, but will be sent abroad for detention the practice even with the Axis' encouragement, will cease.[52]

Rabbi Wise tried to have the French approve the transit of Jews from Syria to Palestine. But the French refused to cooperate.[53]

Two years later, after nearly four million Jews had been murdered by the Nazis and their collaborators, Ben-Gurion observed that American officials had been subjected to anti-Zionist "poisonous propaganda" that had come from pro-Arab circles, the British Colonial Office, as well as anti-Zionist Jewish circles.[54]

On March 19, 1942, Undersecretary Sumner Welles advised Rabbi Wise that some American officials believed that the Germans were using refugees to transport Nazi agents to Palestine. Wise asked Welles to be more judicious in his thinking. Why should the Nazis use such methods of "getting into Turkey and Palestine?" There were much "more pleasant ways" for the Nazis to get their people there. Moreover, there already was a German colony in Palestine and the Nazis could recruit them easily.[55]

The British White Paper of May 15, 1939, brought Jewish immigration to Palestine to a virtual standstill. To enforce their rule, the British sent out more naval patrols and they built additional radar stations. They took such measures in order to catch Jews who were trying to escape the Nazis and to enter Palestine. In the course of World War II, 1939–1945, some thirty-six ships tried to break through the British blockade of Palestine. Five sank or were sunk and most of the rest were seized by the British. The people on board were seized and detained by the British authorities. Jews who had managed to escape the Nazis were captured by the British and imprisoned in British camps.

On February 26, 1939, Justice Brandeis sent Chamberlain a message to persuade him not to restrict Jewish immigration under the present circumstances, but Chamberlain refused to listen. Brandeis to Chamberlain:

> I cannot believe that your Government has fully considered how gravely shattered would be the faith of the people of this troubled world in the solemn undertakings of even democratic governments if Great Britain so drastically departed from her declared policy in reference to the Jewish National Home. I urge you to consider the cruel plight of the Jews in the world today and not to crush their most cherished and sanctified hopes.[56]

On April 19, 1939, Weizmann urged Justice Brandeis to intervene with President Roosevelt and to ask him to prevent the British from issuing their White Paper. He warned in a telegram that the White Paper would not stop the Jewish people from rebuilding their homeland in Palestine:

> Beg you make last minute effort induce President urge British Government delay publication their proposals and reconsider their policy STOP
>
> Please convey President Yishuv united resolute determination oppose all its strength contemplated new policy STOP
>
> Promised liquidation mandate establishment independent Palestine State coupled with reduction Jewish population to one third total and with restricted area STOP
>
> Jewish hopes and surrender Jewish community Palestine to rule Arab terrorist Junta and as tantamount to establishment Jewish Ghetto in small corner of country STOP
>
> This policy will I am convinced defeat his Majesty's Government's object pacification country STOP
>
> Will compel Government use force against Jews will engender unnecessary bitterness between Jews and Arabs and drive Jews who have nothing to lose anyhow to adhere to counsels of despair STOP

> Jews determined to make supreme sacrifice rather than submit to such regime STOP
>
> If new policy imposed Jews will conduct immigration disregard legal restrictions will settle land without permission even if exposed British bayonets STOP
>
> While abstaining physical attacks upon British forces will place every obstacle in way execution policy even if this involves Jews being shot by Government forces STOP
>
> By violation mandate British Government loses moral and legal title government country and becomes more coercive authority STOP[57]

State Department officials like Wallace Murray found the White Paper to be "as reasonable a compromise between Jewish and Arab aspirations as it is practicable to attempt to affect at this time." Roosevelt seemed unwilling to accept the British interpretation of their Mandate over Palestine, but he would not fight them. He promised Wise that he would do all he could, but when the rabbi asked Secretary of State Hull to persuade the British to postpone implementation of the White Paper, Hull insisted that Roosevelt had done all he could despite the highly nationalistic and isolationist spirit in America. Moreover, the State Department found American Jews greatly divided on the Palestine homeland idea. And if they were so divided why should the American government go out of its way on behalf of an unsupported cause? Murray summed it up this way: anti-Zionist Jews claimed that the great majority of American Jews had no interest in the creation of a Jewish state in Palestine; conservative Jewish leaders like Felix Warburg, Cyrus Adler, and others of the American Jewish Committee were ordinarily opposed to Zionism, but because of the persecution of Jews in Europe they joined Zionists in pressuring Britain into opening up Palestine to Jews. Murray believed that as places of refuge would be found for Jews, the anti-Zionist Jews would revert to "their natural role of opposing the establishment of an eventual Jewish State in Palestine" and the United States would not have to support Zionist claims. On September 17, 1937, Murray observed that in

> view of this clear division of opinion among the representatives of American Jewry it seems to me that we are in a strong position to request that they come to some agreement among themselves before they approach us with a view to our taking any particular line of action. In other words we seem to be in good position to ask Rabbi Wise to produce some proof that he speaks on behalf of all of American Jewry before we comply with any specific requests that he may make.[58]

Roosevelt did ask Chamberlain not to issue the White Paper, but Chamberlain's reply was that Britain would refrain from its new policy only if the United States would contribute a force of five hundred thousand troops to keep the peace in the Middle East. America had no such capability at that time and Roosevelt withdrew his objections to the White Paper.

Leaders of the Jewish communities in America were divided on the question of the future state as they were on the rescue of European Jewry, as people had been through much of history. This division enabled Roosevelt and State Department officials like Murray to find additional excuses for not taking effective steps to fulfill previous U.S. commitments. It was easy for Murray to say "first come to some agreement amongst yourselves, then come to see us."

Throughout the catastrophic Holocaust years, anti-Zionist Jews continued to present their anti-Zionist views to the Roosevelt administration. On September 25, 1943, Morris D. Waldman, executive vice president of the American Jewish Committee, wrote to Murray that

> the promise of a Jewish political nationhood flies in the face of 2,000 years of Jewish history; that it is a denial of the rights won by Jews since their emancipation; that the theory and existence of a World Jewish Congress is a singular innovation in international affairs and that it threatens to work damaging effect upon the status of Jews in all countries; that it is especially obnoxious to American Jews because it is repugnant to the spirit of American democracy which tolerates variety only in religious and cultural institutions but does not tolerate racial and religious political minorities; a democracy that encourages religious, racial and cultural loyalties, but does not suffer hyphenated or divided political allegiance.[59]

If American Zionists felt badly about the British policy, the Yishuv of Palestine felt doubly betrayed. Not only had the British let them down but so did the Americans. According to a confidential report from Palestine the British police were "guilty of such atrocities as to make one wonder why Nazis alone are decried as barbarians. They beat children and made Jews run the gauntlet."[60]

While most American Zionists may have meant well, their continual interference in the life of Palestinian Jewry was too much to bear. A report to Brandeis revealed American Jews as interfering and seeking to mold Palestine in their own image. They placed their influence behind "minority parties" so as to weaken the influence of the Histadrut. "It is ludicrous to use American influence to strengthen the hands of Rabbi Berlin, Separsky, Emanuel Neumann, Mossinsohn and Kolodni as against Ben-Gurion, Shertok, Kaplan, Katznelson, Hartzfeld or Kaplanski." Yet that was exactly what some American Jews were trying to do. They wanted the direction of Zionism to come from America rather than from Europe or Palestine. But in their efforts to reshuffle the Zionist executive they deepened the "divisiveness in the country by their emphasis on Americans *qua* Americans." They believed that "being an American was a virtue" and that it entitled them to "special recognition." Those Americans were "strutting about the country as overweening patrons, rich uncles, big-hearted but also somewhat paunch-bellied" leaders. They constantly overstated their Americanism, and the "large sums American Jewry was contributing to the Yishuv." This was what some American Zionists were reportedly doing in September 1939.[61] This was not useful under the circumstances of war and the Nazi terror in Europe. Instead of helping to unite the Jews and to help save European Jewry, according to this report, they were fostering distrust, divisiveness, and destruction.[62]

The American Zionist movement was weak, timid, and divided and it interfered with the Jews of Palestine. During an executive meeting of the Zionist Organization of America in 1939, Ben-Gurion declared that Zionism was too modest a movement in America and he urged the American Zionists to change and have courage, and that they should "court the Jewish people." He wanted them to at least appear united.[63]

Ben-Gurion found that Palestine had been "left out of Zionism because the Jews did not dare" to "appear under the Zionist flag and raise money only for Palestine." A united and strong stance was especially important in view of the forces behind the Arab world. "We must mobilize what we can" for "we have only the unorganized stateless Jewish people." He believed that America was the one "logical place" to organize the Jewish people since Europe was under siege by Nazis and Fascists; and England was "largely dependent" on the United States in case of war.[64]

One approach to the challenge that faced the American Zionist movement was the formation of an Emergency Committee for Palestine whose main task it was to "create a strong pro-Zionist public opinion in the United States and to transform it into effective political support."[65]

The program of activities as far as American Zionists were concerned was to include: the cultivation of friendships of influential people and leaders of public opinion in all walks of life; establishment and maintenance of good relations with important American groups, associations, churches, and religious institutions; the formation of non-Jewish pro-Zionist and pro-Palestine groups; the publication of literature dealing with Jewish issues such as Zionism by such authors as Dorothy Thompson, Stefan Zweig, and John Gunther; and the promotion of cooperation among all Zionist organizations for a common plan and assistance to the Haganah.[66]

In his statement before the American Zionist Emergency Council on November 14, 1940, Ben-Gurion urged that the Jews proceed with their efforts to reestablish their homeland in Palestine:

> The only realistic Zionist policy at present which could reasonably hope to bring about a change of Britain's policy in Eretz Israel at the end of the war is the development of such adamant Jewish strength during the war as would, at its conclusion make impossible, or at least very difficult, the implementation of the White Paper.
>
> This new strength could in the first place be derived from an increase in our position in Palestine through continued immigration, the establishment of new agricultural settlements and the strengthening of our defense forces in the country. While war conditions and the new legislation clearly impede our efforts in that direction, progress is not impossible, and it is necessary to exert ourselves to the maximum to bring in as many young people to Eretz Israel as possible and to acquire new land and found new settlements.[67]

Meeting with Zionist leaders in America in early December 1940, Ben-Gurion called for the creation of a unified Zionist policy. The lack of "concerted" and "far-sighted policy" was one of the "deepest causes of the calamity" that befell Europe and European Jewry. "We cannot live from hand to mouth." He pleaded for "a clear objective or objectives in the immediate future, during the war and at the end of the war." Ben-Gurion, like some other Jewish leaders outside of Europe, did not seem to have much hope for European Jewry when he added that "for the time being, we are left with only two communities which have any real significance—the Yishuv in Palestine and the Jewry in America."[68]

In July 1941, Weizmann called for a change of relations with Britain. He insisted that the Zionist movement become more assertive and openly proclaim its goals.

Weizmann called for a Zionist conference that would formulate Zionist "demands" and that would establish a "political fund" for such necessities as "a press and books and pamphlets and everything required for the enlightenment of public opinion."[69]

But he found that many of his colleagues and that some so-called Zionists were opposed to such public declarations and open gatherings.

Nahum Goldmann, of the World Jewish Congress, opposed Weizmann's suggestions and called for a quiet meeting with no public pronouncements on Zionist goals. He believed that for as long as there was no democratic military victory in sight and the Arabs still had "their great nuisance value it would be very bad to proclaim our aims." He believed that by January or February 1942, the Near East might be threatened by the Nazis again and that this would provide the Arabs with much more of a "nuisance value than they have had." The time for proclaiming "our aims," said Goldmann, would be when the Allied victory would be at hand.[70]

Rabbi Israel Goldstein and Neumann supported Weizmann. Goldstein believed that "the great majority of American Jews were not yet convinced of the Zionist thesis that Palestine was virtually the only solution," and he felt that an open proclamation and an open conference would help bring them closer to that realization.

Weizmann felt that Goldmann and his crew had swallowed up the British point of view that since they were at war nothing should be done to embarrass them. Weizmann was unwilling to sit tight and do nothing. He wanted to see the British win the war, but he would not accept the British argument that the "Arabs have a nuisance value and that their nuisance value may increase." Weizmann wanted to see a "Jewish nuisance value" created. Weizmann felt that Goldmann and his crew were echoing the British viewpoint. "The British . . . have got us where they want us," they created a climate of opinion that nothing could be done to embarrass them since they were at war. Weizmann was no longer willing to sit tight and do nothing. After working with the British for more than twenty years he concluded that the British were not afraid of the Arabs, but of the Jews. It was about time that the British stopped playing with the White Paper and the Arab question. As he saw it, "for two years we sat tight and swallowed every possible ignominy. We did not want to embarrass them. But we believe we have a contribution to make to victory and that they should know what we want to do for the Jews in Palestine." He insisted that the Zionist movement openly proclaim its goals. As he saw it,

> whatever the Arabs will have, will be due to the efforts of England and America, so that if England and America really both had political acumen, courage, and a desire to settle the Jewish problem decently, they can do it now. Therefore, it reduces itself to an effort on our part to make clear to England and America what they have to do in order to bring about what I call a decent solution to the Jewish problem. Perhaps I ought to define. . . . I mean the opening up of Palestine in a way that it should absorb, within . . . 20 years . . . about three million Jews, particularly the younger generation. The older generation is either broken or doomed to be broken.[71]

Weizmann proposed a confederation with the Arabs. Jews would have Palestine minus the triangle, "in other words, the cutting out of the district which is absolutely purely Arabic." Only Palestine would do and he believed that the great powers would soon realize "that all of their prospects for sending Jews to South America, and here and there was just . . . a soap bubble."[72]

Weizmann believed that support and sympathy would come from President Roosevelt, Secretary of State Hull, Undersecretary of State Welles, as well as members of Congress. But he anticipated that there would be trouble from State Department people who were "definitely against" and who took "their cue from the British." It was therefore necessary to pull all resources together to meet the forthcoming challenges.[73]

The British continued their blockade of Palestine and they maintained strict censorship. When the *Patria* sank, they censored all reports from the Palestine homeland. Many American officials, including Secretary of the Treasury Henry Morgenthau, appeared to be unaware of the facts. Bernard Joseph of the Jewish Agency advised him on March 4, 1941, of how the British had prevented immigrants from entering their homeland, and how the British high commissioner had planned to keep survivors of the *Patria* in concentration camps outside of Palestine if not for Weizmann's intervention with Prime Minister Winston Churchill. After hearing this, Morgenthau said that he was prepared "to spank the British for their stupidity" and then he wanted to know how the Jews of Palestine felt towards the new immigrants. Would they welcome more immigrants? There were no restrictions as far as the Yishuv was concerned, said Joseph. They were prepared to welcome as many Jews as would come. They were "only too glad to be able to help them from their persecution in Europe." Morgenthau promised to help.

Justice Brandeis called for firmness and determination:

> We must not waiver or yield one iota of our position. Assuming that the Germans will do their worst, invade and obliterate part of what we have created, they cannot destroy Jewish ideals and aspirations with regard to Palestine. There are 500,000 Jews in Palestine now, but there are millions of others prepared to go . . . to continue.
>
> It has been established that the Jews require a state of their own for their continued existence. The Germans have established that fact.
>
> The Jews have established their capacity to build such a state. That is the essential ground work for the future effort.[74]

Neither the American nor the British governments would cooperate with the Brandeis, Weizmann, Ben-Gurion, or Jabotinsky elements of the Zionist movements. Adolph A. Berle, assistant secretary of state, insisted that the Arabs would not support the Allies if they feared "increased political dominion by the Zionist groups." He advised Weizmann to see the main point "namely, that if the Mediterranean is closed, the extermination of the Zionists in Palestine is only a question of time." Perhaps, suggested Berle, a deal could be made with the Arabs. Perhaps the United States could get King Ibn Sa'ūd to promise the Jews protection. He thought that it would be wise for the Jews to come to terms with the Arabs since the British might be forced to evacuate the area. If the Jews would give up their plans to build a Jewish state in Palestine and choose to move to Africa, the Allies might help them achieve a token state in Palestine as well as a refuge in the highlands of Ethiopia.[75] But Murray, assistant secretary of state for Middle Eastern Affairs, doubted that the Arabs would make any deal with the Jews as long as they felt that they had the power to exterminate them.[76]

NOTES

1. Chaim Weizmann, *Trial and Error* (New York, 1966), p. 395.
2. Chaim Weizmann, interview with Colonial Secretary Ormsby-Gore, February 25, 1938, Robert Szold Papers, Box 26, File 22, Zionist Archives, New York.
3. Ibid.
4. Ibid.
5. Ibid.
6. Ibid.
7. Ibid.
8. Stephen S. Wise to Robert Szold, March 1, 1938, Robert Szold Papers, Box 26, File 18, Zionist Archives, New York.
9. Ibid.
10. Ibid.
11. Rose Jacobs to Moshe, March 27, 1938, Robert Szold Papers, Box 26, File 18, Zionist Archives, New York.
12. Emanuel Neumann to Robert Szold, September 13, 1938, Robert Szold Papers, Box 26, File 22, Zionist Archives, New York.
13. Ibid.
14. Benjamin V. Cohen to Robert Szold, September 12, 1938, Robert Szold Papers, Box 26, File 22, Zionist Archives, New York.
15. Ibid.
16. Ibid.
17. Benjamin V. Cohen to Robert Szold, September 6, 1938, Robert Szold Papers, Box 26, Files 22, Zionist Archives, New York.
18. Benjamin V. Cohen to Robert Szold, September 29, 1938, Robert Szold Papers, Box 26, File 22, Zionist Archives, New York.
19. Ibid.
20. Notes of meeting between Pincus Rutenberg and Horace Wilson and Lord Hirst, November 9, 1938, Robert Szold Papers, Box 25, File 16, Zionist Archives, New York.
21. Notes on meeting between Pincus Rutenberg and Ramsay MacDonald, November 17, 1938, Robert Szold Papers, Box 25, File 116, Zionist Archives, New York.
22. Minutes of meeting between Pincus Rutenberg and Ramsay MacDonald, October 5, 1938, Robert Szold Papers, Box 25, File 16, Zionist Archives, New York.
23. Ibid. Earlier, in March of 1935, Morris Margulies, secretary of the Zionist Organization of America advised Leo Herman of the United Jewish Appeal, that some nineteen thousand dunams of land in Transjordan were open for purchase. The land was some twenty minutes by car from Amman, and he wanted to know if American Zionists were prepared to purchase it. Herman believed that Zionists were interested in such a proposition, but that the attitude of the Transjordanian

government was in such a state of flux that he did not know if such a deal could be concluded. Morris Margulies to Leo Herman, March 22, 1935, Individuals Files (Small Collections, Leo Herman Files), Zionist Archives, New York.

In 1933 Emanuel Neumann had planned a Development Corporation for Transjordan. This plan aimed to help initiate the creation of Jewish settlements there. King Emir Abdullah of Jordan and the British seemed to have been in agreement with this project and Neumann even received some financial backing from such individuals as Justice Brandeis. But the unsettled conditions within the Zionist movement made it virtually impossible for him to continue with the project. Perhaps Neumann was referring to the division within the Zionist community after the Peel report of 1936. See Emanuel Neumann, *In the Arena* (New York, 1976), p. 134.

24. Minutes of meeting between Pincus Rutenberg and Ramsay MacDonald, October 10, 1938, Robert Szold Papers, Box 25, File 16, Zionist Archives, New York.

25. Minutes of Pincus Rutenberg interview with King Emir Abdullah, December 29, 1938, Robert Szold Papers, Box 6, File 19, Zionist Archives, New York.

26. Minutes of Pincus Rutenberg and Ramsay MacDonald conversations of October 5, 1938, Robert Szold Papers, Box 25, File 16, Zionist Archives, New York.

27. Ibid.

28. Ibid.

29. Notes on meeting between Secretary of State for the Colonies Ramsay MacDonald and Pincus Rutenberg, October 19, 1938, Robert Szold Papers, Box 25, File 16, Zionist Archives, New York.

30. Notes of Ramsay MacDonald meetings with Pincus Rutenberg and Chaim Weizmann, November 17, 18, 1938, Robert Szold Papers, Box 25, File 16, Zionist Archives, New York; Pincus Rutenberg to Justice Louis D. Brandeis, November 25, 1938, Robert Szold Papers, Box 25, File 16, Zionist Archives, New York.

31. Ibid.

32. Ibid.

33. Ibid.

34. Pincus Rutenberg to Justice Louis D. Brandeis, January 6, 1939, Robert Szold Papers, Box 6, File 19, Zionist Archives, New York.

35. Stephen S. Wise to Justice Louis D. Brandeis, December 6, 1938, Robert Szold Papers, Box 25, File 16, Zionist Archives, New York.

36. Internal Press Review, January 2, 1939, World Zionist Organization Papers, Zionist Archives, New York.

37. Ibid.

38. Confidential Report of "Developments on Palestine Discussions, March 9, 1939." Jewish Agency Papers, Zionist Archives, New York.

39. Chaim Weizmann to Field Marshall Jan Smuts, August 15, 1941, Robert Szold Papers, Zionist Archives, New York.

40. Stephen S. Wise Memo, May 22, 1939, Robert Szold Papers, Zionist Archives, New York.

41. Ibid.

42. Solomon Goldman to Chaim Weizmann, June 20, 1939. Jewish Agency Papers, Zionist Archives, New York.

43. Ibid.
44. Ibid.
45. Ibid.
46. David Ben-Gurion to Justice Louis D. Brandeis, June 6, 1939, Robert Szold Papers, Unsorted Materials, Zionist Archives, New York.
47. Statement by David Ben-Gurion to the Emergency Committee for Zionist Affairs, November 14, 1940, Robert Szold Papers, Addendum Box #5, Unsorted Materials, Zionist Archives, New York.
48. Rabbi Abba Hillel Silver to Robert Szold, November 28, 1940, Robert Szold Papers, Box 27, Zionist Archives, New York.
49. Leo Herman's Report of illegal immigration to Mayer Steinglass of Zionist Organization of America, November 27, 1934, Individual Files, Zionist Archives, New York.
50. Richard Lichtheim to Kaplan, March 31, 1940, Jewish Agency Papers, Zionist Archives, New York.
51. Rabbi Abba Hillel Silver to Robert Szold, November 28, 1940, Robert Szold Papers, Box 27, Zionist Archives, New York.
52. Neville Butler to Stephen S. Wise, November 25, 1940, Robert Szold Papers, Zionist Archives, New York.
53. Stephen S. Wise to Gaston Henri Haye, November 14, 1940; Haye to Wise, November 22, 1940, Robert Szold Papers, Zionist Archives, New York.
54. David Ben-Gurion Memorandum of January 1942, Individuals Files A-C, Zionist Archives, New York.
55. Notes of a March 19, 1942, meeting at the State Department, State Department Files, Zionist Archives, New York.
56. The Robert Szold Papers, Unsorted Boxes, Robert Szold Home, Westchester, New York.
57. Robert Szold Papers, Unsorted Boxes, Zionist Archives, New York.
58. U.S. Department of State, *Foreign Relations of the United States, 1937*, Volume II, (Washington, D.C., 1954) September 17, 1937, pp. 909–992.
59. Morris D. Waldman to Wallace Murray, September 25, 1943, State Department File No. 867N.01/1993, National Archives.
60. Confidential Report to Justice Brandeis, September 5, 1939, Jewish Agency Papers, Unsorted Boxes, Zionist Archives, New York.
61. Ibid.
62. Ibid.
63. David Ben-Gurion before executive meeting of Zionist Organization of America 1939, Files, Box 1940, Zionist Archives, New York.
64. Ibid.
65. Memo on Program of Work and Organization of Palestine Emergency Committee, September 12, 1940, Robert Szold Papers, Box 30 XIV/14, Zionist Archives, New York.
66. Ibid.
67. American Zionist Emergency Council Papers, Zionist Archives, New York.
68. Individuals Files, Zionist Archives, New York.
69. Notation of meeting held on July 17, 1941, at the Astor Hotel, New York, Benjamin Akzin Papers, Zionist Archives, New York.
70. Ibid.

71. Notation of July 17, 1941, meeting at the Astor Hotel, New York, Benjamin Akzin Papers, Zionist Archives, New York.

72. Ibid.

73. Ibid.

74. Justice Louis D. Brandeis to Emanuel Neumann, April 15, 1941, Robert Szold Papers, Zionist Archives, New York.

75. Emanuel Neumann, *In the Arena*, pp. 157–159.

76. Ibid.

4

"Illegal" Aliyah

In 1939, the British issued their White Paper that closed Palestine almost entirely to Jewish immigration. No more than one hundred thousand Jews were to be admitted to Palestine from 1939 to 1944. At a time when Germany sought to eliminate Jewry from the face of the earth, the British closed the one place that could have offered them asylum. At a time when the British needed their forces to defend Britain's shores from a German invasion, they sent army, navy, air, and other vital defense forces to patrol the frontiers of Palestine and to keep Jews from finding refuge in Palestine.

Aliyah Bet or "illegal immigration" to Palestine was promoted by almost every branch of the Zionist movement and the Palestinian Jewish community. Especially active were the Irgun and the Jewish Agency. To date there stirs controversy between the descendants of the Revisionists and the Labor Zionists as to who did the utmost to help rescue the Jews of Europe during the war. While the controversy prospers, the disputants forget one vital fact of the wartime: not David Ben-Gurion's group, Menachem Begin's Irgun, or any other Jewish group had the power, military or otherwise, to combat the military and diplomatic might of the British Empire and the German Nazis. In the end, no matter how much they may have wanted to rescue the Jews, the possibility to do so was inhibited by the circumstances of the war and the power of the belligerents.

Despite all the obstacles that the Arabs and British placed in the way of Jewish immigration, Ben-Gurion campaigned for the Jewish people to continue their efforts to reestablish their homeland in Palestine. He urged that they work to increase their strength in Palestine so that during and after the war the British would see great "Jewish strength" and it would be "impossible, or at least very difficult" for the British to continue implementing the White Paper. This had to be done through increased immigration, the establishment of new agricultural settlements, and the "strengthening of our defense forces in the country." "We need to exert ourselves to the maximum to bring in as many young people to Eretz Israel as possible and to acquire new land and found new settlements." In his address before the American Zionist Emergency Council on November 14, 1940, Ben-Gurion appraised British-American policies realistically when he said that a reversal of the 1939 White Paper policy could not be expected since the British were preoccupied with the war effort and with the factors that led to the issuance of the White Paper.

The "maximum" effort had to be exerted to "bring in as many young people to Palestine as possible and to acquire new land and to found new settlements." Under the circumstances of the war it would be unthinkable if the Jewish people did not help the Allies defeat the Nazis. The Jewish people would not be absolved from "the judgment of history" unless they as Jews contributed to the "destruction of the greatest enemy that had ever arisen against the very existence of the Jewish people."[1]

One of the leading proponents of a massive Aliyah (immigration to the land of Israel) was Zeev Jabotinsky. While the Ben-Gurion–Chaim Weizmann group tried to exercise great caution when dealing with the British Mandate power, Jabotinsky's Revisionists wanted more direct action irrespective of British rules and regulations. Jabotinsky had tried to encourage Europe's Jews to emigrate to Palestine, even though few Jews had taken him seriously and by 1939 it was too late. In March 1940 he spoke to American Jews of the need to rescue the Jews of Europe, but again they did not listen to him. While on a speaking tour he died in Hunter, New York, on August 5, 1940.

But at times some of the Zionist leaders and bureaucrats called for selective immigration. Even Ben-Gurion's June 6, 1939, letter to Justice Louis D. Brandeis reflected selective immigration thinking:

> We have in the minimum of time to bring the maximum of immigrants, but immigrants of the right type, well trained, devoted and ready to make sacrifices in order to ensure the defeat of the policy now adopted by the Government. We can depend only on ourselves.
>
> The establishment of a force strong enough to decide the issue when the time comes.[2]

Among some of the Zionist leadership there seemed to have been an antipathy to illegal and unselective immigration as far back as 1934, five years before the British and their White Paper killed Jewish immigration to the Land of Israel almost completely. Leo Herman, one of the American Zionist bureaucrats, complained in November 1934 that east European travel agents, such as in Warsaw, were making small fortunes by forcing Jews to pay three times the ordinary passage rates and then unloading them onto the shores of Egypt, Syria, or the Land of Israel, leaving them to their "fate." He stood opposed to illegal smuggling. He strongly opposed bringing in illegal immigrants in place of legal immigrants who had prepared for the life of the Land of Israel and waited "for years and years for a visa." Herman warned that the Zionist executive should "not be involved in illegal smuggling, otherwise the Zionist Organization would be unable to negotiate with the Palestine Government on the question of legal immigration." He wanted to see "an enlargement of legal immigrants who would prepare themselves for work in Palestine."[3]

One of the most bitter critics of illegal immigration was Richard Lichtheim, a representative of the Zionist Organization in Geneva, Switzerland. Lichtheim, who was a refugee himself that had found refuge in Switzerland, insisted on March 31, 1940, that it was "a fact that the majority of those who came during the last months are not fit for life in Palestine and are a burden on the community." What was the "good" of such immigrants, asked Lichtheim, if the British deduct "the number of illegals from the next schedule." He preferred "5000 carefully chosen legal immigrants to 7,000 or 8,000 illegals"[4]:

> I know what arguments are advanced in favor of illegal immigration. It is said that this is the only way to save a few thousand Jews from Germany and German occupied territories. This could be said during the first months of the war in respect of younger people belonging to the Chalutz type and a certain number of genuine refugees. But then the whole business has degenerated into a very ugly commercial affair conducted by some dozens of private agencies, by the Revisionists, whose organization is living on the money they are getting from their clients, and last but not least by the Gestapo who are now the real "organizers."
>
> If the Jews in America want to help a number of Jews from Germany to leave the country, they should try to get a certain number of visas for America and other neutral countries, but they should not get enthusiastic about the idea of dumping, in company with the Gestapo, ill-fitted refugees into Palestine in the teeth of British resistance and to the detriment of the Zionist cause.[5]

Lichtheim had accepted the British Colonial Office notion that the Germans were smuggling their agents among the refugees. For bureaucrats like Lichtheim there was no room for Jews in the Land of Israel unless they were very carefully selected.

At one point in November 1940, the British had apparently even persuaded Weizmann that the Nazis were smuggling their agents into the Land of Israel. Weizmann sent Ben-Gurion the following telegraph on November 19, 1940:

> Lord Lloyd informs me ships now at Haifa are being followed by another contingent about 1800 now at sea which may be followed by yet others.

Government opinion is that this action may be prelude to wider and more systematic efforts by Nazis now in control of Romanian ports.

This aims first at getting rid of Jews, second at embarrassing British by creating conflicts between Government and ourselves by introduction of German agent provocateurs and using this for propaganda among Arabs.

You must try to prevent rise of feeling which may complicate situation.[6]

Ben-Gurion concurred with Weizmann and said that it was necessary to avoid embarrassing His Majesty's Government. Moreover, if Lord George Ambrose Lloyd's facts were correct, then the simplest way for Britain to avoid embarrassment would be the interception of emigrant ships at the Turkish straits before they even reached the coast of the Land of Israel. But

Regarding 1771 already Haifa first I am reliably informed comprise mainly trained Chaluzim[7] and capitalists who transferred money before war, hundreds having relatives in Palestine. Having already reached Palestine their deportation must inevitably produce great bitterness with undesirable consequences.

Interest already aroused as arrival these boats published. . . .

Urge therefore very strongly their immediate landing.

In order to avoid danger of presence of Nazi agents children and only those adults whose bonafides established beyond reasonable doubt in cooperation with Jewish Agency Jerusalem should be released all others interned for duration.[8]

Such were the opinions of some within the Zionist communities.

British officials worked to persuade Americans that illegal Jewish immigration was bad for the Allies. Neville Butler of the British embassy in Washington D.C., advised Rabbi Stephen S. Wise that the

Axis powers are encouraging an influx of Jews to Palestine giving them the choice of embarking on a ship for Palestine or of remaining in a concentration camp. Their object being not only to embarrass His Majesty's Government by inflaming Arab sentiment, but to introduce enemy agents into Palestine and the Middle East. His Majesty's Government are persuaded that to admit into Palestine any further shiploads of illegal immigrants and to allow the law of Palestine to be openly flouted would undoubtedly involve risk of serious trouble with the Arabs and jeopardize the whole British military position in the Middle East.[9]

In January 1942, Ben-Gurion observed that American officials had been subjected to "poisonous anti-Zionist propaganda" that originated from pro-Arab circles, the British Colonial Office, as well as anti-Zionist Jewish circles.[10] In March 1942, Undersecretary of State Sumner Welles informed Rabbi Wise that some American officials believed that the Germans were using refugees to transport Nazi agents to Palestine. Rabbi Wise asked Secretary Welles if he thought it possible that the Nazis would choose such a way of getting into Turkey and Palestine, and whether he did not think that there were "more pleasant ways."[11]

The British White Paper restrictions of 1939 brought Jewish immigration to a virtual standstill. The British sent out more patrols and built additional radar stations to catch Jews trying to enter Palestine and thereby escape the Germans. From 1939 to 1942, some thirty-six ships tried to break the blockade. Five sank or were sunk and most of the rest were seized by the British. Jewish people had gone through torture and tragedy only to be captured and encamped by the British.

British and American officials claimed that they could not support Jewish immigration to Palestine because the Arabs might be aroused to the point of seeking to kill the Jews of the Land of Israel and endanger the Allied war effort. To Weizmann those arguments seemed no more than convenient excuses. As Weizmann saw it, the British seemed more fearful of helping Jews than of losing Arab cooperation. As he wrote to Marshall Jan Smuts, the Allies were afraid that the war would be called a Jewish war and that was why the Allies refused to help the Jews:

> Developments in the Middle East have been utilized by the Arab leaders to achieve a very advantageous position; when loyal they have to be rewarded; when rebellious they have to be placated, and it would be tactless to mention the case or the rights of the Jews. This is a situation in which the Jewish people and their leaders cannot acquiesce.[12]

As Weizmann saw it, after the war some four million uprooted Jews would seek refuge in Palestine and not in the impractical, nonoperative dream of "neo-territorialist projects." The Jewish people would never permit the Land of Israel to be an Arab country nor would they let America disclaim its responsibilities there. Pressure, said Weizmann, would be brought to bear to make the United States help create a Jewish Land of Israel.[13]

On August 3, 1939, the S.S. *Tiger Hill* ran aground on the shores of Tel Aviv. On board were some fourteen hundred Jews. They were met by thousands of Tel Aviv residents. Some three hundred of the passengers managed to mix with those on shore before the British authorities arrived. The Haganah removed two men killed by shots from British ships. Those who did not make it to shore before the British soldiers arrived were placed in Sarafand, a detention camp. A few weeks later on August 21, another ship ran aground on a beach north of Tel Aviv. Sirens pierced the night air for more than half an hour. Thousands of Jews came to the shore to meet and mingle with the 850 "illegal" immigrants. The landing was successful. The British made a house to house search in order to find the "illegals," but they did not find the newcomers.[14]

During the fall and winter of 1939, the Irgun—Revisionist Zionists—

helped some two thousand Jews from German-occupied territories go down the Danube River to Romania. The Romanian government did not permit them to disembark since they did not have visas to Romania. Jabotinsky, the leader of the Irgun, pleaded their cause with the British government, but the British refused to grant them the right to enter Palestine. His son, Eri Jabotinsky, had chartered the S.S. *Sakarija*, a Turkish ship, and he successfully brought the two thousand people to Haifa. The British permitted them to disembark, but then placed them in a detention camp. Most were released, but Eri was jailed while the British annulled a corresponding number of immigrant visas.[15]

Eri, kept in jail, was sentenced to a year's detention by a British administrator rather than by a court. In a public appeal his father asked: "Is it decent to prosecute a man for helping to save fugitives, in a crisis?" Is it "decent when the British government officials obviously admit that there was nowhere else to take them but to Palestine?"[16]

On March 19, 1940, Vladimir Jabotinsky warned that if the democracies failed then "Jewish fate seems hopeless." If France would fall then Europe's main window to "fresh aid" would fall. Europe would be enveloped in "medievalism right up to the Atlantic shore." It was obvious to Jabotinsky that the Allies did not want Jews as an "ally." Some 130,000 Jews had volunteered to serve in the British armed forces and the British failed to accept them. But he felt that the Allies must make room for a Jewish army and "some kind of Jewish Embassy." Jabotinsky called for the unification of all Jewish organizations and the "uninterrupted free immigration of Jews into Palestine."[17]

THE *ST. LOUIS*

In June 1939, the *St. Louis*, another ship with Jewish refugees, was prevented from reaching Cuba, its destination. The *St. Louis* was a Hamburg Line ship and the 943 passengers were German Jews who had tourist visas for Cuba. Some 743 had quota numbers that would admit them to the United States within a few months. But Loredo Bru, president of Cuba, would not permit them to land unless the Joint Distribution Committee would provide him with a sum of nearly a million dollars. In essence, President Bru wanted bribe money. At first the committee refused, but then it yielded. When the deadline set by Bru passed and the money was not provided, he insisted that the Jews on board the *St. Louis* could not disembark. The United States would not grant the 943 even temporary asylum. It asked U.S. ambassador Joseph P. Kennedy, in London, to help the 943 refugees find asylum in Europe. Kennedy found them refuge in Belgium, France, Holland, and Great Britain.

Kennedy had also tried to persuade the British to make a part of their

African empire available to Jews. While Zionists like Brandeis doubted the sincerity of Ambassador Kennedy, other representatives of the Zionist community believed him to be sincere. On November 2, a few days before the infamous Krystalnacht of November 9 and 10, 1938, when Nazi Germans and Nazi Austrians attacked Jews in the streets of Germany and Austria, set fire to synagogues, and arrested some twenty thousand Jews, a Jewish representative spoke with Ambassador Kennedy.

Kennedy appeared worried about the future of European Jewry and he wanted to help them. He observed that while people "were busy trying to make a better world, the Jews might well be wiped out." He said that he knew how the Jews felt because "as a Catholic in Boston he had reason to know what discrimination meant." He recalled how his father had been unable to find any entree in Boston and how he had "been forced to look elsewhere for a livelihood." But then if it had been difficult for others in the past, the position for the Jews "was a hundred times worse."[18]

Ambassador Kennedy suggested that he might go see Adolf Hitler and discuss the Jewish question with him. The Zionist representative, identified as Mr. X, did not seem to think that it was such a good idea. Mr. X "had heard that this subject was an obsession with Hitler, so that he became virtually insane when it was raised." But Kennedy still said that he "had more than half a mind to pay him such a visit. It might light up a few bonfires in the United States, but all the same he was tempted to intervene."[19]

Weizmann did not have much confidence in Kennedy. Weizmann wrote to Solomon Goldman on May 30, 1939: "I have not much faith in Kennedy."[20] Goldman wrote back on June 20, 1939, that Kennedy had "given us much concern."

Benjamin V. Cohen wrote out of friendship to Ambassador Kennedy and advised him that stories unfair to Kennedy were being circulated in London and that he should "scotch" them.[21]

Kennedy was dismayed that some American Zionists had been so ungrateful to him "after my work for their cause." But he was "getting used to this type of experience." Goldman then sent Kennedy a telegram saying that he had seen the correspondence with Cohen and he felt it his duty to say that "American Zionists have always regarded you as a devoted friend" and that they felt "indebted for the earnestness with which you have furthered the interests of American Jews and the cause of a people whose fate must be of deepest concern to you."[22]

Kennedy appreciated Goldman's message: "I can't tell you how pleased I was to receive your cable. I was really frightfully upset by the one I got from Ben, because while realizing he sent it in the most friendly spirit, it seemed to me that it was another one of those unfortunate things that happened to me no matter how much work I did on the Jewish problem."[23]

On November 20, 1940, the British declared that any refugee who entered or tried to enter Palestine would be interned on the tropical island of Mauritius. With this decree the British were advising the Jews that under no circumstances would they be permitted to live in their homeland. But despite this British move to deny them their rights, some Jews dared an exodus from Europe to their homeland.

As early as November 14, 1940, Ben-Gurion addressed the Emergency Committee for Zionist Affairs on the need for militant action. He observed that everything had to be done to help the British destroy Hitler, but every possible measure had to be taken to "reverse" the White Paper policy so as to absorb a "maximum number of Jews from Europe in the shortest possible time." Ben-Gurion considered it folly to "suppose that the British government would of its own accord risk a quarrel with the Arabs" or that the United States would side with the Jews against the will of the British government. He advised that the only way to save the future would be to build up Jewish strength during the war so that at war's end it would be "impossible, or at least difficult" for the British to implement the White Paper. It was therefore necessary to build up defenses and to "bring in as many young people to Palestine as possible and to acquire new land and furnish new settlements." It was absolutely necessary to have a Jewish army. The army was "a political and moral necessity from a purely Zionist as well as from a general Jewish point of view." The Jews would help defeat Hitler with this Jewish army and at the same time play a major role in the Middle East theater of operations during the war.[24]

The leaky and rundown steamers *Pacific* and *Milos* were intercepted off the coast of Palestine in November 1940, and their nineteen hundred passengers were transferred to the S.S. *Patria,* a captured rusty French ship. The Jews of Palestine asked the British not to ship these people out of the country.

When such appeals proved fruitless, the underground force known as the Haganah decided to forcibly prevent the *Patria* from sailing. Haganah planned to blow a hole in the ship, while Zionists in America, Palestine, and Britain tried to persuade the British to let the Jews stay in Palestine.

On November 25, the Haganah smuggled a bomb on board the ship and detonated it. The *Patria* began to sink almost immediately. The Haganah did not realize that the ship was so completely unseaworthy or that any damage would sink it. Thousands of people in the Haifa Bay area rushed to help. Boats, launches, rowboats—all scurried to save the people. Despite all these efforts, some 250 people were killed. Survivors as well as an additional seventeen hundred passengers that had arrived on board the *Atlantic*, on November 24, were sent to Athlit detention camp, a few miles south of Haifa.

When Haganah discovered that the British planned to transfer these people to the island of Mauritius, some of its leaders like Manya Mardor called for direct action against the British. He proposed that the Jews of Palestine line up along the roads from Athlit to Haifa, the route where the British planned to transport the convoy of immigrants. Jews were to sit on the road and prevent the trucks from passing. Haganah military units would engage the British and help the immigrants escape. Both the Jewish Agency and the Haganah command rejected Mardor's recommendation for direct action against the British.

On December 8, the refugees were told to pack up their belongings and be ready to depart Athlit by 4 A.M. But instead of packing, they stripped and locked themselves in their quarters. The British had bolted the barracks of the refugees from the *Patria* as well as the Jewish policemen of the camp. British soldiers were posted around the perimeter of the camp with loaded machine guns and rifles. They then brought in special police detachments called "toughies." Most of the "toughies" were drunk as they went into the camp to drag out the Jews. But the Jews would not surrender. They barricaded themselves in their quarters and lay there sobbing, crying, and lamenting. This lasted from 4 A.M. to 6 A.M. British soldiers, who could not take the screaming, began to sing as loud as they could. The Jews responded with even louder songs and lamentations. As the British clubbed and carried them out, the Jews screamed: "Where are our brethren? Is there none to help us? Wild beasts are not handled like this. Go tell the world. Tell America!"[25]

Some of the Jews believed in America. But did America care about the Jews? Had President Roosevelt shown that he cared for the Jews of Europe and the Jews of Palestine?

America wanted to remain free of international commitments and involvements. President Roosevelt was concerned with relief, reconstruction, reform, and reelection. Perhaps he was aware of the suffering Jews were going through because individuals like Wise and Brandeis had talked to him about it, but he did little to help. As for American Jews and American Zionists, they continued to be badly divided and they lacked the power to help the Jews of Europe or the Jews of the Land of Israel.

Seventeen hundred Jews were forced to board two Dutch ships bound for the island of Mauritius.

In December 1940, another group tried to make it to shore. The seventy-five-foot sailing ship with 350 passengers from Bulgaria reached the Turkish coast. They were transferred to the ship *Atlantic* and forced out to sea. The ship sank. Two hundred and thirty people lost their lives. Survivors were brought to Istanbul. The British would not let them enter Palestine before March 1941.

Weizmann reminded the British that Palestinian Jews were fighting the Nazis and that Britain was in violation of the Mandate when it prevented Jews from entering Palestine. But British officials rejected his interpretation of the Mandate and they refused to accept the notion that they owed the Jews anything at all for their resistance to the Nazis. The British claimed that they did the Jews the greatest possible service by getting rid of the "present German regime." Britain continued to blockade Palestine and they prevented such ships as the *Struma* from bringing Jews to their homeland.

THE *STRUMA*

The *Struma* left Constanta, Romania, for the homeland in December 1941. Its captain found the ship incapable of making it all the way and he tried to dock at Istanbul, Turkey. The seven hundred sixty-nine survivors of Nazi persecution on board the *Struma* hoped that the Turks might grant them at least temporary asylum. The ship remained in Istanbul for two months in 8 degrees below zero temperature while the Jewish Agency and spokesmen for the American Zionist community like Wise tried to obtain Palestine certificates for the passengers. The British refused to grant the certificates and they worked on the Turks so that Turkish authorities would not permit the Jews to disembark. The British claimed that there were Nazi agents on board the ship. This was a far-fetched notion since the people had come from homogeneous communities where everyone knew everyone else. Although the *Struma* calamity was reported in the newspapers, few political leaders except for a few Jewish personalities protested to help save the Jews on board the *Struma*.

After being anchored at Istanbul harbor for some two months, the *Struma* was towed, by Turkish police boats, some five miles outside the harbor and then cut loose. Jews on board had tried to resist the Turkish police, but they were overcome. The boat's engines were not operational, the sea was mined, and there were submarines in the area. There was an explosion and the *Struma* sank. In all, 768 women, men, and children drowned. One person, David Stoliar, survived. He recalled what had transpired on board that terrible journey:

> The Romanian customs officials still managed to rob most of the passengers of their clothes, linen and jewelry, as well as the canned goods and other food that many had brought along for the journey in case of emergency. Each passenger was allowed only 20 kilograms of baggage. A Romanian ship escorted the *Struma* until it left the mined waters.

On the ship the day began at four or five a.m. because no one could sleep. With the morning light, those who had the privilege went up the deck to get a little water for washing—seawater of course—which they hauled up in pails. It was mostly the men who went up to the deck, while the women remained below, in the dormitories. Some of these were large, for 120 persons, while others were small, for forty. They slept on wide berths, four to a berth. Each person was allotted a space of about 60 centimeters.

Time crawled. After eight days at anchor in the port, the Turkish Government sent health inspectors to the ship. They asked whether anything had happened, and soon left without doing anything. The Turkish police were constantly on the ship, and they were upset by what they saw.

In order to obtain lunch—soup was cooked twice a week—everyone lay in his berth, for that was the only way in which the food could be distributed; otherwise there was no way to pass. The people were weak and irritable. Nevertheless, there were frequent arguments and considerable friction over nothing at all, as is likely to happen among a group of desperate people.

Supper was at five o'clock—again, an orange and some peanuts.

Night fell. It was impossible to sit on the deck, since there were many people forced to sleep there for lack of berths in the dormitories. So everyone went to bed. At this hour, milk was distributed to the children.

The children on the ship were models of good behavior. At night, waiting on their berths in the dark for their portion of milk, they did not cry. Only from their parents' eyes did the tears flow. One little girl, who shared a berth with me, would tell me her dreams. She used to dream about a long train carrying all the people.

The ship was towed out to the Black Sea.

We sensed a plot, and objected to the untying of the ship. The few policemen were no match for us and left the ship. A little later about eighty policemen arrived on motorboats and surrounded the "Struma." The Ma'apilim did not permit the policemen to come onto the ship and struggled against them for about half an hour. The policemen succeeded in coming on by force, disconnected the anchor and tied the "Struma" to the tugboat.

At 10 p.m. the ship reached the Black Sea, about five kilometers from the shore. Here we were untied from the tugboat, whose men shouted, as they left us: "You are going to Burgas! To Bulgaria!"

The ship did not move from its place. The sea was completely quiet. Suddenly, a little before 9 a.m., I heard a loud explosion. Within a few minutes the ship sank. I was thrown into the air, and when I fell into the sea, I saw only a few dozen of the Ma'apilim struggling against the waves. The terrifying shouts of men and women pierced the air. Various parts of the ship could be seen floating on the sea. Some of the Ma'apilim grabbed such pieces, and I did the same. The sea was cold as ice. From the cold and exhaustion, those who tried to hold on to pieces of the ship lost their grip and disappeared into the depths of the sea, one after another.[26]

Stoliar was rescued, brought to a hospital, and, once he was found to be in good health, they jailed him. Months later he was allowed to enter Palestine.

Undersecretary of State Welles told Mrs. David de Sola Pool that he considered the *Struma* incident "one of the most appalling and shocking things of the whole war," and he promised to register a protest with the British authorities. Welles was the same State Department official who had told Rabbi Wise that British officials believed the Germans were using the refugees to transport Nazi agents to Palestine. Wise had asked him if he "thought it possible that the Nazis would choose such a way of getting into Turkey and Palestine, and whether he did not think that there were more pleasant and easier ways" for the Nazis to penetrate Allied lines. After American officials had apparently protested to Britain, the British still claimed that there had been foreign agents on board that ship and that it was all the fault of the Turks, since they had towed the ship out to sea.[27]

In mid-1943, Rabbi Meyer Berlin met with some of the members of the U.S. Congress and asked why they had remained silent about the slaughter of Europe's Jews. Even though the prime minister of England had not helped, Parliament had condemned the Nazi German atrocities. Congress had not yet issued such a condemnation. Senate majority leader Alben W. Barkley said that he favored such a resolution, but Joseph W. Martin, the House minority leader, had not yet given his support. Rabbi Berlin advised Barkley that some fifty thousand Jews of Romania could be saved if they only had some place to go. Jewish leaders and Jewish people of Palestine believed that "if a place of refuge were offered to the remaining suffering Jews in Nazi lands, they would be allowed to emigrate." Senator Barkley was aware of the Romanian situation and he expressed full sympathy with Zionism. He had talked with President Roosevelt regarding the request that the Jews of Palestine be permitted to form an army to fight the Nazis and the president had said "that for many reasons the issue could not be pressed." When Berlin asked Barkley as to the possibility of bringing Jews to America, he answered that in view of the present restrictions there was no chance of "opening the doors."[28]

Barkley seemed impressed and interested when Rabbi Berlin spoke of the many Jewish men and women who had volunteered and fought for the Allies. He listened most attentively as Rabbi Berlin spoke of the ancient Hebraic belief "that nations who subjected Israel to torture and persecution, sooner or later feel the full measure of God's wrath, and that even the British government was made to suffer because of solemn and sacred promises made to the Jewish people which they did not fulfill." Berlin explained that the Jewish people could no longer depend on

Great Britain and they turned to the United States to achieve the "historic goal" of a restored Israel.[29]

When Rabbi Berlin met Senator Robert F. Wagner of New York, he stressed the need for America to offer the Jews asylum, either permanent or temporary, within the quota laws or by special legislation. Once again he urged that Britain be convinced to open the doors of Palestine to the Jews and not just to Arabs. It seemed that "if horses were being slaughtered as are the Jews . . . there would now be a loud demand for organized action against such cruelty to animals," but somehow when it came to the Jews "everybody remained silent, including the intellectuals and humanitarians and enlightened America." Berlin was not much impressed by Senator Wagner. He was a "fine gentleman" but rather "lukewarm in general political questions," and he knew little about Zionism or Jewish problems even though he was chairman of the so-called Pro-Palestine Committee.[30]

Rabbi Berlin found Joseph Martin very much to the point, but Martin seemed unsure when it came to details regarding the Jewish situation in Europe. Berlin explained that the United States could save a great many Jews if it agreed to admit them and if it would persuade the British to admit them to Palestine. Martin asked Rabbi Berlin if he was familiar with the immigration laws. Berlin said that he was and that he believed that the quotas would permit at least seventy-five thousand Jews to enter the United States. But Martin insisted that Congress had little to say with respect to the immigration quotas, and that it was up to the president. The immigration question, insisted Martin, had "nothing to do with Congress."[31]

This was an extraordinary statement since the president repeatedly claimed that it was all up to Congress. With tears in his eyes and uncontrolled emotions Rabbi Berlin rejected Martin's assertion. "Is it not the duty of men like you to meet together . . . with those who are able to give you the facts about the greatest tragedy in history and to look for a way to prevent the utter annihilation of the Jewish people? Is it merely a question of formality and division of responsibility?" Those in a position to help and who do not help are in a very real sense "guilty to a great extent in what was going on."

"I suppose you are right in regard to this phase of the question," said Martin, "now what about Palestine?"[32] As Rabbi Berlin described the British White Paper policy, Martin admitted to not knowing anything about it and he wanted to hear all the details of the history and promised to make every effort so that Congress would pass a resolution on behalf of Polish Jewry.[33]

In his report, Berlin observed that people like Martin had been neglected by the American Jewish leaders and that was a "pity." He urged that the Jewish "leaders" provide such individuals with "proper material which will bring home to them some knowledge of our situation."[34]

Rabbi Berlin's most disappointing interview was with Vice President Henry A. Wallace. When Berlin advised Wallace that "without its historic homeland the Jewish nation was definitely threatened with total extinction," the vice president curtly replied that he could not "agree." He could not see that Zionism was "the major solution to the problem of Jewry as a whole." And when Berlin asked Wallace if America might admit "a million additional Jews Wallace said that he could not speak on behalf of the government." He said that he sympathized with the Jewish people and Zionism, but he could not express a "positive opinion when many groups in American Jewry were totally against zionism."[35]

Aliyah to Palestine—legal or illegal—came to a halt after the *Struma* disaster. Such efforts were resumed in the summer of 1945, despite British restrictions and blockades. It was then that efforts were resumed to bring the surviving remnant back to Palestine by the Haganah, the Palmach (an offspring of the Haganah), the Irgun, and the Jewish Brigade. The Jews called this rescue effort *Bricha*. The ships came from Italy, France, Romania, and the United States. During the three years after the war the British continued to do all in their power to prevent the Jews from entering the Land of Israel. When they intercepted the boats and captured Jews they placed them in detention camps in the Holy Land, Cyprus, Africa, and, in the case of the *Exodus 1947*, they brought the Jews back to Germany. But despite all the British efforts to prevent it, some Jews were smuggled back—to the Land of Israel—from 1945 to 1948. The total number of Jews who were brought back to the Land of Israel from 1934 to 1948 was about 120,000. This Aliyah may be considered part of the Jewish resistance against the Nazis and their collaborators. The Aliyah from 1945 to 1948 may likewise be considered as part of the Jewish struggle against Western and in particular Anglo-Saxon anti-Jewish policies.

There was little reason for the surviving Jews of Europe to return to the misery of their European persecution. Thousands of Jews were smuggled to the Land of Israel, their homeland, with the help of the underground and the Jewish Brigade. Many more could have been saved if only the Allies had been willing to help. British and American claims that Jewish immigration to the Land of Israel would arouse the Arabs and endanger the Allied military effort was no more than an excuse as far as Jewish leaders like Weizmann and Begin were concerned. During World War II, the Anglo-Americans would proclaim their concern that the Arabs would support the Nazis. When that war was over they would proclaim their concern that the Arabs would support the Soviet Union and the communists.

The Allies had failed to help rescue the Jews. The Jews learned that power politics was the main commodity of the international arena. Those that had the power would be respected, those that had little or no power would be neglected and remain homeless.

NOTES

1. David Ben-Gurion's statement to the American Zionist Emergency Committee, November 14, 1940, Robert Szold Papers, Unsorted Boxes, Robert Szold House, New York.

2. David Ben-Gurion to Justice Louis D. Brandeis, June 6, 1939, Robert Szold Papers, Robert Szold House, New York.

3. Leo Herman's report of illegal immigration to Meyer Steinglass of the Zionist Organization of America, November 27, 1934, Individuals Files, Zionist Archives, New York.

4. Richard Lichtheim to Kaplan, March 31, 1940, Jewish Agency Papers, Zionist Archives, New York.

5. Ibid.

6. Robert Szold Papers, Unsorted Boxes, Robert Szold House, New York.

7. Pioneers.

8. Robert Szold Papers, Unsorted Boxes, Robert Szold House, New York.

9. Neville Butler to Stephen S. Wise, November 25, 1940, Robert S. Szold Papers, Robert Szold House, New York.

10. David Ben-Gurion Memorandum, January 1942, Individuals Files A-C, Zionist Archives, New York.

11. Notes of March 19, 1942, meeting at State Department, State Department Files, Zionist Archives, New York.

12. Chaim Weizmann to Field Marshal Smuts, August 15, 1941, Robert Szold Papers, Zionist Archives, New York.

13. Ibid.

14. Bracha Habas, *The Gate Breakers* (New York, 1963), p. 109.

15. Zeev Jabotinsky Memo, Individual's File, Zionist Archives, New York.

16. Ibid.

17. Address given by Vladimir Jabotinsky, March 19, 1940, Individual's Files, Zionist Archives, New York.

18. Short Note of Mr. X's report on his interview with Joseph P. Kennedy, November 2, 1938, 11 A.M. Jewish Agency Papers, Unsorted Boxes, Zionist Archives, New York.

19. Ibid. Mr. X might have been Miss X or Mrs. X because in a letter dated November 4, 1938, Rose G. Jacobs recalled that Kennedy had "made a profound impression" during her recent visit with him. She found him sincere and with a "genuine desire to be helpful." Kennedy had also referred to "the attacks that are being made on him by the newspapers and Jewish columnists in America, because of his suggestion that efforts be made to come to terms with Hitler on the Jewish problem." Rose G. Jacobs to Robert Szold, November 4, 1938, Jewish Agency documents, Unsorted Boxes, Zionist Archives, New York.

20. Chaim Weizmann to Solomon Goldman, May 30, 1939, Jewish Agency Papers Unsorted Materials, Zionist Archives, New York.

21. Solomon Goldman to Chaim Weizmann, June 20, 1939, Jewish Agency Papers Unsorted Materials, Zionist Archives, New York.

22. Ibid.

23. Ibid.

24. Statement by David Ben-Gurion to Emergency Committee for Zionist Affairs, November 14, 1940, Robert Szold Papers, Addendum Box, Unsorted Materials, Zionist Archives, New York.

25. Manya Mardor, *Haganah* (New York, 1957), pp. 76–84.

26. Zionist Youth Foundation, *Yom Ha'atzmaut Materials* YH/33 (New York, 1974). An August 10, 2000 *New York Times* report claims there were 778 people.

27. Notes of the meeting with Sumner Welles, March 19, 1942, State Department Files, Zionist Archives, New York.

28. Confidential Memorandum by Rabbi Meyer Berlin, February 23, 1943, American Zionist Emergency Committee Files, Political Files, Zionist Archives, New York.

29. Ibid.

30. Ibid.

31. Ibid.

32. Ibid.

33. Ibid.

34. Ibid.

35. Ibid.

5

Harry S Truman and the Recognition of Israel

On April 12, 1945, Harry S Truman was sworn in as president. He had been a farmer, a soldier, a businessman, a salesman, a county judge, a U.S. senator (representing Missouri for ten years), and, very briefly, a vice president. As senator, he had expressed his understanding and sympathy for the plight of the Jewish people, but he refused to challenge Franklin D. Roosevelt's cautious Middle East policies, as can be seen from his February 16, 1944, letter to the president of the Jewish National Worker's Alliance: "With the difficulty looming up between Russia and Poland, and the Balkan States and Russia, and with Great Britain and Russia absolutely necessary to us in financing the war I don't want to throw any bricks to upset the apple cart, although when the right time comes I am willing to help make the fight for a Jewish homeland in Palestine."[1]

Much has already been said and written about Truman's capacity to fill Roosevelt's shoes. Some have claimed that he was unfit for the job, others have said that he was exactly what the country needed, and still others observed that the presidency made the man.

Whatever the facts may be about his assumption of the presidency, he inherited most of his predecessor's programs, policies, and people, and he tried to work with them.

ROOSEVELT'S RECORD

Roosevelt had directed America's foreign policy and seldom had he shared his powers with Congress, or even with his secretary of state.

In 1944–1945, Congress considered passing a resolution in support of a Jewish commonwealth in the Land of Israel, but it yielded to Roosevelt's pressures and dropped the resolution. Congress accepted the Roosevelt administration's view that such a resolution might be used by German propagandists to injure the Allied cause among the Arabs. As Assistant Secretary of War John J. McCloy insisted, "From a military point of view we would much prefer to let such sleeping dogs lie."[2]

Truman was a student of history and he knew the history of the Jewish people. The tragedies suffered by the Jewish people during the mad genocide created by Adolf Hitler's Germany reminded him of his Missouri-Kansas ancestors who had been displaced by the Civil War. The self-made man from Independence who helped end World War II, who inaugurated the self-help concept in American foreign policy, and who pioneered for civil and human rights in America, would play an important role in the history of the Jews. He believed that the survivors of the Nazi German atrocities represented a challenge to the West, and as president, he "undertook to do something about it." He agreed to the creation of the Nuremberg tribunal to punish Nazis and to record the crimes committed by the Germans and their collaborators so that later generations should not claim that the Holocaust did not happen. Napoléon Bonaparte had been made into a hero and Truman did not wish to see Hitler made into one as well.[3] He called upon the British to open the Land of Israel to Jewish immigrants and he helped reestablish the state of Israel. Truman likewise fought for a revision of American immigration laws. It was Truman who invited the 984 displaced persons encamped in Oswego, New York, to enter America rather than to make them return to Europe as FDR had envisioned in August 1944.

Once Truman discovered that the inmates of concentration camps were still kept in those camps by the victor powers, he ordered General Dwight D. Eisenhower to get them out "and into decent houses until they could be repatriated or evacuated." He also advised Eisenhower that he was "communicating directly with the British government in an effort to have the doors of Palestine opened to such of these displaced persons as wish to go there."[4]

He felt for the survivors and on December 22, 1945, he asked Congress to do something "at once to facilitate the entrance of some into the United States." In this way, America could do something to relieve the human misery and establish "an example to the other countries of the world which [were] able to receive some of these war sufferers." Very few Europeans had managed to come to America during the war years. In 1942, only two percent of the immigration quotas had been used; in 1943, five percent; in 1944, six percent; and as of November 30, 1945, only ten percent of the quotas for the European countries had been used. President Truman believed "that common decency and the fundamental comradeship of all human beings" required that America seek to reduce human suffering.[5]

Truman was aware that the Land of Israel might not be able to accommodate all those that wanted to go there. It was evident that the prospects for admitting a great number of refugees to the United States were slender. As he wrote to David K. Niles on April 10, 1947: "The idea of getting 400,000 immigrants into this country, is of course, beyond our wildest dreams. If we could get 100,000 we would be doing remarkably well and I imagine there is a shortage of coatmakers."[6] On July 7, 1947, President Truman asked Congress to admit the displaced persons to America. He reminded Congress that the United States was a nation founded by immigrants who had fled from oppression and that America had "thrived on the energy and diversity of many peoples." After much deliberation and debate, Congress passed the Displaced Persons Act, which admitted two hundred thousand refugees during a two-year period. Although Truman claimed that the legislation discriminated "in callous fashion against persons of the Jewish faith," and excluded "many persons of the Catholic faith," he signed the measure on June 25, 1948, "in the expectation that the necessary remedial action will follow when the Congress reconvenes."

When Congress did reconsider the immigration laws five years later, it passed the Walter Immigration Act over Truman's veto. It was "incredible," said Truman, that "in this year of 1952, we should again be enacting into law such a slur on the patriotism, the capacity, and the decency of a large part of our citizenry." Truman vetoed it on June 25, 1952, because it repudiated "our basic religious concepts" and "our belief in the brotherhood of man." Congress overrode Truman's veto. The prejudices of the 1920s remained the prejudices of the 1950s despite the Holocaust.

PUNISHMENT OF NAZI CRIMINALS

After the victory in Europe, President Truman was apparently determined that the Nazis had to be punished for their war crimes and their crimes against humanity. In a letter to Senator Burton K. Wheeler dated December 21, 1945, Truman put it this way: "While we have no desire to be unduly cruel to Germany, I cannot feel any great sympathy for those who caused the death of so many human beings by starvation, disease, and outright murder."[7] The Allies could not agree on how to deal with the war criminals. British foreign minister Anthony Eden said that he wanted to see them executed on the spot. Truman called for court trials, while Joseph Stalin wanted to link the trials to well-known Nazis.[8]

The International Military Tribunal at Nuremberg, and later at Tokyo, was organized with judges from the United States, Great Britain, France, and the Soviet Union. Nazi and Japanese defendants were tried for "crimes against peace," "war crimes," and "crimes against humanity." The Nuremberg, Tokyo, and auxiliary tribunals brought a few, but by no means all, of the war criminals to justice.

At those trials, the record of these unspeakable crimes was officially inscribed and the principle was established that no person could say that they could not be held accountable because they were following orders. Each and every defendant was held accountable for their own actions.[9]

President Truman had apparently favored prosecution and punishment of all war criminals, but by 1947, McCloy, Truman's U.S. high commissioner for Germany, had exonerated some two hundred thousand young Germans from any culpability for political activities, amnestied eight hundred thousand Germans of low economic status, and pardoned forty thousand Germans who were at least 50 percent disabled. Of the three million who could have been charged with criminal behavior as part of Hitler's Third Reich, most were never examined, only two hundred thousand were identified on record, and few were ever brought to a formal trial. Almost all the Nazis who brought death to millions of people through starvation and massive executions went unpunished. Indeed, West Germany and Austria prospered. They soon found their way back into governments within the occupied sectors of West Germany and Austria where they assumed positions of authority in both civil and military administrations. In Bavaria, the cradle of Nazidom, some 85 percent of the Nazi-era civil servants were reinstated. This was a consequence of the so-called cold war, wherein the West and the East competed for German missile and atomic experts, scientists, and civil servants, and they sought to have them on their side.

In 1948 the United Nations prepared and adopted a convention against genocide. President Truman asked Congress to ratify it. "We must do our part to outlaw forever the mass murder of innocent people."[10] But Congress did not follow Truman's advice.

From the outset of his presidency, Truman was advised by State Department officials to be most cautious on the issue of Palestine. He was warned that Zionists would use every possible tactic to obtain his support for unlimited immigration to the British Mandate of Palestine. Secretary of State Edward R. Stettinius cautioned Truman of "Zionist leaders who sought to press for unlimited Jewish immigration into Palestine and the establishment of a Jewish state." Stettinius urged Truman to exercise "the greatest care" and to keep "the long-range interests of the country" in mind.[11] Acting Secretary of State Joseph C. Grew's memo to President Truman urging him to be cautious and to do no more than to thank Zionists for the information they might provide was typical of the kind of advice Truman received from the State Department on the Palestine issue.[12] But while elements of the American establishment affiliated with the influential Council on Foreign Relations and various industrial, oil, and missionary interests tried to keep the doors of the Land of Israel closed to Jews; the Yishuv,[13] the American community, and various members of Congress would not let them monopolize Truman's thinking with their anti-Jewish and anti-Zionist sentiments. David Ben-Gurion made it clear soon after World War II ended that the doors of the Land of Israel would not be closed to Jews. He advised the State Department that the Jewish people would wait no longer. They would reestablish their homeland regardless of broken Balfour Declaration promises, aborted congressional resolutions, and insincere presidential pronouncements. The Jews would "fight if necessary, in defense of their rights and the consequences would be on Great Britain's head."[14]

Truman was suspicious of the views and attitudes expressed by the "striped pants boys" of the State Department who were so coldly indifferent to the Jews. He felt that America's long-range goals for world peace would "be best served by a solution that would accord justice to the needs and the wants of the Jewish people who had so long been persecuted."[15]

By July 3, 1945, Truman heard from some Americans and their representatives on the question of the reestablishment of a Jewish homeland when Senator Robert F. Wagner sent Truman a letter, supported by 54 senators and 250 representatives, which asked him to urge England to open the doors of the Land of Israel and reestablish a Jewish commonwealth there. He could not afford to ignore such a manifestation of popular will. While Truman followed Roosevelt's example and promised Arab rulers that the United States would take no action without consulting both Arabs and Jews, he sent Dean Earl G. Harrison of the University of Pennsylvania Law School to Europe as his personal investigator to report on Europe's displaced persons.

Harrison's report was heartbreaking. Refugees were still in the German camps and they had little hope for the future. Few wanted to remain in Europe, most wanted to go to Palestine. Harrison recommended that they be admitted to the Land of Israel. He reported that anyone visiting the concentration camps would find it "nothing short of calamitous to contemplate that the gates of Palestine should be closed."[16]

After reading Harrison's report, Truman asked Winston Churchill to lift the 1939 White Paper restrictions "without delay," and at the Potsdam Conference he disregarded State Department working papers and urged Churchill to support the establishment of a Jewish homeland in Palestine. Delay would only compound the difficulties. He asked for Churchill's views so that they could "at a later, but not too distant date, discuss the problem in concrete terms." Churchill preferred to see such a Jewish homeland in Tripoli. When reporters asked Truman if any progress had been made, he replied that the matter was still being discussed. And when they asked whether Stalin had been consulted, he replied that there was nothing Stalin could do about it. Truman had hoped that Stalin would have nothing to "say" or "do" about Palestine. Truman said that he wanted to see as many Jews as possible enter Palestine, and he believed that it could be worked out diplomatically with the British and the Arabs. In reality, that was only wishful thinking.[17]

On August 31, 1945, Truman urged Clement Attlee, the newly elected prime minister of England, to open Palestine to one hundred thousand Jews. While the Nazi German extermination policies had killed many of the prewar Jews who might have wanted to emigrate, there were still those that wanted to go to Palestine, and Truman firmly believed that Britain should not bar a reasonable number of these survivors from settling in their ancient homeland. No claim was "more meritorious" than of the Jews "who for so many years have known persecution and enslavement."[18] Truman's remarks upset the Arabs. The Iraqis protested that it would be unwise for the United States to fall from favor with the forty million Arabs in the Middle East.[19]

Attlee rejected Truman's suggestion. He called for the establishment of an Anglo-American Committee to investigate conditions for Europe's Jews and recommend where they might go. Truman agreed to such an inquiry, provided attention would be focused on Palestine and that it would work quickly.

Members of Congress endorsed Truman's approach with pro-Zionist resolutions. Senators Wagner, Robert A. Taft, and David I. Walsh as well as House Republican leader Joseph W. Martin introduced resolutions that called upon the United States to secure unrestricted immigration and colonization to ensure a "free and democratic commonwealth." Truman favored the move, but during his November 29, 1945, press conference, he expressed his reservations, saying that the resolutions might make the Anglo-American Committee's work superfluous. Truman's hesitations did not stop Congress. A concurrent resolution was adopted by the Foreign Relations Committee by a vote of 17 to 1, the Senate passed it on December 17, and two days later the House followed.

Truman could not ignore such congressional consensus. Nor could he forget the impression Chaim Weizmann had made on him during their meeting of December 4, 1945. Weizmann described the agricultural and industrial progress Jewish settlers had made and he reassured Truman that the Jewish state would be based on "sound democratic foundations with political machinery and institutions on the pattern of those in the U.S."[20]

When the American members of the Anglo-American Committee ran into obstinate opposition from their British counterparts, Niles suggested that Truman send the following message to the American delegation:

> The world expectantly awaits a report from the entire Commission which will be the basis of an affirmative program to relieve untold suffering and misery. In

the deliberations now going, and in the report which will evolve from them, it is my deep and sincere wish that the American delegation shall stand firm for a program that is in accord with the highest American tradition of generosity and justice.

On April 18, Truman wrote Niles: "Thanks for . . . the suggested message. It was sent."[21]

The Anglo-American Committee recommended that one hundred thousand Jews should be admitted immediately. Attlee had promised to accept its findings but he refused to do so. Instead, he called for the establishment of still another committee to examine "Forty-three subjects" that had not been studied. Foreign Minister Ernest Bevin urged a delay in the publication of the commission's report. He complained that the Jews were smuggling people into Palestine capable of bearing arms. He accused the "aggressive" Jews of "poisoning relations between our two peoples." He insisted that the Jews of Palestine disarm and that the United States start preparing for military as well as economic assistance to the areas because His Majesty's Government was considering complete withdrawal from Palestine.[22]

Truman welcomed the committee's report.[23] He was especially pleased that the document called for "the abrogation of the White Paper of 1939."[24]

The Chiefs of Staff advised Truman to stay out of the Middle East. They warned that if the United States entered the Middle East, it would alienate the Arabs and foster Soviet penetration into the area.[25]

Many Americans had lost patience with the British. Congressman Herman P. Eberhalter illustrated that feeling. There had been enough procrastination. He believed that it was time for action. "One cannot fail to have some suspicion that delay is being purposely used with the hope that perhaps some other solution rather than the actual transference may be accomplished."[26] Truman agreed.

When the British called for further discussion of some "Forty-three subjects" concerning the Land of Israel, Truman replied that the one hundred thousand Jews must first be admitted to that land, and then the experts could be brought in to split hairs.[27]

On June 5, he advised the British that the United States was prepared to assume all expenses and provide the ships to transport the one hundred thousand Jews to Palestine.

The British responses greatly displeased many people in America. Abba Hillel Silver, Stephen S. Wise, Emanuel Neumann, Robert Szold, and various members of Congress including Chet Holifield, Emanuel Celler, and Bill Barrett called on Truman to withhold all loans to England unless the British would admit one hundred thousand Jews to Palestine. Barrett demanded an apology from Bevin. Andrew Biemiller found Bevin's remarks "uncalled for and insulting."[28] There was no way Bevin or the entire British Empire could halt the legitimate aspirations of the Jewish people, said Biemiller, and he demanded that the British "immediately cease their Gestapo tactics."[29]

On June 11, Truman announced the establishment of a Cabinet Committee on Palestine that would help determine and implement U.S. policies on Palestine. Bevin accused Truman of wanting to push the Jews into Palestine because he did not want them in America.

Politicians were engaged in a war of words. The Jewish people of the Land of Israel were in the midst of great strife and real war.

On June 17, the Haganah, one of the key Jewish underground forces, blew up eight bridges along the Palestine frontiers. A week later the British government retaliated by placing Jerusalem under curfew and arresting twenty-six hundred Jews. President Truman again called for the admission of the one hundred thousand Jews "with all dispatch" and he promised "technical and financial" support for the "transportation of the immigrants from Europe to Palestine."[30]

The torture and imprisonment of thousands of Jews by the British reminded Celler of the "Spanish Inquisition days and the Gestapo." While the British accommodated the former Nazi collaborator Haj Amin el-Husseini in an Egyptian palace, they imprisoned Moshe Sharett (Shertok), a man who had recruited well over twenty-five thousand Jews for service in the British army during World War II. But as Celler said, British tactics had not succeeded against India and Ireland and they would not succeed against the Jews.

Celler asked if the Truman government was doing anything to help the Jews. It had done nothing to help save them during World War II and it was spending four and a half billion dollars to assist England. All America did was "to permit a thousand (984) out of the perishing millions" to enter America and then locked them up at Camp Oswego, New York.[31]

Former senator Guy M. Gillette reminded Bevin that America had not fought two world wars to "support disintegrating empires." England had not asked Jews and New Yorkers to stay home during World War II. Nor was England advising American Jews not to pay taxes for loans to England. The Middle East battle was not between "the oppressed Arabs and the persecuted Jews." It was a conflict between the "interests of empire and the happiness of peoples," and Americans could not remain neutral under those circumstances.[32]

"The people of America are as disgusted by Bevin's words as they are impatient with his inaction," said Senator Elbert D. Thomas. Palestine was not England and the British had no right to exclude the Jews from there.[33]

Under these circumstances, Truman met with American members of the Jewish Agency and confided that he was determined to see the transfer of 100,000 Jewish immigrants to Palestine and the president promised "technical and financial" aid to transport the immigrants from Europe to Palestine."

The Jewish Agency representatives got back to Truman within a week, writing him about their concern over reports that the British were insisting on an "exhaustive diplomatic schedule" before any action would be taken on the admittance of the one hundred thousand. They found "the statements emanating from London inimical or hostile to the whole spirit of the constructive proposals contained in the report of the Anglo-American Committee."

American and British cabinet committees met to discuss the Anglo-American Committee's recommendations, but since Truman refused to assume military responsibility for Palestine, he had little bargaining power. The Morrison-Grady Plan was just another British "White Paper" that called for a strong central government to rule over two autonomous states; fifteen hundred out of the nine thousand square miles of West Palestine were to be under Jewish control; the central government was to maintain control over Jerusalem and Bethlehem as well as the Negev; and Arab approval would be needed before the one hundred thousand Jews could be admitted into that Promised Land.

Concerned with this development, American Zionists asked James G. McDonald to see the president. When McDonald saw him on July 27, 1946, he found Truman very angry and unhappy with the pressures he had to cope with on this question. McDonald advised Truman that "if we get the 100,000 at the price of this you will go down in history as anathema." Truman "exploded" at that remark, but McDonald was not intimidated. He again told Truman that even "if indirectly he gave assent to this thing he would be responsible for scrapping the Jewish interests in Palestine."

"Well," said Truman, "you can't satisfy these people." Truman insisted that he would strive to get one hundred thousand Jewish people into Palestine, but the "Jews aren't going to write the history of the United States or my history."[34]

President Roosevelt had understood "some of the imponderables," said McDonald.

"But I am not Roosevelt," Truman shot back. "I am not from New York. I am from the Middle West."

"I have no object in coming to see you except to tell the truth," McDonald pleaded.

"I want to hear it," Truman replied. "I hear it too seldom."

"Well," continued McDonald, "the moderation of the Jewish leaders is shown by the fact that they have asked me to see you."

"They knew I wouldn't receive some of them," answered Truman.

McDonald found Truman "hell-bent on the 100,000," but he would not "assume any more responsibility than the $45 million obligation." Truman had told McDonald that he did not care about the partition of Palestine. "It is not my business. You can't satisfy the Jews anyway. You have got to get the British to agree."[35]

"Well, Mr. President," McDonald said, "you can make them agree at too high a price."

"We got them to agree," Truman said.

"Yes, but it was too high a price. I think you can get the British to agree if you will be firm and insist on it and refuse to have anything to do with these other matters."

McDonald tried to follow a prepared memorandum, but Truman often interrupted him to complain about how ungrateful everybody was, and how badly served he was: "I can't get the right people."[36]

But Truman still could not find his way clear on the Palestine issue. Britain had ignored the Anglo-American recommendations and his own requests that one hundred thousand Jews be admitted. Moreover, the cabinet committees had failed and Thomas Dewey, the Republican Party leader, issued strong statements in favor of Jewish immigration to Palestine.

Various members of Congress likewise protested against the new plan. They found it to be unjust. While the Arabs had obtained more than 1.2 million square miles since Lord Arthur Balfour had issued his declaration, the Jews had been excluded from the land of their forefathers.[37]

By August 12, Truman rejected the Morrison-Grady Plan as unfeasible and he wrote Attlee to that effect.

On October 3, Truman advised the British prime minister that he would soon issue a statement in favor of Jewish immigration to Palestine. A day later was Yom Kippur and as he wished the Jewish people a happy holiday he again called for the admission of one hundred thousand Jews to Palestine. Soon thereafter he wrote Senator Walter F. George revealing a depth of understanding and sympathy for the Jewish people that surpassed the statements of previous American presidents. He wished that all members of Congress could visit the displaced persons camps to witness what was happening to five hundred thousand human beings "through no fault of their own." "These people had to be properly located" and there was no reason "in the world why 100,000 Jews could not go to Palestine," nor was there any reason why the unused north European quotas could not be used by them.[38]

The British and the Arabs did not care for Truman's viewpoint and they told him so. King Ibn Sa'ūd of Saudi Arabia insisted that the Jews were aggressors and was astonished by Truman's remarks.[39] Truman's response was that all parties had "a common responsibility" to work for a solution that would allow those who must leave Europe to find a home and to "dwell in peace and security." While Truman supported the entry of Jews into Palestine, he promised to consult with both Arabs and Jews.[40]

When Attlee threw the question into the laps of the United Nations on February 18, 1947, he accused Truman of using the issue to gain votes in the 1946 elections. The White House replied that America's interest in Palestine was "of long and continuing standing" and that it was "a deep and abiding interest shared by our people without regard to their political affiliation."

This British attitude and approach unsettled many Americans. Some even suggested that the United States should not assist Britain with its problems in Greece and Turkey. Holifield suggested that the United States strike a bargain with Britain: "We support Britain if it admits the 100,000 Jews to Palestine."[41] Some urged the president to delay the loans to Britain so as to show them that they could not get whatever they pleased.[42]

The United Nations received Britain's request for UN General Assembly action on the Palestine situation on April 2, 1947, and on May 15, a special committee called United Nations Special Committee on Palestine (UNSCOP) was ordained to study the Palestine question.

UNSCOP was composed of representatives from Australia, Canada, Czechoslovakia, Guatemala, India, Iran, the Netherlands, Peru, Sweden, Uruguay, and Yugoslavia. All governments and peoples were asked to refrain from using force or any other action that might prejudice a settlement.

Secretary of State George C. Marshall advised Truman to issue a statement calling upon all Americans to abide by the UN request. He anticipated that such a statement might irritate certain groups who actively supported illegal immigration to Palestine, but he felt that the United States should not support "activities of American citizens or residents of a character which might render more difficult the task which the U.N. has assumed."[43] Truman agreed and issued the statement on June 5, 1947.

EXODUS 1947

The story of the *Exodus 1947* began in 1934, when the first immigrant ships secretly landed their passengers in Palestine in defiance of British restrictions. A number of Zionist bureaucrats were unhappy that the immigrants were not carefully selected, but the Jewish people of Palestine did their best to help save the lives of their brethren.[44]

Palestinian Jewry refused to heed some British and Jewish Agency officials who advocated a curtailment of immigration. Early in 1938, a new immigration campaign was inaugurated.

Financial assistance was needed for this undertaking, but rich and powerful Jewish organizations in America and Europe remained indifferent and inept. When the British issued the White Paper of May 1939, Jewish leadership from the Jewish Agency to the Irgun called for increased illegal immigration in order to disregard the artificial quotas and restrictions created by the British. But that unity of sentiment came too late. World War II sealed the fate of European Jewry. Six million Jews died because they were not allowed into Eretz Israel or anywhere else.

By July 1947 there were some five hundred thousand Jews, most were survivors of the Holocaust who wanted to leave Europe. They wanted to return to that place for which they prayed on such days as Passover and the High Holy Days: "Next Year in Jerusalem!" Between May and December 1945 some forty-four hundred Jews were smuggled into Palestine. In January 1946 one ship brought nine hundred passengers. In March two ships arrived with two thousand and in May another brought three thousand, so that by December 1946, twenty-three thousand survivors tried to enter Palestine illegally. Some swam ashore under cover of darkness, while many others were captured and transported to such British internment camps as those on Cyprus.

And then there was the *Exodus 1947*.

The Haganah Jewish underground purchased an old four-thousand-ton Mississippi River steamer, *The President Warfield*, and after refitting the ship they sailed into the small Riviera port of Sete in July of 1947. The ship took on more than forty-five hundred Jewish refugees who hoped to go to the Land of Israel.

Five minutes before the ship was to cast off for Israel, the British intervened. A British official warned France that if the ship was permitted to leave port, Anglo-French relations would be damaged irreparably. Paris sent an eight-word message to Sete: "Halt, the ship is not permitted to sail." The Jews tried to bribe a French port pilot with a million francs, but the British blocked the deal. The Jews then defied the British and cast off the mooring lines and set sail without a pilot.[45]

Despite the many hazards the ship made it out to sea where it was confronted by British destroyers in international waters, twenty-two miles off the coast of Israel. The crew painted a new name to the ship: *Exodus 1947*. The blue and white Jewish flag was raised, just in case the British might mistake the ship's identity.

The British destroyers were at general quarters and ordered the *Exodus* to stop engines and prepare for towing. The Jews replied: "On the deck of this boat, the *Exodus*, are 4,500 people, men, women and children, whose only crime is that they were born Jews. We are going to our country by right and not by permission of anyone. . . . we shall never recognize a law forbidding Jews to enter their country."[46]

The British flotilla drew up alongside the *Exodus* and, without warning, opened fire with machine guns aimed at her bridge. Two destroyers rammed against the wooden sides of the refugee ship, and they sent a boarding party of sailors and Royal Marines aboard to take control of the wheelhouse. In the battle, Bill Bernstein, an American sailor, was killed.

The refugees and the Haganah counterattacked, retook the wheelhouse, and captured the British boarding party. Three British sailors were taken captive and the rest were forced to retreat. The *Exodus* continued towards shore.

The British destroyers continued to ram the *Exodus* and again they sent a boarding party aboard. This time they bombarded the immigrant ship with gas bombs that sent dozens of refugees sprawling across the deck, killing two people. There was another counterattack. Thirty British sailors were captured by the Jewish fighters. Throughout the fighting, *Exodus* radio transmitted to Palestine an account of what was happening on board.

Three hours after the first encounter, water started to flood into the battered *Exodus*. With his ship beginning to sink and his decks cluttered with exhausted, wounded, and dead refugees, the commander of the *Exodus* had no alternative but to surrender to the British. *Exodus* was towed to Haifa where the refugees were immediately transferred to three deportation ships. Once at sea, the British informed the refugees that they were not going to British camps on Cyprus. They were going back to Germany.

British officials intended to teach the Jews a lesson. But what had the Jews done to deserve such harsh treatment? They had survived the Nazi Holocaust. They had dared to return to their homeland and escape the brutality of Western civilization. Was that why Foreign Minister Bevin said that he wanted to teach the Jews a lesson?

Jews in Palestine responded with violence when they learned of the fate of the *Exodus* passengers. British military installations were attacked, oil pipelines were sabotaged, and British troops were shot at. A radar installation on Mount Carmel was destroyed and a British transport was sunk. But the British still brought the Jews back to Germany.

After weeks on board the *Exodus*, many were too weak to resist, but those who had some strength left did fight. The *Exodus* left an impact on the world, and on members of UNSCOP who were brought to watch while the British transferred Jews to the prison ships. The UNSCOP committee never forgot the "very tired and poor" refugees who were manhandled by British troops.[47]

UNSCOP REPORT

American diplomats were generally opposed to the partition of Palestine. UNSCOP recommended that the British Mandate in Palestine should be terminated without delay and two states should be established, one Jewish and the other Arab. These two states were to be tied by an economic union. The Negev was to go to the Jews, and Jerusalem was to be placed under UN trusteeship. The Arabs rejected UNSCOP's recommendations and prepared for war. Some Jews had mixed feelings about this plan since they considered all of Palestine to be their homeland, but most saw the partition plan as an opportunity to realize the dream of a Jewish state.

President Truman favored it. He was much more partial to the creation of a Jewish state than were the British, who incidentally had issued the Balfour Declaration, which viewed "with favor" the creation of a Jewish homeland in Palestine back in 1917. Truman sought peace and he believed that it could be achieved if world leaders kept their promises and agreements.

State Department officials continued to work against Truman and they used every conceivable tactic to prevent partition and the rebirth of the Jewish state. While UNSCOP's majority report recommended the partition with the Negev and the Port of Eilat going to the Jewish state, some State Department officials allied themselves with Arab and British interests in opposition to the creation of a viable Israel. The U.S. delegation to the United Nations was adamantly opposed to the boundaries recommended by UNSCOP.

According to Eliahu Elath, who was director of the Jewish Agency's political office in Washington and a member of the Jewish Agency delegation to the UN General Assembly, the British wanted to maintain control of the route through the Negev and the Gulf of Eilat to Sinai. American military and political officials were likewise very much concerned with Soviet expansion in the Middle East and they favored strong British bases there rather than to extend U.S. military commitments.[48] Thus, the U.S. delegation to the United Nations was instructed to help improve Galilee boundaries in favor of the Jews in return for a concession in the Negev.[49]

The Jewish Agency refused to yield the Negev and, as the United States was not prepared to support the UNSCOP recommendations on boundaries, it appeared as if the necessary two-thirds majority for the General Assembly to adopt partition would not be secured. Prospects for the future Jewish state were dim and on November 17, 1947, a delegation representing the future Jewish state asked Weizmann to call on President Truman as soon as possible to secure his help. A call was made to the White House and within an hour Weizmann was informed that President Truman would be pleased to see him on November 19.[50]

Justice Felix Frankfurter met Weizmann and his party at Washington's Union Station and accompanied the group to the Shoreham Hotel. The next day, Elath gave Weizmann the aide-mémoire on the port of Eilat, a document that set the port in a geographical perspective of being Israel's only sea access to Asia, east Africa, and Australia. A map of the Negev, with a plan for future development, was appended to the aide-mémoire, which Weizmann took with him when he went to see President Truman.

Weizmann was advised to take up only one issue with the president: the fate of Eilat. It was felt that there would not be time for a serious discussion of several issues and, if he presented the president with only one matter, and there was time to explain it fully, there would be a better chance for success because Truman might not want to see Weizmann leave empty-handed.[51]

When they entered the White House at noon, Weizmann was invited to proceed directly to the president's office while Elath and the rest of the party remained outside with Clark Clifford and David Niles.

Weizmann talked with Truman for half an hour, and when he came out of the session "his face showed signs of great satisfaction."[52]

Weizmann talked with Truman about the importance of the Negev to the future Jewish state. He spoke of the agricultural plantations, of carrots, potatoes, and bananas that have been grown with success in the arid desert. Truman had been a farmer and he was fascinated by the agronomy involved and he sympathized with Israel's agricultural plans. Weizmann showed Truman a map of the future Israel with a circle drawn about the Gulf of Eilat. He explained that the waterway was of little use to anybody at this point, but that the future Jewish state planned to expand the area and make it into an important trade route.

President Truman found the Negev-Eilat question interesting "in its widest aspects" and he promised to do all he could to help provide a constructive solution.[53] Weizmann asked for U.S. support in the boundary questions and the president agreed to give that support. He also said that he would personally give clear instructions to his delegation at the United Nations about the Negev and Eilat.[54]

But while Truman assured Weizmann, the State Department instructed Herschel Johnson, chief of the U.S. delegation to the United Nations, that he should inform the Jews that the United States would not support the inclusion of Eilat within the territorial frontiers of the future Jewish state and that the Negev would be part of the future Arab state.

At 3 P.M., November 19, Johnson saw Sharett (Shertok)[55] of the Jewish delegation in the lobby of the United Nations at Lake Success. Johnson approached Sharett and was about to deliver the bad news when he was interrupted by an aide. At first Johnson said that he did not wish to be bothered. But the aide persisted: "The President is on the line." Johnson went to the phone and returned a few minutes later, apologizing to Sharett for making him wait for a conversation, which, he said, "could be continued on another occasion."[56]

Members of Congress kept a close watch over UN developments and they were most supportive of partition. Thirty members of Congress wrote Marshall on May 9, 1947, asking him to support partition.[57] But State Department officials had different ideas. They wanted to prevent the rebirth of a Jewish state.

The vote on partition came before the General Assembly on November 29, 1947. Thirty-three states, including the United States, favored partition, thirteen opposed, and ten abstained (with England being one of the ten). The Arab states denounced the resolution and declared their determination to block its implementation by all means at their disposal. While the United Nations debated, Palestinian Arabs and others openly recruited by neighboring states of Syria, Lebanon, Transjordan, Iraq, and Egypt planned the liquidation of the Jews of Eretz Israel.

On November 30, eight Jews were killed. The British were still in charge of keeping order, but they failed to do so. At every opportunity they confiscated weapons gathered by the Haganah, Irgun, Lehi, and others of the Jewish defense forces. An Arab general strike was called and violence erupted in nearly all the cities and towns of the Land of Israel.

On January 9, 1948, the armed invasion of Palestine began by an "Arab Army of Liberation" based in Syria. By mid-January there were hundreds of Jewish and Arab casualties, and by February 11, Truman had reports that the Arabs would start full-scale military operations against the Jews in March. He appealed for peace and tried to bring an end to the fighting through the Security Council, but with little success.[58]

The Jews of the Land of Israel had hoped that America might sell them weapons, but that hope was shattered by a strict U.S. adherence to a UN embargo on weapons destined for the Middle East. American weapons reached the Arabs indirectly through Turkey, Saudi Arabia, and even France.[59] The Turks did not wish to see a Jewish state established and they supported the British view that if such a state were established it would only serve as a base of operations for the Russians.

As early as December 1947, Weizmann appealed to Truman directly for weapons: "Our people are being attacked, but we have no weapons. Help us. The other side [has] no shortage."[60] The United States refused to help even after the embargo was no longer in effect once the Mandate came to an end.

Israel turned to Russia for help. Since the Russians hoped to see an end to Anglo-American rule in the Middle East, they sold Israel weapons through Czechoslovakia. However, the Russians also sold weapons to the Arabs.[61]

Congressman Arthur G. Klein observed that the Arabs received supplies from England and indirectly from the United States, but the Jews got nothing. This was an "illogical, indefensible, and untenable" policy. Congressman Donald L. O'Toole, called on his fellow congressmen to show concern for "humanity and the cause of freedom by taking immediate action to lift the arms embargo."[62]

But those like Congressman John E. Rankin, who had been opposed to partition, were likewise against sending weapons to the Jews. Rankin claimed that an "international Sanhedrin" at the United Nations was "attempting to subordinate the U.S. to its domination."

> The mothers and fathers and the servicemen of this nation who just fought two wars in the last 30 years do not want that outfit dragging us into a race war in Palestine. I am speaking now for the real Americans. They have no more right to go in there and set up a racial state in Palestine than they have to set up an Indian state in Ohio or Pennsylvania than they have to set up a Negro state in Virginia, Texas or Mississippi. We are not going to let this Zionist group, this branch of the Communist movement drag us into another world war to sacrifice probably five million American boys.[63]

Lawrence Smith supported the antipartitionists and claimed that the Russians would conquer the Middle East if Palestine were again partitioned. Quoting Secretary of Defense James Forrestal, he insisted that America would be dragged into war and that it would lose two million barrels of oil for each day the war lasted.[64]

Celler attacked those U.S. officials who frustrated "the will not only of the Executive but of the people." He accused Loy Henderson, the "misguided chief of the Middle East State Department, of intriguing behind the scenes to avoid decisions made on higher levels." Celler wanted Truman to investigate the motives and connections of State and Defense Department officials and to end the arms embargo.[65] (The investigation into State Department motivation took place only after the department had impeded the implementation of the president's partition decision.)

Pressure on Truman mounted. Both pro-Arab and pro-Israeli spokesmen courted his favor. Truman did not wish to see any of them.

Weizmann wanted to see Truman again because the enemies of partition were collecting UN votes to revert to trusteeship. Weizmann asked people of the American Jewish community to intervene on his behalf. All were unsuccessful in their attempts. However, they eventually discovered that Eddie Jacobson, a Jewish storekeeper in Independence, Missouri, was a longtime friend of Truman. Although Jacobson was not very involved in Jewish affairs or Zionism, he was concerned with what had happened to the Jewish people. Truman and Jacobson had been friends since the time they had both served in the army during World War I and after the war they were partners in a men's wear shop in Independence. On February 21, 1948, Jacobson wrote Truman: "I have asked you very little in the way of favors during all our years of friendship, but am begging of you to see Dr. Weizmann as soon as possible."[66]

Truman replied a few days later that there was not anything that anyone could say on the Palestine question that he had not already heard. Jacobson went to Washington anyway. The B'nai B'rith organization offered to pay his way, but Jacobson refused to take their money. He was going to see his friend and no one had to pay him for that. Jacobson recalled what had happened when he went to see Truman:

> I came to the White House on Saturday, March 13, and was greeted by Matt Connelly who advised and begged me not to discuss Palestine with the President. I quickly told Matt that that's what I came to Washington for and I was determined to discuss this very subject with the President. When I entered the President's office, I noticed with pleasure that he looked well, that his trip to Florida did him good. For a few minutes we discussed our families . . . and other personal things.
>
> I then brought up the Palestine subject. He was abrupt in speech and very bitter in the words he was throwing my way. In all the years of our friendship he never talked to me in this manner.[67]

At this point it was hard for Jacobson to talk with Truman. But he continued. He reminded Truman of his warm feelings for Weizmann. Truman had often told Jacobson as to how much he admired Weizmann. Now Jacobson informed Truman that Weizmann had come to America to see the president even though he was a sick man. Truman did not budge. Jacobson glanced at a small statue of Andrew Jackson that was on the mantle and he was inspired to say:

> Harry, all your life you have had a hero. You are probably the best read man on the life of Andrew Jackson. I remember that when we had our store together and you were always reading books and papers and pamphlets on this great American. Well, Harry, I too have a hero. I, too, studied his past and I agree with you as you have often told me, that he is a gentleman and a great statesman as well. I am talking about Chaim Weizmann. . . . Now you refuse to see him because you were insulted by some of our American Jewish leaders . . . It doesn't sound like you, Harry, because I thought that you could take this stuff they have been handing out to you.[68]

Jacobson stopped talking. Truman began to drum his fingers on his desk and to stare out the window into the rose garden, just over his family pictures. Then silence. The seconds seemed more like hours for Jacobson.

Truman looked at his old friend square in the eyes and said: "You win, you baldheaded SOB, I will see him."[69]

President Truman saw Weizmann.

They talked for almost three quarters of an hour. Weizmann talked about the possibilities of developing the Land of Israel and about the scientific work that had been done that someday would be used for industrial innovation in the Jewish state. He spoke of the need for land if the future immigrants were to be absorbed and he stressed the need of the Negev. Truman recalled that he had told Weizmann "as plainly" as he could why he had at first put off seeing him. Weizmann said that he understood. Truman "explained to him what the basis of my interest in the Jewish problem was and that my primary concern was to see justice done without bloodshed. And when he left my office I felt that he had reached a full understanding of my policy and that I knew what it was he wanted."[70]

Weizmann felt that President Truman had reassured him of his support.[71]

But the day after Weizmann saw Truman, Ambassador Warren Austin announced a reversal in the U.S. position. Austin said that the General Assembly vote of November 29, 1947, was merely a "recommendation" and not a binding decision. Since peace was at stake, he proposed the establishment of a UN trusteeship for Palestine in which Great Britain would continue to hold the Palestine Mandate. Austin's speech apparently was a rude awakening for many, including President Truman.[72]

Some officials of the State and Defense Departments had honest differences of opinion with the president, but as Truman observed in his calendar, there were individuals who always wanted to cut his throat, and with this act, they had succeeded.[73] Still others were just plain bigots. "I am sorry to say," Truman wrote in his memoirs, "there were some among them who were also inclined to be anti-Semitic."[74]

After the partition vote, those State Department officials who had opposed Truman predicted that the United States would lose bases, oil concessions, and trade and religious institutions, and that the Marshall Plan for European Recovery would suffer a setback because there would be a loss of oil. Moreover, cold war warriors like George F. Kennan and Forrestal insisted that the Soviet Union would increase its influence in the Middle East and Europe because of U.S. support for the Jewish state.[75] Dean Rusk, who led the State Department's UN division called for a reversal of the partition vote.[76]

At a National Security Council (NSC) session on February 17, 1948, General Alfred Gruenther estimated that between 80,000 and 160,000 American soldiers would be needed to enforce the partition of Palestine.[77] The NSC also considered a State Department draft report that said any solution of the Palestine problem that brought the Russians into the picture, or resulted in continued hostility, would be a danger to American security. Some of the American military officials wanted to dump the partition idea and they generally agreed with State Department officials who wanted to abandon partition and place a British trusteeship over the area.

The Central Intelligence Agency (CIA) misled the NSC with a false report that said that the British had been impartial in their efforts to curb Arab-Jewish hostilities.[78] With CIA backing, the NSC adopted Rusk's proposal for the creation of a trusteeship that would receive U.S. military support to "maintain internal order."

President Truman had seen a proposed draft of a UN speech that mentioned trusteeship as a temporary solution. He glanced at it and remarked that it looked all right, but he had not formally approved of it as a "final draft on the question."[79] Furthermore, he had tried to make it clear to Secretary Marshall that "nothing should be presented to the Security Council that could be interpreted as a recession on our part from the position we took in the General Assembly." He instructed Marshall to send him the "final draft of Austin's remarks . . . for his consideration."[80] This was not done.

Some like Clifford, a White House advisor, became alarmed by the antipartition sentiment among the Departments of State and Defense, and CIA officialdom. In early March he submitted a memo presenting arguments in favor of partition to President Truman. Delay, Clifford warned, could only result in a more unstable world situation and, unless the United Nations implemented partition, the Soviets might intervene on the pretense of preserving world peace and defending the UN Charter.[81]

Soviet minister Andrei Gromyko had on December 30, 1947, called for measures to ensure the "speediest and most effective implementation of Partition."

There were some who claimed that the Arabs would not sell their oil to the West if the United States would support partition, but the Arabs needed the United States more than the United States needed them. With or without partition, the Arabs would continue selling oil to the West. Clifford observed that the Arabs "must have oil royalties or go broke." The Arab "social and economic structure would be irreparably harmed by adopting a Soviet orientation" and they would be "committing suicide." Moreover, the experiences of World War II had taught the United States that strategic supplies like oil need to be available closer to home. It was time to develop oil resources in Colorado, Utah, and Wyoming. Clifford's memo also claimed that a failure to implement the UN's partition decision, because of U.S. diplomatic indecisiveness, would damage the reputations of both the United Nations and the United States. America's world image was already damaged, said Clifford, and he could not see how Russia or any other state could treat the United States with anything but contempt because of its "shilly-shalling appeasement of the Arabs."[82]

We would give the appearance of having "no foreign policy," of not knowing "where we are going," of presidential bewilderment, of "trembling before threats of a few nomadic desert tribes." The Arabs themselves would have greater respect for the United States if it appeased them less, Clifford argued. Arab opposition to partition was not so much a defiance of the UN partition vote as it was a "deliberate and insolent defiance of the United States."[83]

Furthermore, he said, Britain was economically exhausted and, to make up for its inability to keep an adequate military force, it turned to making alliances with Moslems from Pakistan to North Africa, but those alliances were not that important to the United States. Finally, Clifford observed that according to "competent military authorities," the Jews of Palestine were well trained and capable of coping with "any forces the Arabs could throw against them," provided they could get equipment. The Jews were strongly pro-American, while the Arabs were not. And the Jews would keep that position unless the Soviets undertook unilateral intervention.[84]

Clifford concluded his memo by proposing that the United States call on the UN Security Council to invoke economic and diplomatic sanctions against Arab states because of their acts of aggression, that the U.S. embargo on arms to the Middle East be lifted, that Britain be compelled to cooperate with the implementation of partition, and that an international security force be established to enforce partition. He was sure that, under any circumstances, President Truman would do what was "best for America," even if it meant "the defeat of the Democratic Party."[85]

Truman discovered the details of Austin's speech by reading the morning newspapers and called Clifford for an explanation. The president was shocked and could not understand how Austin could have made a speech that reversed American policy. Moreover, he was upset because it seemed to reverse everything that he had said to Weizmann. "Isn't that hell," said Truman, "I am now in the position of a liar and a double crosser. I've never felt so in my life."[86]

Those third- and fourth-level State Department officials who tried to sabotage Truman's Middle East policy were also trying to block his anti-Soviet expansion programs. Truman had hoped to "clean them out" of the State Department.[87] One wonders on what other occasions they managed to interfere with the president's foreign policy and what their motives may have been.

If Truman was as angry as he indicated to his staff and later wrote in his diary and memoirs, why did he not stop the State Department's campaign to assassinate Israel before it was born? Was he ready to accept trusteeship as a way out of the Holy Land mess? Were State and Defense Department circles so out of control that Truman could not manage them? Some say that he vetoed the activities of the "pin-stripped boys" by recognizing the state of Israel. But from at least March 19 until May 14, 1948, they seemed to have had a free hand in their combat against the establishment of a Jewish state.

Truman asked Clifford to investigate how America found itself in such a fix.

Clifford discovered that on March 16, Secretary Marshall directed Austin, on the advice of Robert Lovett, to deliver his speech at the earliest appropriate moment. He also learned that the secretary of state had made no provision to inform the president as to when the speech was to be delivered. While the president had seen the substance of the speech he had not approved a "final draft on the question." Furthermore, Truman had made it clear prior to the Austin speech that "nothing should be presented to the Security Council that could be interpreted as a recession on our part from the position we took in the General Assembly." Truman had not seen the "final draft" of Austin's speech and he had never cleared it.[88] So ended Clifford's report.

The memo dated May 4, 1948, that described these developments was in Clifford's own handwriting:

> Marshall to Austin March 16—directs Austin to make speech. Marshall says Austin is to make speech as soon as possible as Austin believes appropriate.
>
> Austin and Rusk were not instructed to delay speech until final vote in Security Council.
>
> Marshall and Lovett left no word that President was to be informed when Austin was to speak.
>
> Text of Austin's speech was not submitted to President for his approval. It was the same substance as the draft previously submitted to President.

In total disregard of Arab infiltration into Palestine, State Department officials insisted that "Jews in Palestine should be made to understand they will receive no United States backing in case they persist in following a course of violence."[89] On March 25, Truman issued a statement supporting Austin's speech. Truman said that since partition could not be carried out peacefully at the present time, the United States proposed a temporary trusteeship. This was not to be construed as a "substitution for the partition plan but as an effort to fill the vacuum soon to be created by the termination of the mandate on May 15." This reversal remains one of the many unresolved puzzles of Truman's White House years. From the recently published Israel State papers, we learn that the State Department had advised such countries as France and Belgium of Austin's statement before he addressed the United Nations on America's reversal. They had been informed, but Truman apparently was not.[90]

Despite the American reversal on partition, the Jews of the Land of Israel were determined to go ahead with their plans to establish a Jewish state. Sharett told Secretary Marshall that the Yishuv planned to fight indefinitely, even though it was "in desperate need of arms." Trusteeship, he said, was out of the question.[91]

Weizmann met with the U.S. delegation to the United Nations shortly after Austin had made his speech. He asked what had brought about the change. Were they afraid of Soviet infiltration, an oil embargo, or Arab military power? He reassured them that there were no grounds for such fears, that the Soviet Union could not succeed in establishing a foothold in a Jewish state, that the Arabs needed to sell their oil to the West, and that Arab military strength was so disorganized that it should be assigned a factor of "zero."[92]

Austin's speech caused many to be disappointed with President Truman. He seemed to be so indecisive when it came to the Palestine question that even some of Truman's good friends did not know how to handle the situation.[93]

Jacobson was distraught by what had happened. Weizmann tried to reassure him of President Truman's sincerity, but Weizmann's April 9, 1948, letter to President Truman seemed to show that even Weizmann was uncertain as to what Truman might do:

> Arabs believe that an international decision has been revised in their favor purely because they dare to use force against it. Mr. President, I cannot see how this belief can honestly be refused. The practical question now is whether your Administration will proceed to leave our people unarmed in the face of an attack which it apparently feels it is unable to stop; and whether it can allow us to come directly or indirectly under Arab domination which is sworn to our destruction.
>
> The choice for our people, Mr. President, is between Statehood and extermination. History and providence have placed this issue in your hands, and I am confident that you will yet decide it in the spirit of the moral law.[94]

Jacobson told the president that the reversal had been a "terrible shock," and he wanted to visit with Truman to talk the whole thing over and "maybe we can work something out."[95]

Truman wrote back to Jacobson. He said that he appreciated Jacobson's letter "very much and sometime or other when we have an opportunity I'll sit down and discuss the situation. . . . My sole interest in that problem now is to stop the bloodshed and see if we can't work the matter out on a peaceful basis."[96]

Members of Congress were dismayed by this apparent equivocation and indecision. Representative Leo Isacson, a member of the American Labor Party, called for a congressional investigation to determine how American investors had been able to "twist the policies of this nation." Forrestal and Undersecretary of State William Draper had been recruited from the Dillon Reed Company, which floated ARAMCO–Standard Oil bonds. Isacson wanted to know with what other Arab-connected companies did the Truman administration have ties?[97]

Representative Helen G. Douglas referred to the reversal as a "betrayal of people everywhere" and it showed "a lack of courageous and intelligent leadership."[98] Vito Marcantonio, a member of the American Labor Party from New York and a harsh critic of Roosevelt and Truman, spared no effort to condemn the reversal as just another Wall Street trick. In 1938, "stop communism was the pretense of the cartelists to appease Hitler." That "cost the lives of six million Jews." In 1948, the "same cry is raised by our Wall Street monopolies to appease the Hitlerite Arabs."[99]

The usually circumspect Jacob K. Javits found the American reversal replicative of an old "bankrupt British line" and based on a misguided and oft-disproven premise that the Arabs would be a "buffer" against Soviet expansion. Javits asked that officials like Lovett, Forrestal and Henderson "come forward and lay their cards on the table."[100]

Appeasement was a worthless policy said Eberhalter. It was a "worthless effort to impose a trusteeship upon all of Palestine." Arabs violated their UN obligations by refusing to accept trusteeship and by their invasion of Palestine. The United Nations aided and abetted that aggression by imposing an arms embargo aimed against the Jews. The Arabs obtained all the arms that they wanted from England. Unless President Truman would take decisive action, "we will later regret the horrible sacrifice and bloodshed which will inevitably occur."[101]

On March 5, the UN Security Council adopted a resolution calling on "all governments and peoples" to prevent or reduce disorders from taking place in Palestine. The resolution had no effect. On March 30, the United States introduced another resolution that called upon "Arab and Jewish armed groups to cease acts of violence immediately." The Jewish Agency representatives opposed the U.S. resolution because it conveyed the impression that the fighting simply involved the population of Palestine and that Jews and Arabs were equally guilty of violence. Sharett, the Jewish Agency representative, reminded the United Nations that Arab states had sent their forces into the fight. Before a truce could be accepted, Sharett insisted, Arab invaders had to leave the Land of Israel. "No people anywhere in the world," he said, would "voluntarily sign a truce with invading forces converging upon it and posed to strike. This would not be a truce, it would be a capitulation."

Despite such objections, the Security Council adopted the U.S. resolution. It did not prevent the Arab states from their invasion of Palestine. The State Department had detailed reports of "Arab irregular" forces invading Palestine. Some sixteen thousand troops had been recruited in Syria as of January 1, 1948, and the CIA documented that by February some eight thousand Arabs had slipped into Palestine from Syria, Lebanon, and Transjordan.[102] On April 16, the Security Council passed a third resolution that asked the belligerents to cease fighting. This time the resolution also called upon the neighboring Arab states to stop supplying the Arab guerrilla units. The resolution was ignored; the fighting continued unabated.

On April 23, Samuel Rosenman telephoned Weizmann to advise him that the president would recognize the new Jewish state as soon as it would be proclaimed. This information had to be kept absolutely secret.[103]

Truman secretly promised recognition, but the State Department kept pressuring the Yishuv not to declare independence. Undersecretary Lovett threatened to expose Zionist activities and pressures exerted on behalf of the future Jewish state. He threatened to impose an embargo on money and oil as well as munitions against the Jews of the Land of Israel. State Department officials wanted Arabs and Jews to meet for roundtable discussions at some desert location to examine their differences and work out an accord. Rusk accused the Jews of "armed aggression" and suggested a three-way split of Palestine with the northern half going to Syria and Transjordan, the southern half going to Saudi Arabia, and the Jews receiving "a coastal state from Tel Aviv to Haifa."[104]

Sharett (Shertok) advised Marshall, Lovett, and Rusk that Palestinian Jews opposed the "somewhat spectacular proceeding" of a meeting in the desert[105] and that they would "strenuously" oppose any prolongation of the British Mandate, *de jure* or *de facto*.[106] Sharett made it very clear to Marshall that there would be no more postponement.[107] Peace could be achieved through an unconditional agreement for an immediate cease-fire, but the Yishuv could never agree to another Mandate—British, United Nations, or otherwise.[108] For the Jewish people it was now or never. If they would give up the UN-endorsed Jewish independence, they might not get another chance in perhaps two thousand to five thousand years. Furthermore, American officials had gone back on their word for partition and they had even refused to permit Israel to purchase American sheet metal to protect buses from Arab attacks. Such officials had no business advising the Jews what to do. Sharett advised the Marshalls, Lovetts, and Rusks of the State Department that all their pressures and power politics would not diminish the Yishuv's will to live as a free and independent nation.[109] No doubt that show of determination on the part of the Yishuv had an impact on the Truman administration and it may have helped Truman decide in favor of recognition.

Rusk insisted that trusteeship was far more desirable than partition. As he saw it, the Jews were in control of only one-third of the area of the Jewish state as described in the UN resolution of November 29, and he preferred a truce that excluded the proclamation of a Jewish state.[110] Rusk's call for a truce was one of at least two dozen expedients that

American diplomats had tried in order to bring about a settlement. They tried everything except consideration of a Jewish state. The energy and time expended on equivocation was unprecedented in American history. In the UN Security Council, American diplomats proposed that the council carry out its responsibilities under the November 29 resolution if a threat to peace was involved; that a committee representing the world's five major powers develop a program to be presented to the council; that a temporary trusteeship for Palestine be established; that a truce between Jews and Arabs be reached; that a special session of the General Assembly consider the future of Palestine; that a truce commission composed of United States, French, and Belgian consuls be created in Jerusalem; and that Britain be persuaded to agree to trusteeship and to furnish troops. Those same diplomats worked to obtain British cooperation for a short extension of the mandate's life. They invited Judah Magnes, president of the Hebrew University and an anti-Zionist, to meet with Truman. They also tried to persuade the Jewish Agency to accept trusteeship and to agree to a ten-day "stop-the-clock" truce with a temporary continuation of the British Mandate; to negotiate a ninety-day truce; and to dissuade the Jewish Agency from declaring a Jewish state after May 15. In addition, the State Department officials worked hard at enforcing an arms embargo and they sought to discourage all other countries from furnishing military supplies to Israel. They even tried to prevent Jewish immigration to the Land of Israel.[111]

Washington officialdom had used every imaginable argument against the Jewish state idea. The importance of oil and the danger from Russia was the most often repeated argument against the Jewish state. Max Ball, director of the oil and gas division of the Department of Interior, presented the typical argument. Oil meant social progress, a higher standard of living, education, and the promotion of democratic government and as far as he was concerned it could help prevent Europe from "falling to communism or the dogs."[112] Lovett, Forrestal, Rusk, and Henderson, among others, used the same line. Because of the serious U.S. oil shortage, they said, the United States could not afford to antagonize the Arabs. They not only advocated appeasement of the Arabs, but Lovett warned Zionists of an increased anti-Semitism in America if it became necessary for the United States to send troops into the Middle East.[113] They likewise threatened to cut all private assistance to the Jewish community of the Land of Israel if it declared its independence. The American loan Truman had promised in the summer of 1948 would not be forthcoming until the winter of 1949.

Officials like Lovett saw trusteeship as advantageous to Israel. For them the fact that the United States voted for partition was not binding on the United States. If the United States would have to implement all the General Assembly decisions, "we would have to send our troops to

Kashmir, to Indonesia and to half of the whole world." Were the General Assembly to implement its political decisions "it would mean a world government," but "we haven't yet reached that point." Lovett thought that the Jews should have negotiated with the Arabs in January when Israel's position was "very strong politically" and Israel should have tried to "improve" their relationship with Great Britain. The British were "a most decisive factor" and the Jews should have tried to "reach some *modus vivendi* with them." Lovett insisted that the Jews should accept a truce, and if they did not, their situation would become very tough for them. Unless the Jews would be more forthcoming, "we will wash our hands of the whole situation and will prevent any help from being given to you." Lovett threatened to publish a White Paper that "will incriminate the Arabs and the British, but not less the Jews." He spoke of anti-Semitism as mounting in America and that his White Paper "would do great harm to the Jews in this country." Once published, Lovett warned, "I am not sure that outstanding Jewish leaders who are helping you today would go along with you." Lovett warned that the United States would "not allow the Arabs or the Jews to go on fighting with the help of American dollars."[114]

On May 9, 1948, Lovett warned the Jewish Agency not to proclaim an independent state on May 16. He said there would be sanctions if it did. Sharett advised him that if that happened "it would force Israel into the Soviet orbit."[115]

Nahum Goldmann likewise advised Lovett that if the United States and Britain would abandon Israel, it would turn to the Soviet Union for help. Lovett was greatly upset. He warned that if the Jewish people wanted "to commit suicide nobody could prevent them." But the United States would take the necessary measures. The Jews should "not believe for a moment that we will sit quietly and see the Russians come into Palestine." And this he warned would not be handled by the State Department, but by the Defense Department.[116]

State Department officials complained that Americans pressured the Truman administration to favor Israel. Lovett seemed unable to accept the notion that in a democratic society the people had a right to express their will and opinions. Israeli officials were advised by the State Department "that the only way of influencing American policy" with regard to Israel was through diplomacy rather than through "the use of sympathetic groups inside the United States."[117]

Israeli representatives advised their American counterparts that there was "nothing illegitimate in the desire of Jewish and non-Jewish groups in the United States to give all possible help to Israel in its fight for peace, territorial integrity and prosperity." The Irish, Poles, Germans, Italians, and others in America gave their support to their countries of origins and there existed all sorts of pressure and lobby groups in Washington.

Why should friends of Israel be denied the right to support Israel in Washington?[118]

State Department officials disregarded Arab infiltration into Palestine and they insisted that the "Jews in Palestine should be made to understand that they will receive no United States backing in case they persist in following a course of violence."[119]

Republican politicians were approached by American Zionists in the hope that they could persuade the Truman administration to be more helpful. By February 1948, leading Republicans like Taft, Arthur Vandenberg, John F. Dulles, and Thomas E. Dewey had given their private assurances of support, but Zionists felt that such words were worth "a dime a dozen" in the struggle against the many officials of State and Defense Departments.[120] Those officials had not only maneuvered against presidential policy, but they had campaigned successfully to persuade elements of the American press and media against the establishment of a Jewish state.

Almost the entire editorial board of the *New York Times* seemed against the Jewish state idea when Jewish Agency representative Eliahu Elath (Epstein) talked with them on March 5, 1948. Editorialist James Reston seemed to reflect the attitude of the *Times* when he said that a proclamation of independence would only bring further bloodshed to the area. Only Arthur H. Sulzberger seemed to disagree with Reston and then he complained that American Zionists had boycotted his paper. Elath reminded him that the anti-Zionist articles of the *Times* had not only harmed the Yishuv and the cause of Jewish independence, but they had also endangered the lives of Jewish displaced persons in Europe who needed Palestine.[121]

There had been previous interventions with the *Times*. In early February 1948, two American Zionists, Abe Tuvin and Joseph P. Sternstein, met with Julius Ochs Adler of the *Times*. They objected to the way the *Times* reported the news concerning Israel and Zionism. Adler read their written protests and claimed that the charges were debatable. He rejected the accusation that the *Times* "Letters to the Editor" column had been unfair in its inclusion of letters against Zionism. As to the assertion about Reston's claim that American officials were determined to reverse the UN partition decision, Adler asked, "Well, isn't that true?"

Adler informed his guests that Secretary of War Forrestal was vigorously opposed to partition. Tuvin and Sternstein strongly rejected Herbert L. Matthews' stories from London regarding Jewish communists. When Adler insisted that it was important news and that it had to be reported, he was told that many readers felt that the *Times* had become an "enemy of the Jewish people and the mouthpiece of the British Colonial office and that an increasing number of people doubted the veracity of the *Times*."[122]

American Zionists had various complaints against the *New York*

Times's style of reporting the news. When it reported the partition resolution of November 30, 1947, its editorial noted, "Many of us have long had doubts on another score: doubts concerning the wisdom of erecting a political state on the basis of religious faith." Why did the *Times* fail to comment on the Syrian invasion of the Holy Land? Why did it fail to comment on Britain's refusal to leave Palestine on time? Why did the *Times* tolerate "misleading and fallacious" statements by such correspondents as Reston? In his January 26 report Reston had claimed that pro-Zionists in America had tried to "induce the Government to send United States troops to Palestine to assist in implementing the U.N. partition." But this was not true. American Zionists had made no such effort. This had never been part of Zionist policy and it "never will be." Matthews, in a dispatch from London, had reported that "illegal" vessels namely the *Pan Crescent* and the *Pan York* had carried a large group of communist agents to Israel and the *New York Times* radio station WQXR broadcasted this canard as if it were true. The *Times* also printed an equal number of pro and con letters on Zionist issues. The assumption was that an equal number of pro-Israel and anti-Israel letters had been received by that paper. As Elath noted, newspapers had a responsibility to indicate truthfully how readers responded to national and international issues. The letters should have been selected on a more "proportional basis."[123]

Partition was an accomplished fact as Clifford explained it to President Truman on May 9. The British acknowledged that fact from the reports of British military commanders in Palestine and Egypt, as well as their heavy investments in Jewish enterprise in the Land of Israel. The Jews organized and maintained essential governmental services and proclaimed their intention of confining the Jewish state to areas assigned them in the UN partition plan, even though they could have extended military control to other areas. The president had a choice, said Clifford: he could either recognize a Jewish state or he could seek a reversal by using force, sanctions, threats or persuasion. But since those methods had not succeeded in the past, there was no reason to believe they could work in the future. By extending recognition, Truman could regain some of the prestige he had lost during the previous weeks and months of equivocation. American prestige in the Arab world would likewise increase since the Arabs respected "reality rather than sentimentality." American prestige would likewise be enhanced vis-à-vis the Russians. It was expected that the Russians and their satellites would recognize the Jewish state and if they were the first to do so, American recognition might be regarded as "begrudging," and this "would represent a diplomatic defeat for the United States." At home, Republicans would be pressing Truman "before, during and after their convention" for recognition, but that pressure could be eliminated from the Republican campaign provided Truman recognized the Jewish state before May 16.[124]

By May 12, 1948, Clifford received field reports indicating that the Jews could defend themselves successfully. Major George Eliot, a writer for American papers, reported that the efficiency and strength that the Jewish army had displayed in the field during the past few weeks raised some grave doubts as to whether a concerted invasion by all the Arab armies could be successful after May 15. Daniel DeLuce, of the Associated Press, reported that the Jewish state was a reality. Regardless of the exaggerated pronouncements issued after each Arab conference, there were strong indications that the old jealousies among the Arab potentates and premiers ran on unabated.[125]

Despite the optimistic evaluations of the Jewish position in Palestine during May 1948, it was far from good. They had few men and hardly enough equipment with which to face the challenges of well-armed enemies. According to published sources, the total number of men and women in the Haganah forces on May 14, 1948, was between 28,760 and 35,000. This included the mobilized infantry, the home guard, air force, navy, and special services units. They had 22,000 rifles, 11,000 submachine guns, 105 three-inch mortars, 682 two-inch mortars, 16 Davidkas, 75 Piats and anti-tank rifles, and four 65 mm artillery pieces. The Arabs had far more men and substantially more equipment of every sort.[126]

Jewish leaders had expected the West to provide the future state with supplies and they believed that they could succeed with those supplies. The supplies never came from the West because of the Anglo-Arab blockade and the UN sponsored embargo. On April 17, 1948, the UN Security Council passed a resolution that imposed a general arms embargo, and a ban on immigrants of fighting age to the Palestine area. While some UN members like the United States upheld the resolution, Britain continued to furnish arms to Egypt, Transjordan, and Iraq. Using the communist bogeyman threat, the British claimed that their treaty obligations required them to ship arms to the Arabs. Ambassador Archibald Inverchapel argued that unless the British provided the Arabs with arms, they would not be able to prevent internal disorders caused by communist subversives.[127] The State Department continued to advise Truman not to lift the arms embargo. If the United States provided Jews with weapons, it would "evoke hostile and violent mob reactions against the United States and thereby damage American-Arab relations." Moreover, it would "result in the destruction of American tactical and strategic security throughout the entire Near East."[128] Russia and Czechoslovakia ignored the UN embargo resolution and sold arms to both Jews and Arabs.[129]

On May 13, Weizmann wrote President Truman, suggesting that the United States, "the greatest living democracy be the first to welcome the newest into the family of nations." But Lovett and Marshall still maintained that such a move would be "injurious to the Prestige of the President." Lovett charged the president with trying to "win the Jewish vote" with recognition of the Jewish state. Clifford advised President Truman to recognize the Jewish state. Lovett complained that Palestine was filled with "Jews and Communist agents from the Black Sea area." Marshall said that "if the President were to follow Mr. Clifford's advice . . . he would vote against the President" in the next election. President Truman responded to all his advisors that he was fully aware of the difficulties and dangers of the situation and the political risks he would face.[130]

While the Arabs rattled their swords and State Department officials prophetized the coming of Armageddon, the Palestinian Jews asked the world to persuade the Arabs not to make war. On May 13, 1948, Sharett telegraphed Truman: "Urge immediate strongest effort secure immediate direct sternest warning by President personally to King Abdullah" not to commit his armies to the conflict.[131] "Hours count," said Sharett.[132]

Some have made it seem as if Truman's decision to recognize Israel was a move shrouded in secrecy. It was no secret. The possibility of U.S. recognition and the timing of Israel's proclamation was known and endorsed by various members of Congress. On the day Truman would recognize Israel, Celler announced: "Independence will be declared at 6 p.m., this evening. Take hold of yourself," said Celler to Truman, "push back some of your misadvisers and do what your heart prompts you to do."[133] "I always felt that the only ultimate solution of this age-old question," said Congressman John McCormack, "was the establishment in Palestine of a free and independent Jewish commonwealth." The sooner that Jewish state would become strong the better the chance for peace in the Middle East.[134]

As Israel prepared to declare its independence, Clifford asked Elath of the Jewish Agency if the Jews were still determined to proclaim their independence. "There wasn't the slightest doubt," said Elath. Clifford then asked him to draft a letter requesting U.S. recognition.[135] With the help of Benjamin V. Cohen, he drafted the following request:

> With full knowledge of the deep bound of sympathy which has existed and has been strengthened over the past thirty years between the Government of the United States and the Jewish people of Palestine. I have been authorized by the provisional government of the new state to tender this message and to express the hope that your government will recognize and will welcome Israel into the community of nations.[136]

The letter was rushed to the White House and President Truman responded with the following statement of recognition some ten minutes after Israel proclaimed its independence:

> This Government has been informed that a Jewish state has been proclaimed in Palestine, and recognition has been requested by the provisional Government thereof.

The United States recognizes the provisional government as the *de facto* authority of the new Jewish State of Israel.

Harry Truman

Approved,
May 14, 1948
6:11[137]

At 5:45 P.M., Clifford gave Rusk a call to tell him that President Truman would recognize Israel at 6 P.M. Rusk was still opposed. He claimed that recognition would "cut across what our Delegation has been trying to accomplish in the General Assembly under instructions and we have a large majority for that approval." They sought to establish a British trusteeship over Palestine. "Nevertheless," said Clifford, "this is what the President wishes you to do."[138]

Clifford called Ambassador Austin, who was addressing the UN General Assembly. Austin left the rostrum to speak with Rusk. When he heard that the president had decided to recognize Israel, he refused to return to the General Assembly that day.[139] Some officials in the State Department threatened to resign, but it was only talk; no one resigned.[140]

Truman's move was enthusiastically received by Israel and its backers. Expressions of support could be heard throughout Congress. Thomas applauded Truman and echoed Henry Morgenthau's suggestion that the European Recovery Program, the Export-Import Bank, and the International Bank should "consider sympathetically any applications that may be submitted by the new state."[141]

Some of the congressional declarations of approval were rejected with requests that Truman lift the arms embargo against Israel. Congressmen John J. Rooney, Klein, and James J. Hefferman were among the members of Congress that supported an end to the arms embargo since Israel had to face enemies that were far better armed and superior in numbers.[142]

Javits, Celler, Holifield, Abraham J. Multer, Barkley, Vandenberg, John Joseph O'Connor, Ralph Owen Brewster, Irving Ives, and Warren G. Magnuson applauded Truman's decision to recognize Israel. They indicated their appreciation for his ability to "finally" grasp "the realities of conditions" as they were, and they commended him for taking the "proper step" but they all said that he had to do more than just recognize Israel *de facto*.[143]

What was it that persuaded Truman to support the Jewish state and to be the first to recognize it? Was it the strong almost overwhelming endorsement Israel received from Congress? Perhaps the members of Congress may have had an impact on his thinking. Truman had been in Congress for ten years and he respected the constitutional right of advice and consent that Congress offered.

Was it the presence of Russia in the Middle East that persuaded Truman to seek out Israel? The Arabs were greater in number and they had far more land, but they were still feudalistic and asleep atop their oil resources.

Was the 1948 election a factor? Truman wanted to win that election and all issues concerned him, but the Republicans were as much for Israel as the Democrats in and outside of Congress. He was concerned with getting votes, and yet at times, he pursued policies with respect to Israel that alienated many voters. He sustained a one-sided arms embargo and failed to make good the promise of a loan to Israel until January 1949.

There were many factors that helped influence Truman, but there was still one more factor that is often ignored. The attempt on the part of Washington officialdom to make U.S. foreign policy and to kill his policy decisions helped direct him against their viewpoints. Who, after all, was president? By what right did Lovett instruct Austin to dynamite America's support for partition or recognition? He had permitted officials in the State and Defense Departments to have free reign in the Middle East. He had to reassert his credential as president and formulate American foreign policy or he might have had to resign. The study of Truman's policy towards Israel is interesting not only because it indicates how difficult it was for a president to establish policy, but also to overcome opposition from within his own administration even after policy goals were set. It was not easy to be an effective and decisive president. He had to both cope with the challenges and issues that faced the United States, and be aware of his own people who wanted to be the decision makers and who wanted to be president.

During all of Truman's studies of American history and his ten years in the Senate, he had never seen such disregard of the presidency. Regardless of his pledged word, regardless of the Democratic platform commitments, and regardless of Soviet threats, such Washington officials as Rusk, Ball, Kennan, Lovett, Dean Acheson, Henderson, and Forrestal tried to conduct their own version of American foreign policy. At times they refused to follow Truman's policies even after he had specified what those policies and programs were to be.

Even after Truman had extended recognition, some of these individuals pretended that America's recognition was tentative and they wanted to see England maintain a mandate over the Land of Israel. They continued to appease Arab extremists and they wanted to do away with the Jewish state. Truman could not afford to ignore them. He had to fight them and win, not just for the sake of his presidency, but for American democracy.

Some of the officials in the State and Defense Departments expressed surprise when Truman recognized Israel. But they need not have been surprised had they followed his policies instead of trying to sabotage them.[144] While the men and women of Israel made partition a reality and recognition added to that reality, peace and security for Israel was still very far away. Israel would continue to face opposition from such sources as the State Department and the British Foreign Office. They would have to face the Bernadotte Plan, arms embargoes, foreign interventions, factionalism within Israeli society, and meddling Jewish politicos outside of Israel.

Truman appointed McDonald as the U.S. ambassador to Israel. He did so independently of the State Department. Truman appointed McDonald because he had a high regard for him and because McDonald was independent of the State Department bureaucracy that had tried to redirect Truman's foreign policies.[145]

On June 24, 1948, Ambassador Elath reported that the Republican Party platform was weak in its support of Israel. He believed that it was because of Senator Vandenberg. Dulles, the foreign affairs advisor to Dewey, had drafted a more favorable document. Among the Republicans who were more supportive of Israel that Elath mentioned there were: Ives, Brewster, Raymond E. Baldwin, C. Wayland Brooks, Edward Moore, Forrest Donnell, Javits, Klein of the Jewish War Veterans, journalist George E. Sokolsky, New York attorney general Goldstein, and Rabbi Silver.[146]

In mid-July 1948, the Israeli ambassador reported that there had been a tough and bitter debate at the Democratic platform committee hearings as they worked on a pro-Israel plank. Democrats pledged full recognition of Israel; support of the November 29, 1947, boundaries and that they could be modified only if Israel agreed; support of Israel's membership in the United Nations; appropriate economic aid to Israel; and revision of the arms embargo and the internationalization of Jerusalem.[147]

When it was suggested that Jerusalem might be turned into an international city, Weizmann advised Truman that the idea was repulsive to Israel. "The only interest the world has in Jerusalem is the holy shrines" and they constitute "only two percent of all of Jerusalem" and the "bulk of this sacred area is not in our possession but in that of Abdullah." While he agreed that such places should be given "special safeguards" and "protection," he could not agree that "our ancient Mother-City should be severed from the new Commonwealth of Israel."[148] "How can any right thinking man demand that the Jews of Jerusalem, who last year went through hunger, thirst and deadly peril in defense of their city, should now be placed under alien rule?" asked Weizmann. "We are trying to live up to the hopes which you placed in us when you gave us your generous support . . . but to fulfill that task we need peace. I pray that you may do what you can to help preserve it."[149]

Ambassador Elath asked Jacobson to intervene with Truman. Truman told Jacobson that the United States would not support any Arab or British demands on Israel's territories as defined by the UN resolution of November 29, 1947. He said that he was "bitter sick about Bevin and he condemned the British intrigues responsible for his personal difficulty to settle the Palestine problem."[150]

Israel's Washington embassy experts anticipated that Dewey would win the 1948 election. Moreover, they concluded that Truman had been more influenced by "departmental recommendations" than by his "personal attitude." They likewise predicted that Dulles would become Dewey's secretary of state. Dulles had "never been particularly friendly nor intimately concerned with the Palestine problem." It was expected that Dewey would be "more decisively controlled by Dulles than Truman was by Marshall." They observed that while both the Republican and Democratic platforms had been "exceedingly friendly" to Israel, it would be wise to "discount their importance" in the long run.[151]

On January 26, 1949, the United States extended *de jure* recognition to Israel and it granted Israel a loan for $100 million. Ambassador Elath observed that this would give Israel the "right to view the future with a little more optimism" but this did not mean that "we are out of the woods."[152]

The man from Independence had moments of hesitation when it came to the question of Israel. Like Roosevelt before him and the many presidents after him, Truman tried to follow a middle-of-the-road policy between the Arabs and the Israelis, something that neither side appreciated, but he did support the new state and he saw great hope for all the people in the Middle East. He envisioned Israel as a beacon of light that would help stimulate economic and industrial growth throughout that part of the world. Through the Truman Doctrine, the Marshall Plan, and Point Four self-help programs, he provided aid to all those states that were prepared to help themselves. As he stated in a 1962 interview, America had sent a team of Tennessee Valley Authority engineers and experts to help advise the Iraqi government on how to develop the Tigris and Euphrates Rivers. Those experts came up with a plan to develop that region, which could sustain sixty million people. Iraq made no use of that plan. "The plan is in my library. They can have it for free."[153]

On November 29, 1948, Truman wrote Weizmann: "I was struck by the common experience you and I have recently shared. We had both been abandoned by the so-called realistic experts of our supposedly forlorn causes. Yet we both kept pressing for what we were sure was right—and we were both proven to be right."[154]

NOTES

1. Individual's Files, Zionist Archives, New York.

2. McCloy was the same official who had rejected various pleas to bomb the Auschwitz concentration camp and the railroads leading to that death camp. See

U.S. Department of State, *Foreign Relations of the United States, 1944*, Volume V (Washington, D.C., 1965), February 2, 1944, pp. 574–576.

3. Interview with Harry S Truman, August 1, 1962, Independence, Missouri.

4. Judah Nadich, *Eisenhower and the Jews* (New York, 1953), pp. 113–114.

5. *Public Papers of the Presidents of the United States, Harry S Truman, Containing the Public Messages, Speeches and Statements of the President*, April 12 to December 31, 1945 (Washington, D.C., 1961), December 22, 1945, pp. 572–576.

6. Harry S Truman to David K. Niles, Official File 204, Harry S Truman Library, Independence Missouri. According to Saul S. Friedman, *No Haven for the Oppressed* (Detroit, 1973), the Stratton Displaced Persons Bill of 1947 resulted in the admission to the United States of only 2,499 Jews out of a total of 220,000 admitted.

7. Samuel I. Rosenman Papers, Harry S Truman Library, Independence, Missouri.

8. U.S. Department of State, *The Conference of Berlin (Potsdam Conference)*, Volume II, (Washington, D.C., 1960), July 31, 1945, pp. 537–539.

9. Interview with Judge Samuel I. Rosenman, New York, April 19, 1961.

10. *Public Papers of Harry S Truman*, January 1–December 31, 1950 (Washington, D.C., 1965), June 17, 1950, pp. 494–96.

11. Harry S Truman, *Years of Trial and Hope* (New York, 1956), p. 69.

12. Ibid., p. 134.

13. The Jewish community of the Land of Israel.

14. U.S. Department of State, *Foreign Relations of the United States, 1945*, Volume VIII (Washington, D.C., 1969), June 27, 1945, pp. 713–715.

15. Truman, *Years of Trial and Hope*, pp. 134–135, 162, 164, 165; Margaret Truman, *Harry S Truman* (New York, 1973), pp. 388–389.

16. Truman, *Years of Trial and Hope*, p. 137.

17. *Potsdam Conference*, Volume II, p. 1407; *Foreign Relations, 1945*, Volume VIII, August 18, 1945, p. 722; *Public Papers of Harry S Truman*, p. 228.

18. Harry S Truman to Clement Attlee, August 31, 1945, President's Official File 204, Harry S Truman Library, Independence, Missouri.

19. *Foreign Relations, 1945*, Volume VIII, August 20, 1945, pp. 723–724.

20. Chaim Weizmann to Harry S Truman, December 12, 1945, Jewish Agency Papers, Individuals Files, Zionist Archives, New York.

21. Papers of Harry S Truman, Official File 204, Harry S Truman Library, Independence, Missouri.

22. U.S. Department of State, *Foreign Relations of the United States, 1946*, Volume VII (Washington, D.C., 1969), April 27, 1946, pp. 587–588.

23. *Public Papers of Harry S Truman*, January 1–December 31, 1946 (Washington, 1962), April 25, 1946.

24. *Foreign Relations, 1946*, Volume VII, May 1, 1946, pp. 589–590.

25. Papers of Harry S Truman, President's Official File 204, Harry S Truman Library, Independence, Missouri.

26. Herman P. Eberhalter to President Harry S Truman, May 23, 1946, President's Official File 204, Harry S Truman Library, Independence, Missouri.

27. Truman, *Years of Trial and Hope*, p. 148–149; *New York Times* May 5, 1946; *Foreign Relations, 1946*, Volume VII, June 21, 1946, pp. 632–633.

28. *Congressional Record*, June 27, 1946, A3784.

29. Ibid., July 12, 1946, A4139.

30. Truman, *Years of Trial and Hope*, pp. 150–154; *Public Papers of Harry S Truman*, July 2, 1946, June 18, 1946, p. 335; *New York Times*, June 18, 1946.

31. Ibid., July 2, 1946, p. A3894.

32. Ibid., July 3, 1946, pp. A3894–3895.

33. Ibid.

34. James G. McDonald interview with President Harry S Truman, July 27, 1946, Benjamin Akzin Files, American Zionist Emergency Council Papers, Zionist Archives, New York.

35. Ibid.

36. Ibid.

37. *Congressional Record*, August 2, 1946, p. A4952.

38. Harry S Truman to Walter F. George, October 8, 1946, Stephen S. Wise Papers, Brandeis University Archives, Waltham, Massachusetts.

39. King Ibn Sa'ūd to President Harry S Truman, October 15, 1946, President's Official File 204, Harry S Truman Library, Independence, Missouri; *New York Times*, October 18, 29, 1946.

40. President Harry S Truman to King Ibn Sa'ūd, October 25, 1946, President's Official File 204, Harry S Truman Library, Independence, Missouri; *Foreign Relations, 1946*, Volume VII, October 25, 1946, pp. 714–717.

41. *Congressional Record*, April 1, 1947, pp. 2995–2996; *New York Times*, April 1, 1947.

42. Interview with Emanuel Neumann (member of the Zionist Executive), May 6, 1971.

43. General George C. Marshall to President Harry S Truman, President's Official File 204, Undated, Harry S Truman Library, Independence, Missouri.

44. Chaim Weizmann to Justice Felix Frankfurter, Henry Morgenthau, and Rabbi Stephen S. Wise, May 1, 1947, Stephen S. Wise Papers, Brandeis University Archives, Waltham, Massachusetts; Jon Kimche and David Kimche, *The Secret Roads* (London, 1954), p. 30.

45. David C. Holly, *Exodus 1947* (Boston, 1969).

46. Ibid.

47. Robert St. John, *Eban* (New York, 1972), pp. 168–169.

48. Eliahu Elath, *Israel and Elath: The Political Struggle for the Inclusion of Elath in the Jewish State* (London, 1966), p. 10.

49. Ibid., p. 13.

50. Ibid.

51. Ibid.

52. Ibid., pp. 19–20.

53. Ibid., pp. 22–23.

54. Ibid.

55. Shertok changed his name to Sharett.

56. Dan Kurzman, *Genesis 1948: The First Arab-Israeli War* (New York, 1970), p. 14.

57. *Congressional Record*, May 9, 1947, p. A2201.

58. G. Yogev, ed., *Political and Diplomatic Documents*, December 1947–May 1948 (Jerusalem, 1979) p. 71.

59. Ibid., pp. 283, 352.

60. Ibid., pp. 40–41.

61. Kimche and Kimche, *The Secret Roads*, p. 70.

62. *Congressional Record*, January 2, 1946, pp. 454–455; February 19, 1948, p. 1418.

63. *Congressional Record*, January 15, 1948, p. 204.

64. *Congressional Record*, January 22, 1948, pp. A434–435.

65. *Congressional Record*, January 13, p. 121; February 3, 1948, p. 1033.

66. Eddie Jacobson to Matt Connelly, Eddie Jacobson Papers, Zionist Archives, New York.

67. From the Harry S Truman Library, Independence, Missouri; the Individuals Files of the Zionist Archives, New York; and B'nai B'rith Archives, B'nai B'rith Headquarters, Washington, D.C.

68. Ibid.

69. Ibid.

70. Truman, *Years of Trial and Hope*, p. 161.

71. Weizmann wrote in his memoirs that the "President was sympathetic personally, and still indicated a firm resolve to press forward with partition." See Weizmann, *Trial and Error*, p. 577.

72. Margaret Truman, *Harry S Truman* (New York, 1973), p. 388. According to Joseph P. Lash, *Eleanor: The Years Alone* (New York, 1972), pp. 122–123, U.S. officials led by Forrestal and Robert Lovett campaigned for a trusteeship over Palestine. Rabbi Israel Goldstein, former president of the Zionist Organization of America, claimed that there were some American Zionists who were ready to accept a trusteeship rather than have a war. Interview with Israel Goldstein on October 2, 1973.

73. M. Truman, *Harry S Truman*, p. 388.

74. Truman, *Years of Trial and Hope*, p. 164; Interview with Emanuel Neumann, May 6, 1971.

75. U.S. Department of State, *Foreign Relations of the United States, 1948*, Volume V, Part 2 (Washington, D.C., 1976), pp. 549–561.

76. Ibid., pp. 593–595.

77. Kurzman, *Genesis 1948*, pp. 84–86; M. Truman, *Harry S Truman*, p. 388.

78. *Foreign Relations, 1948*, Volume V, Part 2, pp. 670–671.

79. M. Truman, *Harry S Truman*, p. 388.

80. Harry S Truman to George C. Marshall, *Foreign Relations, 1948*, Volume V, Part 2, February 22, 1948, p. 645.

81. Clark Clifford Memo, March 8, 1948, Clark Clifford Papers, Harry S Truman Library, Independence, Missouri; *Foreign Relations, 1948*, Volume V, Part 2, March 8, 1948, pp. 687–696.

82. Ibid.

83. Ibid.

84. Ibid.

85. Ibid.

86. M. Truman, *Harry S Truman*, pp. 388–389. That morning the Russians called upon the Arabs to withdraw their forces from Palestine. The Russians called for an end to the bloodshed and war, which had been brought on by the Arabs. See *Foreign Relations, 1948*, Volume V, Part 2, pp. 732–735. According to

Charles Bohlen, of the State Department, Truman "was so much exercised in the matter" because "Austin made his statement without the President having been advised that he was going to make it at that particular time." See Charles Bohlen to George C. Marshall, *Foreign Relations, 1948*, Volume V, Part 2, March 22, 1948, p. 750.

87. M. Truman, *Harry S Truman*, pp. 388–389.

88. Clark Clifford Memo, May 4, 1948, Clark Clifford Papers, Harry S Truman Library, Independence, Missouri.

89. *Foreign Relations, 1948*, Volume V, Part 2, pp. 756–757.

90. Yogev, *Political and Diplomatic Documents*, pp. 482–484.

91. Ibid., pp. 762–763.

92. Ibid., pp. 821–824.

93. Lash, *Eleanor*, p. 130.

94. Chaim Weizmann to President Harry S Truman, April 9, 1948, Zionist Archives, New York. Weizmann's letter was filed away with the following notation: "Not answered RAC (Rose A. Conway, Administrative Assistant in the President's office)," President's Official File 204 Misc., Harry S Truman Papers, Independence, Missouri; *Foreign Relations, 1948*, Volume V, Part 2, pp. 802–809.

95. Personal Papers of the President, File 1656, Harry S Truman Library, Independence, Missouri.

96. Ibid.

97. *Congressional Record*, March 22, 1948, pp. 3239–3240.

98. Ibid., p. 3241.

99. Ibid., p. 3243.

100. Ibid., April 12, 1948, p. 4335.

101. Ibid., April 27, 1948, p. 4900.

102. *Foreign Relations, 1948*, Volume V, Part 2, pp. 798–800, 832–833.

103. Kurzman, *Genesis 1948*, p. 212.

104. *Foreign Relations, 1948*, Volume V, Part 2, pp. 640–648, 894–895; Kurzman, *Genesis 1948*, p. 212; interview with Emanuel Neumann, May 6, 1971; Moshe Shertok to Dean Rusk, May 4, 1948, Clark Clifford Papers, Harry S Truman Library, Independence, Missouri. Every possible means was used by American officials in order to block the Zionist cause. Lovett invited the anti-Zionist Judah P. Magnes, president of Hebrew University, to Washington so that he would speak against Zionism. Magnes met with U.S. officials in May and spoke against the Jewish state idea. Time, he said, was on the side of the Arabs. He urged that the United States impose "financial sanctions" against both Jews and Arabs so as to bring an end to the fighting. He felt certain that "if contributions from the United States were cut off, the Jewish war machine in Palestine would come to a halt." He believed that only trusteeship was the answer. His views fit especially well with the views of State Department officials and of such organizations as the American Jewish Committee of that time. *Foreign Relations, 1948*, Volume V, Part 2, pp. 901–904.

105. Ibid.

106. Ibid.

107. Ibid.

108. Moshe Sharett (Shertok) to Dean Rusk, May 4, 1948, Clark Clifford Papers, Harry S Truman Library, Independence, Missouri.

109. Memo on meeting between Moshe Shertok, Eliahu Elath, George C. Marshall, Robert Lovett, and Dean Rusk, May 8, 1948, Israel State Archives, Jerusalem, pp. 757–769.

110. Clark Clifford conversations with Dean Rusk, May 6 and 9, 1948, Clark Clifford Papers, Harry S Truman Library, Independence, Missouri.

111. Unsigned Memo to Clark Clifford, May 7, 1948, Clark Clifford Papers, Harry S Truman Library, Independence, Missouri.

112. Yogev, *Political and Diplomatic Documents*, pp. 482–484.

113. Ibid., pp. 776, 297.

114. Memo of Nahum Goldmann's conversation with Robert Lovett, April 28, 1948, Z6/2759, Nahum Goldmann Papers, Zionist Archives, Jerusalem.

115. Eliahu Elath to Moshe Sharett (Shertok) (no date given), Israel Foreign Office Papers (Eliav Files) 2308/6, Israel State Archives, Jerusalem.

116. Ibid.

117. "U.S. Foreign Policy and attitudes of the State Department regarding Israel," unsigned memo dated November 17, 1948, Israel Foreign Office Papers, 2479/8, Israel State Archives, Jerusalem.

118. Ibid.

119. *Foreign Relations, 1948*, Volume V, Part 2, pp. 756–757.

120. Yogev, *Political and Diplomatic Documents*, pp. 361–362.

121. Ibid., pp. 393–394, 426–427.

122. Memo regarding the *New York Times* by Abe Tuvim and Joseph P. Sternstein, February 10, 1948, Foreign Office Papers, 70/9, Israel State Archives, Jerusalem.

123. Ibid.

124. Clark Clifford Memo dated May 9, 1948, Clark Clifford Papers, Harry S Truman Library, Independence, Missouri.

125. Clark Clifford Memo dated, May 12, 1948, Clark Clifford Papers, Harry S Truman Library, Independence, Missouri.

126. Jon Kimche and David Kimche, *A Clash of Destinies* (New York, 1960), pp. 160–162.

127. *Foreign Relations, 1948*, Volume V, Part 2, p. 581.

128. Ibid., p. 1060 ff.

129. Kimche and Kimche, *A Clash of Destinies*, p. 157.

130. *Foreign Relations, 1948*, Volume V, Part 2, pp. 972–977.

131. Clark Clifford Memo, May 13, 1948, Clark Clifford Papers, Harry S Truman Library, Independence, Missouri.

132. *Foreign Relations, 1948*, Volume V, Part 2, pp. 972–977.

133. *Congressional Record*, May 14, 1948, p. 5831.

134. Ibid., pp. 5830–5831.

135. *Foreign Relations, 1948*, Volume V, Part 2, p. 959.

136. Eliahu Elath to Moshe Sharett, May 14, 1948, Israel Foreign Office Papers, 2308/6, Israel State Archives.

137. Ibid.

138. *Foreign Relations, 1948*, Volume V, Part 2, pp. 1005–1007.

139. Ibid., p. 993.

140. Interview with Harry S Truman, August 1, 1962, Independence, Missouri.

141. *Congressional Record*, May 16, 1948, p. A3164.

142. *Congressional Record,* May 18, 19, 20, 1948, pp. A3081–3082, A3152, A3157–3158, A3188.

143. *Congressional Record,* May 14, 17, 18, 1948, pp. 5830, 5831, 5836, 5905, 5906, 5907, 5908, 5986, 5987, 5990.

144. Truman, *Years of Trial and Hope,* p. 164.

145. Eliahu Elath to Moshe Sharett, June 24, 1948, Israel Foreign Office Papers, 2308/6, Israel State Archives, Jerusalem.

146. Ibid.

147. Eliahu Elath to Moshe Sharett, July 14, 1948, Israel Foreign Office Papers, 2308/6, Israel State Archives, Jerusalem.

148. Chaim Weizmann to Harry S Truman, January 3, 1950, Yehoshua Freundlich, ed., *Documents on the Foreign Policy of Israel,* Volume 5 (Jerusalem, 1988), pp. 4–6.

149. Ibid.

150. Eliahu Elath to Moshe Sharett, June 22, 1948, Israel Foreign Office Papers, June 22, 1948, E.2308/6, Israel State Archives, Jerusalem.

151. Israel Embassy report to the Foreign Office, July 23, 1948, Israel Foreign Office Papers, 2308/6, Israel State Archives, Jerusalem.

152. Eliahu Elath to Stephen S. Wise, Israel Foreign Office Papers, Israel State Archives, Jerusalem.

153. Interview with Harry S Truman, August 1, 1962, Harry S Truman Library, Independence, Missouri.

154. Yehoshua Freundlich, ed., *Documents on the Foreign Policy of Israel,* Volume 2 (Jerusalem, 1984), pp. 246–248.

6

Recognition Was Not Everything

President Harry S Truman's support of Israel came only after he had seen that it was in America's best interest to extend that support. It came only after he realized that Russia might get there before the United States. Only then did he agree to recognize Israel. But recognition was not everything, and the newly established state of Israel witnessed its so-called American friend join Britain in forcing Israel to withdraw from such strategic positions as the Sinai, Gaza, and from the Old City of Jerusalem.

By May 14, 1948, trusteeship was out of the window. The Israelis had only to fight for their survival. The armies of Egypt, Syria, Lebanon, Transjordan, and Iraq invaded Israel while the secretary general of the Arab League proclaimed: "This will be another war of extermination which will be talked about like the Mongol massacres and the Crusades."[1]

The Arabs wanted all of the Land of Israel, but each Arab faction had its own ambitions, and sometimes these ambitions conflicted. King Emir Abdullah of Jordan wanted to extend his desert kingdom to the Mediterranean and was particularly interested in the Haifa area and the Negev. Syria wanted northern Palestine. The Mufti of Jerusalem, a Nazi collaborator, wanted to liquidate the Jews. Iraq and Syria made several serious threats, but neither was truly prepared for intervention. And although Egypt and Saudi Arabia were preoccupied with domestic difficulties, they were also apprehensive over Abdullah's expansionist ambitions and opted for intervention.

UN Secretary General Trygve Halvdan Lie observed that Egypt was trying "to establish a *de facto* position beyond its frontiers" and if this was not stopped, "the future usefulness of both the United Nations and its Security Council" would be prejudiced.[2] On May 17, two days after

Egyptian forces invaded Israel, the Security Council met and the U.S. delegation proposed a cease-fire. But British ambassador Sir Alexander Cadogen rejected the measure, saying that there had been no clear case of aggression. It was apparent that as long as the Arabs were somewhat successful the British would not endorse a cease-fire.

A week later, on May 22, the United States again claimed that there had been a breach of the peace in the Middle East, and it once again proposed a cease-fire. Again the British rejected the proposal; the Arabs were still advancing. Two days later Israel accepted the proposed "cease-fire," but through the combined efforts of Syria and Britain the question of a cease-fire was still postponed.

On May 29, the Soviet Union proposed, with American and French support, a "cease-fire within thirty-six hours under threat of United Nations sanctions"; but the British vetoed this. They introduced a resolution that might stop the fighting but without the threat of sanctions against the Arabs.

The Jewish Quarter of the Old City of Jerusalem fell on May 30, and a British resolution was accepted by the Security Council. The cease-fire resolution called upon all the parties to accept a four-week truce, and if this was rejected, repudiated, or violated, the United Nations was to consider a course of action as directed by the UN Charter. By the time a cease-fire was arranged on June 11, more than a third of the area allocated to Israel by the United Nations had fallen into Arab hands.

Britain pretended neutrality, but sustained the Transjordanian Arab Legion with guns, money, and officers. It was British advisers who briefed Egyptian pilots before they took off for bombing missions over Israel, and it was the British who dispatched some three thousand Sudanese troops to assist the Arab Legion. In effect, the British used the Arabs as their proxy in their war against Israel.[3]

Why were the British trying so hard to see Israel destroyed? According to Clark Clifford, the British were searching desperately for allies in the Arab world and they hoped to win their friendship by helping to destroy the Jews.[4]

The Israelis were in bad shape despite all their spirit and courage. Representatives of the Jewish state wired Truman on July 1, 1948, for some desperately needed supplies: "rush at least one hundred tons of milk powder and fifty tons of egg powder to Jerusalem before July 9." Israel would pay for these relief supplies.[5]

The situation was well summarized in a letter a Jerusalem Jew sent to his brother in America on August 16, 1948:

Dear Brother,

We received your letter of July 20, 1948, and we wondered that you took such a long time to ask what we are doing here. It is hard to describe all that we have suffered during this time. It is enough that we are still alive. Our apartment was bombarded and we are almost inundated by the attacks. We barely saved our lives. We suffered very much from hunger and thirst and the end is not yet near. All night long there was shooting in the city. The artillery barrage was heavy and we have no roof over our heads now.

The mail comes from America regularly. Some folks received weekly packages of food from America.

Nourishment here is defective and faulty. There is a shortage of all essentials including flour, meat, eggs and milk. But what is worst of all, is the shortage of drinking water. Nobody dreams of washing himself because of this water shortage. The heat becomes greater and greater.

Our so-called Socialist political leaders have obtained their objectives. They are ministers and ambassadors of a Jewish State without Jerusalem and without a Land.

Tel Aviv suffered a great deal, but only from the air attacks. My son Oscar is not doing well. He has no job and our situation is poor. During the whole time of this war it was still possible to write to Tel Aviv.

How goes it with you and your family? Is your son studying well?

Because of hunger and fear, our health has deteriorated greatly. Hopefully God will help and our difficulties will lessen. Do not expect any further letters from us, but write often. Be healthy and strong.

With kisses and best wishes from,

Ever yours,
Shlomo and Malca[6]

Shlomo would not make it through that war, nor would six thousand other Jews.

THE LOAN TO ISRAEL

A loan to Israel promised by the United States was very slow in coming. On May 25, 1948, President Truman assured Chaim Weizmann that Israel would have no difficulty in getting a substantial loan for construction purposes. But after several months and a great many explanations as to what the money would be used for, Israel still had no loan. One reason it took so long was because State Department officials wanted to use the loan as leverage to force Israel into making territorial concessions to the Arabs.

On July 29, the Israeli representative to Washington went to see the president. Truman again expressed great interest in the resettlement of displaced persons and related economic developments. But by August 3, there still was no loan. Ambassador Eliahu Elath then wrote to Clifford. Did the president know "how repeatedly we have been put off on this matter, from week to week, and from month to month? The quota of empty words which we have received in this delaying action must set some kind of record."[7]

On January 31, 1949, the day the United States extended *de jure* recognition to Israel, the loan was finally approved.

THE BERNADOTTE PLAN

Even after recognition and after the Israeli forces had proven themselves in the field as being capable of mounting a viable defense, there were still concerted efforts to reverse history and dismiss Israel from reality. One such effort, sponsored by British and United States diplomats, was the Bernadotte Plan.

Swedish Count Folke Bernadotte was appointed as UN mediator in Palestine on May 20, 1948, by the Security Council. Britain interpreted this appointment as a mandate for the mediator to seek some solution other than partition, and Bernadotte seemed to accept that interpretation. On May 25, before Bernadotte had time to establish himself in his new Paris office, British chargé d'affaires Ashley Clark paid him a visit to advise him that Great Britain was not prepared to accept any sanctions imposed against the Arabs. Bernadotte was also told that the British were continuing to supply the Arabs with military hardware and that their military advisors were actively participating in the war. Moreover, Clark informed him that Britain wanted to put the Negev under Transjordanian control since its only practical use was to serve as a land link between Arab capitals.[8]

Bernadotte felt that it would have been far better if a unitary state had been established in Palestine "with far-reaching rights for the Jews." But as the Jews succeeded militarily and the clock could not be turned back, he thought it necessary to bring about some frontier modifications. As mediator, he made the following recommendations on June 27, 1948:

- The right of residents of Palestine to return to their places of abode without restrictions on their right to regain possession of their property.
- Inclusion of the whole or part of the Negev in Arab territory.
- Inclusion of the whole or part of the western Galilee in Jewish territory.
- Inclusion of the Old City of Jerusalem in Arab territory, with municipal autonomy for the Jewish community and special arrangements for the protection of the Holy places.
- Establishment of free ports at Haifa and Lydda.

According to the Bernadotte plan, the Negev would be given to the Arabs while the western Galilee region would go to the Jews. Israel was to become part of a dual state, to be joined in a union with Jordan, and Jerusalem, with its Jewish majority, was to be in Jordan's hands while the seaport of Haifa and the airport of Lydda were to become free ports.

As a further insult to the concept of Israeli independence, immigration was to be determined by both parts of the dual state. Bernadotte felt that "unrestricted immigration" into Palestine might cause "serious economic and political repercussions beyond the control of any Jewish Government. It cannot be ignored that immigration affects not only the Jewish State and the Jewish people but also the surrounding Arab world." While he conceded that Jerusalem was of great concern to the Jews, he insisted that the city "was never intended to be a part of the Jewish state." He seemed to advocate that Jerusalem was a separate question from that of the boundaries of a Jewish state.

Israel rejected the Bernadotte Plan. On July 6, Foreign Minister Moshe Sharett (Shertok) responded to Bernadotte's proposals. Israel "noted with surprise" that his suggestions ignored the resolution of the General Assembly of November 29, 1947, which still was "the only internationally valid adjudication of the question of the future government of Palestine." Israel found it regrettable that Bernadotte had not "taken into account the outstanding facts of the situation in Palestine, namely the effective establishment of the sovereign state of Israel within the area assigned to it in the 1947 Resolution, and other territorial changes which have resulted from the repulse of the attack launched against the State of Israel by Palestinian Arabs and by the Governments of neighboring Arab States." As for the matter of Jerusalem's future, Israel was "deeply wounded" by the suggestion regarding the future of the city: "The Jewish people, the State of Israel and the Jews of Jerusalem will never acquiesce in the imposition of Arab domination over Jerusalem, no matter what formal municipal autonomy and right of access of the Holy Places the Jews of Jerusalem might be allowed to enjoy. They will resist any such imposition with all the force at their command."[9]

As President Weizmann wrote to President Truman

> We cannot agree and we cannot be expected to agree that our ancient Mother-city be severed from the new commonwealth of Israel. Jerusalem has been our capital since the days of David and Solomon. How can any right-thinking man demand that the Jews of Jerusalem, who last year went through hunger, thirst, and deadly peril in defence of their city, should now be placed under alien rule? The Jews of Jerusalem are determined to remain part of Israel, as they always have been.[10]

The Israelis found Bernadotte's suggestion on Jerusalem to be "disastrous," and they felt that he was "encouraging false Arab hopes and wounding Jewish feelings."

Israel also rejected the suggestion that immigration should be restricted. Israel insisted upon "complete and unqualified freedom to determine the size and composition of Jewish immigration," and it refused to accept any encroachment upon its sovereignty. Peace, insisted Israel, could be achieved only "as a result of an agreement negotiated between the interested parties as free and sovereign States."

Bernadotte was assassinated in Jerusalem on September 17, 1948, just as the United Nations inaugurated debate on his plan. Israel was concerned that it would have to suffer for the actions of a few terrorists. Those fears seemed warranted when various speakers at the United Nations urged that the Bernadotte Plan be adopted in recognition for his work. Acting Mediator Ralph Bunche announced, from his headquarters at Rhodes, that he not only endorsed the plan but he accused Israeli officials of having failed to provide adequate care for the safety of UN personnel. The American ambassador to Israel cabled home on September 17: "Regret report, Count Bernadotte, U.N. observer Jerusalem and Colonel Serat, French officer, killed this afternoon."[11] A week later, George C. Marshall announced his support of the Bernadotte Plan. He said that he found Bernadotte's report "a generally fair basis for settlement of the Palestine question." He "strongly urged the parties concerned and the General Assembly to accept them in their entirety as the best possible basis for bringing peace to a distracted land."[12]

It seemed as if the United States was abandoning Israel. Weizmann asked Eddie Jacobson to remind the president how important the Negev was to the future of Israel since it was suitable for immigration and presently uninhabitable. Unless Israel received the Negev, it would remain a desert and a region from which Israel would be constantly attacked. Israel had already proven how it could bring agriculture to the sands of the Negev. "Please go and see him without delay and remind him of Democratic pledge that no changes in boundaries would take place without consent Government of Israel but above all his own encouragement to me on which we all implicitly rely and for which we shall be eternally grateful."[13]

On September 29, President Truman and his staff prepared a statement that was to be issued on October 1, reaffirming U.S. support for Israel. At the same time, the following memo was prepared for Secretary Marshall's attention:

September 29, 1948

To: Secretary Marshall, Paris
From: The President

Your statement that the Bernadotte report should be used as a basis for negotiations in the settlement of the Palestine question requires clarification.

The government of the United States is on record as having endorsed the action of the United Nations General Assembly of November 1947 as to boundaries. As President I have so stated officially. The Democratic Platform endorsed the findings of the General Assembly.

> I shall have to state that my position as to boundaries has not changed. You should know that my statement will be made on October first.[14]

In his memoirs, Truman wrote that when Marshall returned from Paris on October 9, he talked to him about this matter. Marshall claimed that his observations on the Bernadotte Plan had been made primarily to encourage negotiations between the Arabs and the Israelis. Truman seemed satisfied that Marshall understood his position and found that it was not necessary to issue a prepared statement.[15] He did not wish "to display publicly any difference about specific points as long as there was agreement on the general policy." This was not the time to display disunity in American foreign policy as the Russians were seeking to extend their influence over West Berlin, West Germany, France, Italy, Greece, and Turkey.

On October 28, during the election campaign Truman publicly scotched the unrealistic Bernadotte Plan and declared that "Israel must be large enough, free enough, and strong enough to make its people self-supporting and secure."[16]

The UN Security Council, with British and U.S. backing, imposed cease-fires whenever the Israelis started to gain victories, and the Israelis soon realized that in order to defend their new state, every military action would have to be well-planned and swift. When the second cease-fire expired on October 10, 1948, the Israelis were ready to strike back at the Arab invaders with lightning assaults concentrated in the Negev and central Galilee. In the Galilee, the Israelis broke through the Arab armies and quickly cleared the entire area as far as the Litani River in Lebanon.

David Ben-Gurion wanted to see Jerusalem as capital of Israel. To achieve this end he planned to take the area south of Jerusalem and thereby cut the junction between the Egyptians in the Negev and the Jordanians. He presented the plan to his cabinet on September 26, but it was voted down. In his diary, the Israeli prime minister wrote: "The plan has been dropped. Fortunately for us, most of the offensives we've launched this year were not put to the vote of that lot!"[17]

Israel's next effort was directed at driving the Egyptians from the Negev. During the cease-fire, the Egyptians had refused to abide by the truce agreement that permitted Israel to send supply convoys through Egyptian lines to isolated Israeli units. Israeli intelligence also furnished information that, if hostilities broke out, no Arab armies would be in a position to help the Egyptians. On October 15, a supply column was ordered south to test Egypt's willingness to defy the truce accord. As expected, the Egyptians attacked. And Israel was ready. Operation Jacob had begun.

Israeli troops struck swiftly, but international politicians moved rapidly as well. As Israeli troops were about to liberate the Hebron-Bethlehem area, Britain threatened to intervene and Ben-Gurion ordered his troops to halt. As the Egyptians had been forced out of this area, it was soon reoccupied by Jordanian troops.

Meanwhile, the Israelis were intent on opening the route to the Negev by breaking the Arab salient at Falouja, a pocket that served as an Arab stepping stone between Gaza and the Hebron area. A pincer attack cut Falouja on both sides and effectively isolated it. Pleased with this success against the Egyptians, Ben-Gurion then wanted to strike at the Iraqi forces in the triangle and mop up the remaining Arab forces that threatened to cut the Negev from the rest of Israel.

But first, Ben-Gurion waited for an international response to his Negev offensive. While Marshall visited Greece and Italy, President Truman instructed his UN delegation not to make any statements or to take any action "on the subject of Palestine" without "specific" authorization "from me and clearing the text of any statement."[18]

Ben-Gurion then ordered an attack against the Egyptian troops in the south. One force hit the isolated Falouja pocket and another opened a road to the Dead Sea. Israeli guerrilla activity coordinated with a rapid military attack, shattered the Egyptian defenses south of Beersheba.

Exploiting the victory, Israeli troops pressed on and crossed the border into Sinai on December 28. Abu Ageila, a main crossroads in Sinai, fell to the attacking force, as did Bir-Hassne and Bir-Gafgafa. Advance Israeli troops halted about forty miles from the Suez Canal, which, at that time, was still under British protection.

While the main Israeli attack swung to the northwest and was poised to capture the Sinai capital of El-Arish, another unit was ready to roll into Gaza through the Sinai back door, when Ben-Gurion ordered a withdrawal. This order came because of extreme pressure from Great Britain and especially the United States.

On December 30, 1948, the British informed Acting Secretary of State Robert Lovett that unless "the Jews withdrew from Egyptian territory," the British would have to intervene on the basis of their 1936 treaty obligations to Egypt. They threatened "the gravest possible consequences, not only to Anglo-American strategic interests in the Near East, but to American relations with Britain and Western Europe." During this time, the British representatives seemed unable or unwilling to use the term "Israel," but always used the term "the Jews" to describe Israel. They threatened to send supplies to the Arabs if "the Jews" did not do as Great Britain wished. The British pretended that they had not been sending supplies to the Arabs.[19] On December 31, Ben-Gurion received the following threatening communication from the United States:

> The U.S., which was the first to recognize the State of Israel and which is supporting its application to join the U.N., wishes to draw attention to the Israeli

Government to a fact that its attitude could endanger peace in the Middle East. The U.S. Government would have to re-examine its attitude with regard to the Israeli Government's application to join the U.N., which is presented as the application of a "peace-loving" nation, and would also have to re-examine the character of its relations with the State of Israel.[20]

As proof of Israel's peaceful intentions, the United States expected Israeli forces "to withdraw immediately from Egyptian territory." On receipt of this communication, Ben-Gurion informed the U.S. ambassador that the withdrawal order had already been issued and that Israel had not violated the peace in Palestine. It had been the Arab armies in their invasion of Israel that had violated the peace. Ben-Gurion wondered why the United States, a powerful nation, should choose to address Israel, "a small and weak" nation, in such tones.

Weizmann was dismayed and he expressed his concern to President Truman on January 3. It was, after all, the Egyptian army that had invaded Israel with the expressed intention of destroying the Jewish state. "Israeli forces had no intention of destroying the kingdom of Egypt." The Egyptian army invaded on May 15, it bombarded civilian population centers of Tel Aviv and destroyed Jewish villages and water installations in the Negev. Israel "had not touched the head of any Egyptian." When the United States had tried to have the Security Council stop the Egyptian and other Arab invasions, the British worked to defeat those resolutions and it was Great Britain that had "supplied practically all the arms used by Egypt." How could the United States support the Egyptian application for election to the Security Council while Egyptian forces were "actually invading and attacking Israel" and threatened to withdraw its support for Israel membership to the United Nations?[21]

Foreign Minister Sharett was not at all surprised with the British stance since the British had, in the first place, encouraged the Arab invasions in defiance of the UN Charter. But he was somewhat surprised by the questionable U.S. attitude. The fact that the United States sponsored Egypt's candidacy to Security Council membership made it appear that the Egyptian aggressor was the "custodian of peace." Sharett hoped that the United States could help restrain the Arab aggressors and exercise its good offices in this respect to both the Arab states and the United Kingdom.[22]

The Americans also wanted Israel to respond to reports that Israel had demanded a peace treaty with Jordan and threatened continued warfare unless such a treaty was forthcoming. If that were the case, the United States threatened that it "would have no other course than to undertake a review of its attitude toward Israel."[23]

The Israeli foreign minister assured James G. McDonald that no threat of "peace or war" had been made to Jordan, but that in a secret meeting on December 30, Colonel Moshe Dayan and Reuven Shiloah met with

King Abdullah in the Old City of Jerusalem offering to press negotiations further than a cease-fire. The Israelis wanted an armistice that would lead to peace.[24]

The United States, supporting Britain, forced Israel to withdraw from the Sinai. In the meantime, an Israeli task force established a strong wedge south of Rafah near the Israeli-Egyptian border and cut the Gaza Strip from Egypt. At that juncture, Egypt agreed to armistice negotiations, provided the Israeli troops were withdrawn from the Rafah area.

Israel withdrew, and on February 29, 1949, an armistice was signed with Egypt. The Egyptians were permitted to gain control of Gaza.[25]

Had the United States and Britain not intervened to halt Israeli military operations, the geopolitical situation for Israel would have been far more secure. As a result of their meddling, Gaza was turned over to Egypt, and Jordan gained control of a triangle of territory that included Jerusalem and jutted into Israel like a sharp knife threatening the jugular vein.

NOTES

1. John Kimche and David Kimche, *Clash of Destinies* (New York, 1960), p. 49.
2. Clark Clifford Memos dated May 29 and 31, 1948, Clark Clifford Papers, Harry S Truman Library, Independence, Missouri.
3. Ibid.
4. Ibid.
5. Eliahu Elath to President Harry S Truman, July 1, 1948, Clark Clifford Papers, Harry S Truman Library, Independence, Missouri.
6. Shlomo Druks to Chaim Druks, August 16, 1948, H. Druks Family Papers, New York.
7. Eliahu Elath to Clark Clifford, August 3, 1948, Clark Clifford Papers, Harry S Truman Library, Independence, Missouri.
8. Count Folke Bernadotte, *To Jerusalem* (London, 1951), pp. 6–10.
9. M. Sharett to F. Bernadotte, July 6, 1948, Israel Foreign Office Papers 9303/94/9, Israel State Archives, Jerusalem.
10. President Chaim Weizmann to President Harry S Truman, January 3, 1950, *Documents on the Foreign Policy* of *Israel*, Volume 5, 1950, edited by Yehoshua Freundlich (Jerusalem, 1988), pp. 4–6.
11. James G. McDonald to State Department, September 17, 1948, Clark Clifford Papers, Harry S Truman Library, Independence, Missouri.
12. *New York Times*, September 22, 1948.
13. Chaim Weizmann to Eddie Jacobson, Telegram, September 1948, Clark Clifford Papers, Harry S Truman Library, Independence, Missouri.
14. President Harry S Truman to Secretary George C. Marshall, September 29, 1948, President's Official File 204, Harry S Truman Library, Independence, Missouri.
15. Harry S Truman, *Years of Trial and Hope* (New York, 1956), p. 167.
16. Ibid., pp. 167–168.
17. Michael Bar-Zohar, *Ben Gurion: The Armed Prophet* (Englewood Cliffs, NJ, 1968), p. 150.

18. Truman, *Years of Trial and Hope*, p. 167.

19. U.S. Department of State, *Foreign Relations of the United States, 1948*, Volume V, Part 2 (Washington, D.C., 1976), December 30, 1948, p. 1703.

20. Ibid., p. 1705.

21. Chaim Weizmann to Harry S Truman, January 3, 1949, Israel Foreign Office Papers 2308/1, Israel State Archives, Jerusalem.

22. Moshe Sharett to Eliahu Elath, January 5, 1949, Israel Foreign Office Papers, 2308/1, Israel State Archives, Jerusalem.

23. Ibid.

24. Ibid.

25. Armistice agreements would be signed with Lebanon on March 23, 1949, Jordan on April 3, 1949, and Syria on July 20, 1949. Iraq would withdraw without signing any armistice with Israel.

Franklin Delano Roosevelt. Courtesy of Franklin Delano Roosevelt Library.

Harry S Truman with Winston Churchill and Joseph Stalin at Potsdam, 1945. Courtesy of Signal Corps, Harry S Truman Library.

Harry S Truman with Winston Churchill and Joseph Stalin at Potsdam, 1945. Courtesy of the U.S. Navy.

Dwight D. Eisenhower on French soil. Courtesy of the U.S. Army.

Nuremberg Tribunal. Courtesy of the U.S. Army.

Dwight D. Eisenhower with David Ben-Gurion (left) and Douglas Dillon (right). Courtesy of Dwight

Dwight D. Eisenhower and John F. Kennedy at the White House, 1960. Courtesy of Dwight D. Eisenhower Library.

John F. Kennedy. Photo No. PX65:105:17

Robert F. Kennedy at the United Nations headquarters, January 1964. Courtesy of United Nations.

7

The 1948 Election Campaign and Israel

While President Harry S Truman had to face such challenges as the Russian Berlin blockade as well as the war between Arabs and Israelis, Soviet expansionism in Europe, and a civil war in China, he had to campaign for reelection. Truman tried to keep foreign affairs out of the campaign, but that could not be done in a free and democratic society.

At the opening of the Republican Party Convention, some Republican leaders seemed reluctant to support Israel. One of the key Republican figures was Senator Arthur Vandenberg. He used his influence to make sure that the Israel plank of the Republican platform would not strongly endorse Israel, but Senator Robert A. Taft and Governor Thomas E. Dewey, front-runners for the Republican nomination, insisted that there should be a strong declaration in favor of Israel. Dewey's foreign policy advisor, John Foster Dulles, drafted the final and more favorable Israel plank.[1]

Ultimately, the position taken by Taft and Dewey helped influence the Democrats to draft a plank that was likewise favorable to Israel.[2]

The Republicans were anxious to see Dewey in the White House and they worked hard to get him there. Republican leaders tried to discredit Truman's stand on Israel. Dulles and Dewey met with Zionist leaders on July 28, 1948, and promised them everything: full recognition of Israel, an end to the arms embargo, and a loan to Israel. All this for their support of the Republican candidate. If Truman would override George C. Marshall on the Bernadotte Plan, the Republicans would accuse him of weakness. If Truman failed to override the secretary of state, then the Republicans, with the help of some British officials, would blast Truman as an inept diplomatist.

By October 1948, Dewey planned to issue a strong statement against the Bernadotte Plan. Bartley Crum, of the Anglo-American Committee, and Bob Howard McGrath, the Democratic national chairman, advised Truman to speak in favor of *de jure* recognition, the Israeli borders, and the $100 million loan, before Dewey could make his speech.[3] Truman did not follow their advice. He felt that foreign affairs should be kept out of partisan politics. On the occasion of the Jewish New Year, Truman issued a public statement to Israel's president: "May the New Year bring peace to Israel and to its citizens the opportunity to dedicate themselves in tranquility to furthering the prosperity of their country."

On October 22, Dewey issued his statement repudiating Truman's policies with respect to Israel. But Dewey did not commit himself to a full support of Israel. He did call for aid to Israel and full recognition of the Jewish state and its boundaries as sanctioned by the UN vote; but he failed to specify which UN vote, that of November 1947 or some future vote.[4] Since Dewey declared that Truman had gone back on the Democratic platform promises, Truman issued the following statement on October 24, 1948, reiterating his support of the platform:

> So that everyone may be familiar with my position, I set out here the Democratic Platform on Israel:
>
> President Truman, by granting immediate recognition of Israel, led the world in extending friendship and welcome to a people who have long sought and justly deserve freedom and independence.
>
> We pledge full recognition of the State of Israel. We affirm our pride that the United States, under the leadership of President Truman, played a leading role in the adoption of the resolution of November 29, 1947, by the United Nations General Assembly for the creation of a Jewish state.
>
> We approve the claims of the State of Israel to the boundaries set forth in the United Nations' resolution of November 29 and consider that modifications thereof should be made only if fully acceptable to the State of Israel.
>
> We look forward to the admission of the State of Israel to the United Nations and its full participation in the international community of nations. We pledge appropriate aide to the State of Israel in developing its economy and resources.
>
> We favor the revision of the arms embargo to accord the State of Israel the right of self-defense. We pledge ourselves to work for the modification of any resolution of the United Nations to the extent that it may prevent any such revision.
>
> We continue to support, within the framework of the United Nations, the internationalization of Jerusalem and the protection of the holy places in Palestine.[5]

Four days later, President Truman attacked Dewey for introducing foreign affairs issues into the arena of domestic politics. "The subject of Israel," Truman insisted, "must not be resolved as a matter of politics in a political campaign. I have refused, first, because it is my responsibility to see that our policy in Israel fits in with our foreign policy throughout the world; second, it is my desire to help build in Palestine a strong, prosperous, free and independent democratic state. It must be large enough, free enough, and strong enough to make its people self-supporting and secure."[6] With or without Dewey's interferences, Truman aimed to fulfill the pledges of the Democratic Party platform, and according to the following undated presidential memo, Truman wanted American officials involved with the Middle East and Israel to carry out those pledges:

Recognition: Truman wanted full and complete de jure recognition announced "at least one week before the opening of the meeting of the General Assembly in Paris."

Boundaries: He approved the boundaries established in the United Nations resolution of November 29, and he intended to stress Israel's boundary claims.

Admission to the U.N.: He assumed that the U.S. would "actively and unconditionally sponsor the admission of the State of Israel to the U.N. at the forthcoming meeting of the General Assembly at Paris."

Aid to Israel: As the $100 million loan to Israel was still pending, he wondered if there was any way to "expedite prompt favorable action upon this application?" He also wanted to know if there was any other appropriate aid which could be rendered "within the framework of existing legislation?"

Arms Embargo: The President called for a revision of the arms embargo and he wanted to know "to what extent do any resolutions of the U.N. now prevent such revision, and if so, what prompt action can we take to work for their modification?"

Jerusalem: He supported the internationalization of Jerusalem and protection of Holy Places in the area.[7]

President Truman aimed to carry out his campaign pledges. Truman was a man of his word and he expected the individuals working with him to help him keep that word.

On November 29, 1948, after being reelected he wrote the following letter to Chaim Weizmann, president of Israel:

I was struck by the common experience you and I have recently shared. We had both been abandoned by the so-called realistic experts of our supposedly forlorn lost causes. Yet we both kept pressing for what we were sure was right—and we were both proven to be right. My feeling of elation on the morning of November 3rd must have approximated your own feelings one year ago today, and on May 14, and on several occasions since then.

However, it does not take long for bitter and resourceful opponents to regroup their forces after they have been shattered. You in Israel have already been confronted with that situation; and I expect to be all too soon. So I understand very well your concern to prevent the undermining of your well-earned victories.

I remember well our conversation about the Negev, to which you referred in your letter. I agree fully with your estimate of the importance of that area to Israel, and I deplore any attempt to take it away from Israel. I had thought that my position would have been clear to all the world, particularly in the light of the specific wording of the Democratic Party platform. But there were those who did not take this seriously, regarding it as "just another campaign promise" to be forgotten after the election. I believe they have recently realized their error. I have interpreted my re-election as a mandate from the American people to carry out the Democratic platform—including, of course, the plank on Israel. I intend to do so.

Since your letter was written, we have announced in the General Assembly our firm intention to oppose any territorial changes in the November 29th Resolution which are not acceptable to the State of Israel. I am confident that the General Assembly will support us on this basic position.

We have already expressed our willingness to help develop the new State through financial and economic measures. As you know, the Export-Import Bank is actively considering a substantial long-term loan to Israel on a project basis. I understand that our Government is now in process of preparing the details of such projects for submission to the Bank. Personally, I would like to go even further, by expanding such financial and economic assistance on a large scale to the entire Middle East, contingent upon effective mutual cooperation.

Thank you so much for your warm congratulations and good wishes on my re-election. I was pleased to learn that the first Israeli elections have been scheduled for January 25th. That enables us to set a definite target date for extending *de jure* recognition.

In closing, I want to tell you how happy and impressed I have been at the remarkable progress made by the new State of Israel. What you have received at the hands of the world has been far less than was your due. But you have more than made the most of what you have received, and I admire you for it. I trust that the present uncertainty, with its terribly burdensome consequences, will soon be eliminated. We will do all we can to help by encouraging direct negotiations between the parties looking toward a prompt peace settlement.

Very sincerely yours,[8]

ISRAEL'S ADMISSION TO THE UNITED NATIONS

As Israel celebrated the first anniversary of the passage of the UN Palestine Partition Plan, it presented Secretary General Trygve Halvdan Lie with a formal application for UN membership. A few days later, both the United States and the Soviet delegates supported the admission of Israel "as a matter of urgency." British and French delegates objected and called for a postponement, but this attempt was defeated. In the Security Council, the United States and Russia favored Israel's admission, as did Argentina and Colombia. Syria voted against, while Belgium, Canada, Great Britain, China, and France abstained. The application failed to receive a majority vote in the Security Council and the measure was rejected.

After the Israeli-Egyptian armistice was concluded on February 24, 1949, Israel again applied for membership in the United Nations. This time the application was accepted by a wide margin with nine votes in favor, one opposed (Egypt), and one abstention (Great Britain). The application was brought before the General Assembly for ratification.

Just as the General Assembly's Political Committee was to vote on Israel's admission, Dean Rusk called on Eliahu Elath to complain that Abba Eban had not explained what concessions Israel was prepared to make on the Arab refugee question and on frontiers. Rusk warned that unless Israel was prepared to make concessions, its admission to the United Nations would be rejected. Israel did not yield to the State Department pressures. When the Political Committee voted, Israel received more than a two-thirds vote and the question was then placed on the agenda of the plenary session for the following day, May 11, 1949. After that vote, Israel was admitted as a sovereign member of the United Nations.

NOTES

1. Eliahu Elath to Moshe Sharett, June 24, 1948, Israel Foreign Office Papers, 2308/6, Israel State Archives, Jerusalem. Among the Republican leaders that favored a strong pro-Israel plank were Senators Irving Ives, Ralph Owen Brewster, Raymond E. Baldwin, C. Wayland Brooks, Edward H. Moore, and Forrest C. Donnell. Among the Jewish politicos within the Republican Party who worked for a more favorable Israel plank were Congressmen Jacob Javits, General Arthur Klein of the Jewish War Veterans, newsman George E. Sokolsky, and Rabbis Israel Goldstein and Abba Hillel Silver.

2. In an interview with Benjamin Akzin of the Zionist Emergency Committee, I discovered that some Zionists felt that they owed a great deal to Republican senator Robert A. Taft since he was a strong supporter of Israel and thereby indirectly helped influence the Democrats to be more supportive of Israel.

3. Bartley Crum to Clark Clifford, Telegram, October 3, 1948, Clark Clifford Papers, Harry S Truman Library, Independence, Missouri.

4. J. S. Keenan to Matthew J. Connelly, October 23, 1948, Clark Clifford Papers, Harry S Truman Library, Independence, Missouri.

5. *Public Papers of the President of the United States, Harry S. Truman, Containing the Public Messages, Speeches and Statements of the President 1948* (Washington, 1964), pp. 843–844.

6. Harry S Truman, *Years of Trial and Hope* (New York, 1956), p. 168.

7. Harry S Truman Memorandum, undated Official File 204, Harry S Truman Library, Independence, Missouri.

8. Yehoshua Freudlich, ed., *Documents on the Foreign Policy of Israel*, volume 2 (Jerusalem, 1984) (October 1948–April 1949), pp. 246–248.

8

Harry S Truman and Israel's Abandonment of Neutrality

Once the state of Israel was reestablished in 1948, American Jews became more involved with it. Some joined pro-Israel associations, others contributed of their possessions to its growth and development, while still others gave advice as to how it should run its own affairs. Some became involved through a combination of these activities.

But the McCarthy era of the 1950s further complicated the relationship between American Jews and Israel. Senator Joseph R. McCarthy's supporters raised the question of dual loyalty and some American Jews like Jacob Blaustein,[1] of the American Jewish Committee, tried to make sure that David Ben-Gurion's government would not say or do anything that might be interpreted as interfering in U.S. affairs. But at the same time Blaustein joined such personalities as Senator Herbert H. Lehman and Henry Morgenthau in an effort to persuade Ben-Gurion to abandon Israel's neutrality and side with the United States in the cold war conflicts.

In February 1950, the Executive Committee of the American Jewish Committee asked Jewish organizations to "refrain from public discussions" because such discussions might harm the image and position of Jews in America. The American Jewish Committee reaffirmed its position that while it had "an abiding friendship for the new state and a sincere desire as Americans to aid in its development" it had "no political affiliation with the State of Israel" and "stressed unalterable opposition to any concept of world Jewish nationalism." The committee adopted the following resolution regarding American Jews and Israel: Whereas:

> The American Jewish Committee in its 1943 statement of views recorded as axiomatic that American Jews could have no political affiliation with any government created in Palestine; and American Jews . . . have no political affiliation with the State of Israel and that therefore there can be no interference by the

government of Israel in the internal affairs of American Jewry or, of the Jewry of any other country.[2]

In order to resolve differences with the American Jewish Committee, Ben-Gurion issued the following statement on August 23, 1950: "The Jews of the United States, as a community and as individuals have only one political attachment and that is to the United States of America. They owe no political allegiance to Israel. Any weakening of American Jewry . . . is a definite loss to Jews everywhere and to Israel in particular."[3]

But in December 1951, Ben-Gurion would get himself involved with the American Jewish scene. He did not care for the American Zionist leadership. He considered it to be bankrupt and he felt that American society still discriminated against American Jews. Ben-Gurion again called upon American Jews to immigrate to Israel if they truly considered themselves to be Zionists. This brought a strong response from the Jewish Agency and the American Zionist community. One of its political figures, Nahum Goldmann, advised Ben-Gurion that his parliamentary address, which criticized the American Zionists, was inappropriate, unfortunate, and damaging.[4] Benjamin R. Epstein of B'nai B'rith advised Israeli ambassador Abba Eban that he had been "grievously distressed" by Ben-Gurion's speech. He objected to Ben-Gurion's view that "the core of zionism leads to planned immigration to Israel." Epstein concluded by saying that "we cannot leave unchallenged any action or statement harmful to the Jews of America or subversive of the unity of the American people by the cultivation among any of its varied, yet all-American, elements of a sense of insecurity and fear for the American future."[5]

At times, some, like former secretary of the treasury Morgenthau, conducted themselves as if they were self-appointed agents of Israel. Because of Morgenthau's concern for U.S. Middle East interests, he advised Secretary of State Dean Acheson, in February 1950, that Israel would look with favor to the American requests for air bases in the Negev. Apparently, Morgenthau had discussed this idea with Ben-Gurion and, since he had not responded, Morgenthau believed that to mean that Ben-Gurion approved of the idea. Morgenthau recalled that when President Franklin D. Roosevelt had not responded to one of his suggestions it meant that he wanted Morgenthau to pursue the proposed project. Morgenthau recalled that was the way Roosevelt worked when he wanted his "associates to find or do things he did not want to do himself." Morgenthau believed that Ben-Gurion worked in the same fashion.[6]

Ben-Gurion was "surprised" to learn of Morgenthau's offer of bases to the United States. Perhaps Morgenthau acted "in good faith" but it was "in direct opposition" of Israel's policy of neutrality that he had "explained" to him. Ben-Gurion would have likewise "explained" the situation to Acheson had he seen him. "I must implore Morgenthau as a personal and trusted friend not to engage himself in matters relating to Israeli–United States relations or any other foreign policy matters without the prior knowledge and approval of our authorized ambassador in Washington."[7]

Very few Israeli officials appreciated Morgenthau's interference. Foreign Minister Moshe Sharett instructed Eliahu Elath to keep Morgenthau from intervening on behalf of Israel, nothing should be done "without your authority as Ambassador." Elath found that Morgenthau was trying to establish his own "Israeli embassy" in Washington. Elath thanked Morgenthau for his help, asking Morgenthau to work through his ambassadorship in the future.[8]

When Morgenthau was advised by the Israeli ambassador and the Jewish Agency representatives that they did not appreciate his interventionist diplomacy, he seemed "annoyed." Morgenthau believed that it was essential for Israel to identify itself with the United States. It was, he insisted, "right and timely" for Israel to offer the United States bases in the Negev. It would do Israel "a lot of good" to get out of its neutral corner.[9]

Upset as he was with Israel's restrictions on his "diplomatic" endeavors, Morgenthau was prepared to separate from various U.S. organizations supportive of Israel, including the United Jewish Appeal. Goldmann, then a member of the Jewish Agency, observed on March 3, 1950, that matters had reached a breaking point with Morgenthau, but after "a long talk with Morgenthau" he had obtained a promise that the former treasury secretary would "not do things in Washington without consulting with Goldmann."[10]

One of the most demanding of the Jewish critics of Israeli neutrality was Senator Lehman. He claimed that "many Senators" were confused "regarding Israel's position in international affairs" and that there were many who suspected Israel of having a "pro-Russian orientation." Lehman claimed that those senators considered it a "poor bargain for the U.S. to support Israel." He found this development "serious and dangerous from the point of view of our relations with the American public" and he urged Israel to "keep and cultivate closer relations with Congress" as it influenced every aspect of United States foreign policy. He seemed "bewildered by the absence of a press and public relations section" in the Israel embassy. He wondered whether the Prime Minister and Foreign Minister realized that Washington's attitude towards Israel was "decisive." Ambassador Elath found Senator Lehman "extremely kind and ready to assist us whenever necessary."[11]

NEUTRALITY—TO BE OR NOT TO BE

Ambassador Elath favored closer ties with the United States. He called for an end to nonalignment and observed that some American officials, at times, considered Israel to be a "potential ally" and at other times "a very important factor," but more often than not Americans felt that Israel was not a reliable factor "politically." Some Americans believed that the new immigrants were "easy prey for the pro-Russian Communists and Mapam."[12]

American diplomats considered Turkey, Iran, and Egypt to be more useful partners than Israel in the cold war and in the formation of a defensive Middle East Triangle.[13] They believed that Israeli society was "divided" internally and unable to work effectively with the West.[14]

At times it seemed as if some State Department officials preferred to "punish Israel for its neutrality" rather than "reward it for its cooperation." Elath and his successor, Eban, would suggest by May 1950, that Israel should improve its relations with Turkey and Iran so as to "diminish" Israeli isolation in the Middle East. If that should take place then Israel's image with officials in the State and Defense Departments might improve since it would seem as if Israel were an integral part of the Middle East. Then they would be less inclined to consider Israel as an outsider or "alien body without common regional interests."[15] Ambassador Elath urged Israel to abandon its neutrality in favor of making decisions for "specific occasions motivated by our urgent vital interests and not by static concepts which may paralyze our very struggle for progress and survival."[16]

Eban went even further than Elath in calling for an end to neutrality. He suggested that Israel declare its willingness to "fight physically and militarily against an attempt to impose communism whether by subversion or by a Soviet invasion." Only then might the United States consider it beneficial to strengthen Israel. Eban pointed out that democracy and ideology had little to do with the United States lending support to Israel or any other state. It was, he believed, a matter that rested primarily upon strategic considerations. Yugoslavia and Spain were not democratic and yet this did not "disqualify them from United States aid." To get that U.S. aid, "spade work must be done by Israel to persuade the U.S. that Israel could physically resist Communist expansion."[17]

Some Israeli representatives in America found Zionists and so-called Jewish "leaders" in America to be out of touch with reality. Blaustein, Joseph Proskauer, and Frank Goldman, among others, seemed to them to be afraid and timid. They seemed unable to speak forcefully to government officials on behalf of Israel. They preferred to adopt a low profile. From 1949 to 1951, "leaders" of such organizations as the American Jewish Committee and the B'nai B'rith "advised against immediate open public pressure" on behalf of Israel and they repeatedly urged that Israel abandon its neutrality in the cold war. At times, Ambassador Elath was far more encouraged by the help and support provided by Jewish people outside the established Zionist and Jewish organizations. He was especially grateful to such American Federation of Labor and Congress of

Industrial Organizations labor leaders as David Dubinsky and Jacob Potofsky. They were close to the president, and Elath expected that they would provide Israel with some real help in the long run.[18]

Benjamin Akzin was one of several American Zionist leaders who advocated Israeli affiliation with the West even before the state of Israel proclaimed its independence. In early February 1948, he advised American political figures like Taft that Israel might affiliate with Russia. While the Yishuv[19] was grateful for the help Russia had provided in facilitating General Assembly acceptance of partition, it would not covet the status of a Soviet satellite. The Jewish people of the Land of Israel were for a "free enterprise" society and a goodly number of Jews there had escaped communist regimes. Jews who escaped from Poland, Romania, Hungary, and Russia "would not dream of establishing such a system in their homeland or of becoming a Soviet satellite." But Akzin warned American officials that communism would make inroads in the Middle East if they abdicated their responsibilities and thereby helped prolong the Arab-Jewish conflict.[20]

THE KOREAN WAR

The Korean War ushered in another set of circumstances in East-West relations within the context of the cold war, and for Israel it crystallized its own question of East-West affiliations. The events of that war and the actions of Russia were some of the most important factors that motivated Ben-Gurion to swing to the West. It was during the Korean War that American and Russian officials tested Israel's loyalty and pressured Israel for affiliation and support.

When North Korea invaded South Korea on June 25, 1950, Israel tried to steer a neutral course, but Prime Minister Ben-Gurion found it difficult to maintain that neutrality. During the UN debates, there were times when Israel had not voted on the side of the Americans. Israel's UN voting record had been watched with keen interest by both the American and Soviet delegations. While the Americans, at times, hinted that Israeli neutrality might prove detrimental to its future relations with the American people and their government, they offered Israel the tantalizing prospect of "arms and military training" if it voted with the "West."

American pressure on Israel to support U.S. policy in Korea was considerable. When by the first of July Israel had not as yet declared itself in favor of that move, President Truman relayed his "disappointment and indignation" at "Israel's silence."[21]

Minister Moshe Keren, from his vantage point in Washington, advised his government to side with the United States on the UN Security Council resolution condemning the North Korean aggression. His sources of information seemed to indicate that Russia might make a move or retaliation in "Berlin, Iran or some other weak spots." And he warned that if Israel failed to support the United States publicly it would "alienate the good will of the President, Jewry and other friends."[22]

The very next day—July 2—Israel publicly declared its condemnation of the North Korean aggression against South Korea and supported the Security Council resolution "in its efforts to put an end to the breach of peace in Korea."[23]

The Russians were greatly displeased with Israel's support of the UN decision to intervene in Korea. By July 6, the Soviet Foreign Office expressed its unhappiness with Israel's decision.[24] Soviet officials reminded Israeli officials that Russia had been the first to extend *de jure* recognition to Israel and that they had supported its admission to the United Nations. While the Soviet representatives remained "very cordial" to Israeli diplomats at the United Nations and in Washington, they were "vehemently" critical of the United States for "misunderstanding the Asian revolution" and they stressed the fact that the "U.S. was involved in Korea" with the "half-hearted support from a few western powers." The Russians asserted that for the most part, the United States was in it alone and that it had no real support from the rest of the United Nations.[25]

Members of the Israeli Foreign Office establishment had voiced their opposition to Israel's affiliation with the "West" on the Korean matter. Some opposed such affiliation on the grounds that it would be supporting a "corrupt and oppressive" South Korean regime. Foreign Minister Sharett warned that an Israeli stance in favor of the U.S. Korean policy would mean open affiliation with the United States and that it would damage Israeli-Russian relations and endanger the Jews behind the Iron Curtain.[26] Sharett was concerned that if Israel would undertake "a provocative act" the Russians might "write us off as its avowed enemies" and it might "tip the scales against further emigration . . . from the East block states." As Sharett explained it to Acheson, Israel was not "afraid of a rupture" with the Russians for its own sake, but that the Russians might avenge themselves on "their Jews."[27]

The initial Israeli support of the Security Council resolution was not enough for the Truman administration. Washington officials wanted an actual Israeli military intervention and there were members of Israel's Foreign Office, including Arthur Lourie and Keren, both stationed in Washington, that advocated a firmer affiliation with the United States. Keren felt that verbal support was not enough, that the United States expected Israeli armed intervention. By July 24, Lourie wrote Sharett that Israel had "no alternative" but to fully support the U.S. action. Israel's "flat and rather precipitate rejection of any offer to help was interpreted in Washington as an attempt to hedge on our original statement and to retreat again to a more neutral position." Unless Israel would go through with its decision to support the U.S. stance on Korea it "may fall between two stools." "Whether we like it or not, without the funds received from the U.S., Israel cannot at this stage subsist."[28]

During the Korean War, it had come to Israel's attention that the United States planned to transform the Middle East into a base of military operations in case of war with the communists in that part of the world. This plan was part of an effort to protect oil resources and defend freedom of the seas in the Mediterranean. Turkey, Iran, and Egypt were to provide a defensive triangle for U.S. operations in coordination with Great Britain. While the Arabs were not considered to be a contributing element of this military strategy, their friendly cooperation was considered valuable for the preservation of internal security and public service in the region.

Once Ben-Gurion learned of the American plan, he became increasingly concerned that Israel might be left defenseless and stranded in case of a world war. It was towards the end of July 1950, a critical time for U.S. operations in Korea, and a time of great concern in the West that Russia might attempt to make a move in Europe, that Ben-Gurion decided to advise Ambassador James G. McDonald of Israel's readiness to furnish the United States with over two hundred thousand troops in case the Russians might attempt a move in the Middle East.[29] Ben-Gurion asked that Israel be furnished or sold the arms with which to do the job. Apparently, this was a unilateral decision on Ben-Gurion's part because Foreign Office officials like Teddy Kolleck later advised McDonald that Ben-Gurion's views were not those of the Foreign Office.[30]

When Ambassador McDonald relayed Ben-Gurion's message to Washington, Acheson's response was surprisingly cool and reserved. He advised McDonald to thank Ben-Gurion, but not to offer Israel any arms. The very officials who had been displeased with Israel's neutrality appeared indifferent to Ben-Gurion's expressed desire for affiliation. Israel was now in a less than desirable position—dependent on American goodwill. Acheson even vetoed Israel's purchase of World War II tanks from the Philippines.

Some American observers like Richard Ford, U.S. chargé d'affaires to Israel, claimed, in anti-Semitic terms, that the waning economic interests of western Jews had forced Israel to reevaluate its basic policies. Ford claimed that because the Jews were not in a good economic situation, Israel had to reconsider its position and it could no longer afford "strict East-West neutrality." Ford insisted that the Israeli reassessment had come "from the ultimate realization that the hand that feeds will not submit indefinitely to being bitten."

On August 3, at the heels of America's cool response to his offer of two hundred thousand Israeli troops, Ben-Gurion tried to persuade his cabinet and government that Israel should send at least a token force to

Korea. He believed that humanitarian and verbal support was insufficient in the face of this aggression especially since Israel itself had been "a victim of aggression." The cabinet, led by Foreign Minister Sharett, rejected Ben-Gurion's recommendation.[31]

Israel sent ambulances and medical supplies for UN forces, but it was not to send troops to fight in Korea.

Some Israeli diplomats were greatly opposed to Israel's support of the United Nations on the Korean issue. Israeli minister to Poland Israel Barzilai, in protest, resigned from his post in November 1950. He found that Ben-Gurion's decision to support the United States had resulted in Israel's abandonment of its neutrality and had moved the country into the "western camp" "in a warring world which includes warmongers, enemies of progress, and enemies of Israel."[32]

President Truman continued in his efforts to win further Israeli support at the United Nations. When Eban presented his credentials as ambassador to the United States in September 1950, he found Truman to be most friendly and hopeful. Truman "repeatedly" expressed his respect for Weizmann and he spoke "at length of the necessity for regional development schemes for the Near East," and he praised Israel for its work in that field. Towards the end of that first interview with Eban, the president made an "emphatic appeal" for Israel's support of the American stand on Korea. "My main concern," said Truman, "is that international agreements should not be set aside by force and that in view of the general world dangers the states of the Near East should work patiently towards reconciliation."[33]

By November 1951, Foreign Minister Sharett supported Ben-Gurion's pro-West, pro-American orientation. He advised Acheson that Israel could play an important role in the defense of the Middle East, but it needed to exercise considerable caution because of the difficulties Soviet Jews and Jews in other Iron Curtain countries might encounter. "Any provocative act on our part, such as would impel the Soviet bloc to write us off as its avowed enemy, might tip the scales against further emigration" and force governments that permitted Jews to leave to withhold any further exit facilities. While Sharett now favored affiliation with the West he still preferred that Israel pursue its foreign relations most cautiously.[34]

Sharett asked Acheson whether the "Allies were determined to defend the Middle East with their full force." He wanted to know if they "would provide a sufficient force to hold the Middle East against all odds?" Acheson gave no definite answer. Eban watched his reaction to Sharett's question and noticed that Acheson's "unmistakable movement of his eyelids definitely indicated that he could not."[35]

The Arabs bought jets, warships, tanks, and guns of all calibers from every possible quarter: Great Britain, France, Italy, Belgium, Germany,

Russia, the United States, Sweden, and Switzerland. One Foreign Office report dated January 15, 1950, indicated that Egypt purchased forty Vampire and Meteor jets, a destroyer, several frigates and submarines, as well as Centurion tanks and fifteen thousand Lee Enfield rifles from Great Britain. Italy provided Egypt a large number of Sherman tanks. Belgium sold Egypt seventeen thousand semiautomatic guns. Egypt obtained a Krupp ammunition plant from Germany. France sold Egypt a cartridge casing plant, and Sweden set up an explosives factory in Egypt.[36] As Weizmann observed, the Arabs made no secret of their intention to start a "Second round" against Israel and if the "one-sided rearmament continued much longer they will not hesitate to start the "Second round." This would "mean the end of all hopes for an early settlement in the Middle East and it may well threaten the peace of the world."

Weizmann asked the United States to enable Israel to "hold her own against the threatened Arab attack."[37]

Despite America's refusal to assist Israel with critical defensive weapons, the United States called upon Israel to furnish military contingents in the Korean conflict. In early December 1951, American officials again asked Israel to "send a brigade to Korea" and they advised that "such a step would give Israel valuable military experience and political kudos."[38]

What had motivated Ben-Gurion to support President Truman's Korean War position? What was it that had motivated him to swing to the West?

There were many factors. He was sensitive to American public opinion, particularly expressed by Jewish leaders, Zionist as well as non-Jewish American politicians. He was likewise concerned with the growing influence of communists and the Mapam in Israel. He was concerned with the need for American assistance in the development of Israel's economy. He was dismayed by the growing anti-Jewish sentiments behind the Iron Curtain. All these were important factors, but the most critical factors were Soviet expansionism, as evident in the Korean War; and the danger Israel faced if it lost the friendship of the United States and perhaps became isolated from the powerful, democratic West as well as its Jewish populations.

Ben-Gurion could choose to listen to such individuals as Sharett and Barzilai, pursue a policy of neutrality, and risk isolation; or he could choose to follow the path of greater friendship with the United States and perhaps risk the loss of Russian friendship. He chose to side with the United States.

But Ben-Gurion's government would not allow him to send troops to Korea, nor would it allow him to provide the United States with troops in case of a Soviet threat in the Middle East or the Mediterranean. His support of Truman's Korean policy did not bring Israel closer to the United States. Except for President John F. Kennedy's sale of Hawk defensive missiles to Israel, the United States did not provide or sell Israel the defensive weapons it needed until after the Six-Day War. At times, the United States even used its influence to prevent such countries as Canada from selling Israel the weapons it needed for survival.

Israel had abandoned its neutrality—out of what appeared to be necessity—but it did not win American defensive support in return.

One of the most crucial testing times came in 1956 when Egypt—with Soviet weaponry and backing—threatened to destroy Israel. Israel responded with a preemptive war, supported by Britain and France, for their own strategic reasons. Once that victory was achieved, the United States forced Israel to yield its strategic victories for paper promises. Those promises could not be cashed in during the May–June 1967 crisis, as Egypt once again blockaded Eilat and war loomed on the horizon.

Truman remained a friend of Israel even to the last days of his administration. On July 1, 1952, he welcomed Sharett and Eban to the White House "with great gusto." He spoke of the need for peace between Israel and its neighbors and for Israel to become the "industrial backbone of the Middle East." He thought Israel should achieve the position of economic prosperity and leadership "as in the days of Solomon."[39]

Sharett endorsed Truman's sentiments and added that he wished to see Israel become "a living example of a successful democracy."

Truman agreed. He reminded his Israeli guests that Israel had "already been once an example of democracy in antiquity. Were not the judges of Israel the first rulers anywhere to have been elected?"[40]

Sharett invited Truman to visit Israel. Truman thanked him and said that it was nice to know that this was the way some people felt about him. It was "much better than to hear people say 'thank heaven that guy is out.' "[41]

Truman then reminisced of his days as president. He said that he had enough of the presidency, that he was sick and tired of the whole business. "Do you realize that until we went to the Blair House Mrs. Truman had shaken hands with 500,000 people? Oh no, she can't stand it any longer and when I think that something might happen to her, it is more than my life is worth. All we want now is to spend a few quiet happy years together."[42]

Sharett looked around the Oval Office and said, "It was a great epoch, the years you have spent in this room. To us they were most momentous years."

Pointing to the globe Truman responded, "My chief worry has been to prevent this thing from blowing up."[43]

NOTES

1. Blaustein insisted that the Israeli government only speak on behalf of its own citizens and not for Jews living outside of Israel. He advised Israeli ambassador Eliahu Elath that Israel should take greater care to avoid possible misunderstandings that might bring the United States and Israel "headaches." Jacob Blaustein to Eliahu Elath, March 14, 1949, Israel Foreign Office Papers, Israel State Archives, Jerusalem.

Blaustein had served on the National Petroleum Council of the U.S. Department of the Interior. He was president of the American Trading Production Corporation and director of the executive committee of the Pan American Petroleum Corporation and the American Oil Company and a member of various national business corporations in oil, insurance, and banking.

2. Memo on the American Jewish Committee by the Israel Foreign Office dated February 1950, Israel Foreign Office Papers, 85/16, Israel State Archives, Jerusalem.

3. David Ben-Gurion statement, August 23, 1950, Israel Foreign Office Papers, 88/7, Israel State Archives, Jerusalem.

4. Nahum Goldmann to David Ben-Gurion, Nahum Goldmann Papers, December 14, 1951, Z6/659, Zionist Archives, Jerusalem.

5. Benjamin R. Epstein to Abba Eban, December 20, 1951, Israel Foreign Office Papers, A.D.L. Files, 2467/6, Israel State Archives, Jerusalem.

6. Eliahu Elath to David Ben-Gurion and Moshe Sharett, Israel Foreign Office Papers, February 24, 1950, 2308/17, Israel State Archives, Jerusalem.

7. David Ben-Gurion to Eliahu Elath, February 17, 1950, Israel Foreign Office Papers, 2308/15, Israel State Archives, Jerusalem.

8. Moshe Sharett to Eliahu Elath, February 4, 1950; Eliahu Elath to Moshe Sharett, February 13, 15, 1950, Israel Foreign Office 2308/15, 2308/17, Israel State Archives, Jerusalem.

9. Ibid.

10. Nahum Goldmann to Teddy Kollek, March 3, 1950, Nahum Goldmann Papers, Z6/2359, Zionist Archives, Jerusalem.

11. Eliahu Elath to Foreign Office, March 23, 1950, Israel Foreign Office Papers, 2308/17, Israel State Archives, Jerusalem.

12. Eliahu Elath to Israel Foreign Office, March 3, 1950, Israel Foreign Office Papers, 2308/17, Israel State Archives, Jerusalem.

13. Eliahu Elath to Moshe Sharett, August 19, 1949, Israel Foreign Office Papers, 2308/10, Israel State Archives, Jerusalem.

14. Eliahu Elath to Israel Foreign Office, May 23, 1950, Israel Foreign Office Papers, 2308/18, Israel State Archives, Jerusalem.

15. Eliahu Elath to Israel Foreign Office, May 23, 1950, Israel Foreign Office Papers, 2308/28; Eliahu Elath Memo (undated), Israel Foreign Office Papers, 2308/10, Israel State Archives, Jerusalem.

16. Eliahu Elath to Israel Foreign Office, April 14, 1950, Israel Foreign Office Papers, 2308/17, Israel State Archives, Jerusalem.

17. Abba Eban to Moshe Sharett, August 20, 1950, Israel Foreign Office Papers, 2308/18, Israel State Archives, Jerusalem.

18. Eliahu Elath to Moshe Sharett, August 18, 1949, Israel Foreign Office Papers, 2308/10, Israel State Archives, Jerusalem.

19. The Jewish settlement within the Land of Israel.

20. Benjamin Akzin to Arthur Lourie, "Note on Palestine Policy, Problem of Implementation," February 9, 1948, Israel Foreign Office Papers, 7019, Israel State Archives, Jerusalem.

21. Moshe Keren to Moshe Sharett, July 1, 1950, Yehoshua Freundlich, ed., *Documents on the Foreign Policy of Israel*, Volume 5 (Jerusalem 1988), p. 419.

22. *Israel Documents*, pp. 417–418.

23. Ibid.

24. Ibid., p. 162.

25. Eliahu Elath to Moshe Sharett, August 25, 1950, Israel Foreign Office Papers, 2308/18, Israel State Archives, Jerusalem.

26. *Israel Documents*, p. 420.

27. Moshe Sharett's notes on his talk with Secretary Dean Acheson, November 19, 1951, Foreign Office Papers (Eliav Files), 2455/1, Israel State Archives, Jerusalem.

28. *Israel Documents*, July 24, 1950, pp. 443–445,456.

29. U.S. Department of State, *Foreign Relations of the United States, 1950*, Volume V (Washington, D.C., 1978), July 31, 1950, pp. 961–962.

30. Ibid.

31. *Israel Documents*, pp. 172–173.

32. *Israel Documents*, November 2, 1950, pp. 227–229.

33. Abba Eban to Moshe Sharett, September 5, 1950, Israel Foreign Office Papers, 2308/19, Israel State Archives, Jerusalem.

34. Abba Eban Memo regarding Moshe Sharett–Dean Acheson conversations, November 19, 1951, Israel Foreign Office Papers, 2475/3, Israel State Archives, Jerusalem.

35. Ibid.

36. Foreign Office to Eliahu Elath, January 15, 1950, Israel Foreign Office Papers, 2308/15, Israel State Archives, Jerusalem.

37. Chaim Weizmann to Oscar Ewing, January 2, 1950, Israel Foreign Office Papers (Eliav Collection), 2455/1, Israel State Archives, Jerusalem.

38. Walter Eytan to Foreign Office officials in Washington and Paris, December 2, 1951, Israel Foreign Office Papers, 2308/22, Israel State Archives, Jerusalem.

39. Minutes of July 1, 1952, meeting between President Harry S Truman, Moshe Sharett, and Abba Eban, Israel Foreign Office Papers, 2475/3, Israel State Archives, Jerusalem.

40. Ibid.

41. Ibid.

42. Ibid.

43. Ibid.

9

Dwight D. Eisenhower and Israel

The Dwight D. Eisenhower White House years represent a low point in Israel's relations with the United States. President Eisenhower and Secretary of State John F. Dulles entered the White House proclaiming that Harry S Truman had been too pro-Israel and that they would be even-handed in their approach to Middle East diplomacy. The aim of Eisenhower's diplomacy apparently was to forestall communist expansion. He seemed to feel that if colonial powers such as England, France, Belgium, and Portugal would give their territories independence, their actions would prevent communist infiltration and influence. The Eisenhower administration tried to encourage Israel to surrender the Negev, sixty percent of Israel proper, so as to entice the Arabs to make peace. It was a most difficult time for Israel.

Dulles argued that Truman had directed U.S. foreign policy in response to domestic political needs rather than U.S. foreign policy considerations. As Dulles put it, "We are in the present jam because the past Administration had always dealt with the Middle East from a political standpoint and had tried to meet the wishes of the Zionists in this country. That had created a basic antagonism with the Arabs. That was what the Russians were capitalizing on." He believed that unless that policy were changed the Near East and Africa would be lost. From May 9 to May 29, 1953, Dulles toured the Middle East and promised the Arabs a more even-handed American approach to the Middle East. In Cairo he presented the prime minister of Egypt with a .32 automatic pistol, a personal gift from President Eisenhower, and said that "if arms and economic help are justified in the case of Egypt and if Egypt itself desires these things from the U.S., the U.S. would be prepared to consider making the Egyptian Army a real force in the world. Egypt is one of the countries we would like to help with military supplies and equipment."[1]

Ben-Gurion tried to advise Dulles that what the Arabs needed was "economic development and not arms." In the end the Arabs would not use the arms against Russia, as perhaps Dulles believed, but "against Israel." But Dulles felt that the United States had to pursue a new policy because he believed that the Arabs felt that the Roosevelt and Truman administrations had been "subject to Jewish influence" and that the "Arab viewpoint was ignored." Dulles asserted that Eisenhower had been "elected by an overwhelming vote of the American people as a whole and neither owes that type of political debt to any segment nor believes in building power by cultivating particular segments of populations." He advised Ben-Gurion that the United States "would not carry out a policy partial to Israel and that the U.S. would not indefinitely finance Israel immigration."[2]

In Lebanon, Dulles announced that he came to visit the Middle East in order "to seek policies which would be more fair and more just than those of the past." He promised that the United States had "definitely set itself against any aggressive tendencies by Israel" and that Eisenhower would seek congressional appropriations "which would permit the U.S. to be more even-handed in its aid to the area than heretofore."[3]

This attitude was reflected in various testimony presented by State Department personnel in executive session hearings before such committees as the House Committee on Foreign Affairs on July 23, 1953. Arthur Z. Gardiner, a State Department political and economic adviser on Middle East affairs, testified before that committee and maintained that U.S. policy in the Middle East should not be directed by American Zionists. He believed that Israel had become too dependent upon American economic assistance. We cannot "just cast them to the winds, throw in the sea or throw them to the mercy of the Arabs" but they have got "to get along with the Arabs." The Jews "are their own worst enemies on this thing, but on the other hand, if we drive them completely to desperation, it is a very dangerous situation." "They should be pushed back a little. If you push them too far so that you start shooting, then we are in a pickle, I don't want to see American boys go out and fight Jews in Israel. That will be ever so much worse than fighting for the Koreans. It is a very delicate balance there that might be upset any day. We have to do more justice to our Arab refugee problem." But at the same time Gardiner seemed annoyed that Israel was receiving reparations from Germany since those reparations helped Israel to be more independent of the United States.[4]

Support for Saudi Arabia permeated the testimony of such State Department officials as A. David Fritzlan, an official concerned with Arabian Peninsular affairs. "We have a large reservoir of good will in Saudi Arabia, and it must continue to be considered by us in a special category among the countries of the Near East." "We have oil" and "what is equally important, perhaps even more so potentially, Dhahran Airfield." David Robertson, officer in charge of the economic section in the office of Near Eastern affairs, reported that Saudi Arabia was producing some 850,000 barrels of oil a day and providing a revenue of close to $200 million a year to the Saudi government. "The present ownership is thirty percent by Texas Oil Company, thirty percent by the Standard Oil of California, thirty percent by the Standard of New Jersey, and ten percent by Socony-Vacuum." The concession arrangement covers some 400,000 square miles in Saudi Arabia, comparable to the size of Texas and California put together."[5]

But despite the many Eisenhower administration efforts to win Arab friendship, the United States seemed unable to persuade Arab states like Egypt and Syria that the road to peace and reconciliation was the better alternative to the arms race and war, and that the United States was really their good friend. One reason Arab states chose not to follow the path to peace was because they realized that Israel was kept at a military disadvantage and they witnessed the United States pressuring Israel to yield its territorial sovereignty in return for concessions of peace from the Arab states. This would be the essence of U.S. Middle East diplomacy. The pursuit of the so-called "even-handed diplomacy" would fail to improve America's position in the Middle East despite huge U.S. investments and sacrifices on behalf of the Arab states.

Supporters of Israel were suspicious of Dulles and Eisenhower. One of Israel's advocates who had entrance to the White House advised President Eisenhower that many Americans were concerned lest his administration was prepared to sell Israel down the river in order "to placate the Arab world." The individual in question was referred to as Mr. X in Israel Foreign Office papers.[6]

President Eisenhower tried to persuade Mr. X and other supporters of Israel that he would not let Israel down. "Don't worry about our selling the Israelis down the river, we stick by what we believe is right." America had, in its pioneer days, a rather difficult time of it and Eisenhower believed that Israel would have to go through the same kind of thing, "they can't expect the United States to bail them out." Israel "will have to industrialize. That is the only hope for survival." Eisenhower was influenced by establishment individuals like Dulles and John J. McCloy. He was persuaded that "Israel was too concerned about the threat from the Arabs." "Tell the Israelis to woo Arab goodwill," Eisenhower advised Mr. X. One way to do this was to surrender the Negev to Jordan and Egypt.[7]

While Israel could not rely upon the Eisenhower-Dulles team, little more could be expected from the Democratic Party nominee, Adlai E. Stevenson. It was clear to Israel's Foreign Office that Stevenson was not a friend. On a number of occasions he used Arab propagandistic phrases.

While he referred to the Deir Yassin "massacre," he failed to mention the Arab massacres of Jews. He even repeated Glub Passah's accusation that Jews shot themselves in order to show the world that they were in mortal danger in the Holy Land. Israeli diplomats observed that Stevenson did not seem to realize that Israel had not started the war and that Israelis had not bombed such population centers as those of Jerusalem and Tel Aviv.[8]

When Foreign Minister Moshe Sharett met with Stevenson, he heard him say that Israel would have to accept the Arab refugees if it wanted to live in peace with the Arabs. But Sharett advised Stevenson that "nobody in his senses" favored "wholesale repatriation."[9] While some Americans admired Stevenson, there were others, Republicans as well as Democrats, who believed that Stevenson lacked basic good sense.

Some Republicans tried to persuade Stevenson to keep the issue of Israel out of the realm of partisan politics, but Stevenson refused. It was on September 3, 1952, that Eisenhower and Dulles talked with Stevenson about keeping the Israel issue out of the campaign, but he refused. On September 30 and October 3, Abba Eban and Teddy Kollek of Israel's Foreign Office tried to persuade Stevenson to keep Israel out of American politics, but he insisted on the right to preserve his "freedom of action" on this and all other issues.

The 1952 election ushered in the Eisenhower-Dulles team. That team entered the White House proclaiming that it would be much fairer to the Arabs than Truman had been. Dulles traveled to Arab capitals to circulate his "even-handed" proclamation. While Israel needed greater political, economic, and military support, the Eisenhower-Dulles team insisted that Israel admit Palestinian refugees and yield the Negev.

For a time the Eisenhower administration stopped asking for the "territorial integration" of Jerusalem or its internationalization, but it did not show greater support for Israel. In order to win support from Eisenhower, Foreign Minister Sharett once again expressed Israel's willingness to be part of an American-sponsored regional defense pact. But there was "no sign of a positive interest from the United States." Israeli apprehension increased as the United States revealed its intention to establish a Middle East defense pact exclusive of Israel and that the Americans planned to sell arms to Egypt despite Egypt's open belligerency against Israel. When Israel applied for U.S. military assistance it received no reply. Ambassador Eban advised Dulles that if the United States were to sell arms to Egypt it would prove a signal to the Arabs that the United States supported their making war against Israel.[10]

While Israel did not seem to achieve closer relations with the United States, its relationship with the Soviets witnessed a corresponding decline. In early January 1953, Pavel F. Shakov, a Russian senior member of the UN Secretariat, observed that "Israelis were becoming more and more identified with the United States and the West" and in effect Israel has become "an agent" of the United States.[11]

On February 9, 1953, a bomb exploded in the Soviet compound. The Israeli government voiced its profound regrets and promised to apprehend those responsible. The Russians broke relations with Israel stating that the "terrorist act which occurred on February 9, proved the lack of elementary conditions in Israel for normal diplomatic activities"[12] *Izvestia*, Russia's state newspaper, charged on February 25 that Israel had "become the main anti-Communist base in the Middle East" and that this was a consequence of the leadership of David Ben-Gurion and Chaim Weizmann.[13] After a brief rupture in Israeli-Russian relations they were restored.

Pinchas Lavon of Israel's Defense Ministry found it most regrettable that the United States had not accepted Israel's offer of direct defense cooperation. As far as individuals like Lavon were concerned, a Middle East defense pact would be realistic only if it were based on an alliance that included both Israel and Turkey.[14]

From the time of the Korean War, Israeli leaders had advised American presidents of their desire to be part of a mutual alliance with the United States. In February 1953, as Eban advised Dulles of Israel's desire for peace with Egypt and the other Arab states, he reiterated Israel's readiness to be part of an alliance with the United States. Once again Eban informed the Americans that Israel could place "eight divisions into the field," that it could enlarge its airfields and make its armaments industry available to the West. "If the airfields were enlarged and industry increased in advance of an emergency, Israel could then be of great use in the event of an international crisis." Perhaps "others might be hesitant but we are prepared to fight along with the West." The Arabs might join once they would see that Israel was party to such an alliance.[15]

The Eisenhower-Dulles regime, however, failed to accept the Israeli offer. Dulles claimed that the Arab states were against the British, the French, and "to a lesser extent" they were against the United States. He believed that Soviet anti-Semitism presaged more active Russian moves in the area and that this represented the greatest of dangers.[16]

Israel abandoned its neutrality in favor of an association with America and the West, but that did not bring the friendship Israel had anticipated. It served to alienate the Soviets. Soviet official Alexander Lavrichtchev asked the Israeli ambassador to Turkey, Eliahu Sasson, whether the rumor of U.S. bases in Haifa had any substance. He also expressed his concern regarding rumors of a possible Turkish-Syrian alliance.[17]

The Eisenhower-Dulles team seemed to fear the Soviet Communist satan more than anything else. They pressured their allies to liberate their colonies and empires so as to prevent Russia from making inroads with their revolutionary ideas. Whether the colonies of France and England were prepared for independence did not matter to the Eisenhower-Dulles team. What seemed to matter was to find some way to prevent communist infiltration and expansion. They likewise expected Israel to sacrifice everything in order to appease Arab nationalistic aspirations. Eisenhower joined British prime minister Anthony Eden in demanding that Israel give up the Negev to Egypt and Jordan.

Dulles often expressed his concern over the spread of communism as he did in conversations with Sharett and Ben-Gurion on May 13, 1953: "The greatest question was whether the Judeo-Christian civilization was going to survive—whether the moral and spiritual values for which it stood would survive," to which Foreign Minister Sharett responded that Israel was opposed to communism and "an enterprise like ours requires a regime of free creativeness." Prime Minister Ben-Gurion was even stronger in his response to Dulles: With respect to Russia "the free world has to be on guard even more than before," and Israel can provide important assistance to the free world in case of war. If the Suez Canal were to fall "into the hands of the enemy, Haifa and Elath would be important not only for Israel, but for the whole free world." Israel's aim is the "preservation of peace and democracy." He expected the United States and the free world to make every effort to help the Arab world improve the condition of its people. The "liberal people in the Arab countries should be encouraged and not only the rulers."[18]

While speaking with Sharett, Dulles reiterated his usual theme that the United States had to be even-handed, that it had to have the confidence of the Arabs, and that if the Arabs would believe that America's "only concern was with Israel, then the U.S. had no effective part to play in ameliorating conditions between Israel and the Arab states." Dulles said that the "Arabs felt with some justification that the prior administration of Roosevelt and Truman had been subject to Jewish influence and that they had ignored the point of view of the Arabs." And it was known historically that decisions in this matter were taken under direct political pressure by Jewish groups who felt that they had contributed to the election of Roosevelt and Truman. Dulles reiterated an observation the Eisenhower-Dulles team had often made: "We do not owe that kind of political debt."[19]

Not only was it apparent to Israeli leaders that the United States failed to support Israel, but it seemed that the Eisenhower administration was not interested in bringing Israel and the Arab states to the peace table. In 1953 Israel asked Eisenhower to intercede and help bring about an Israeli-Egyptian peace accord, but the United States did not seem interested. Eban told Dulles on February 25, 1953, that Israel believed that once Egypt would make peace, the other Arab states would as well. Eban reported that the United States seemed supportive of the idea of direct Israel-Arab peace talks and that American officials seemed to better appreciate Israel's position with respect to the Arab refugee question. Previously, on October 24, 1952, Eisenhower had said that the Arabs should be "assisted with adequate means honorably to reintegrate themselves in the neighboring countries."[20] Apparently, the Americans no longer called for the "territorial internationalization" of Jerusalem. But in the end little or no American effort was made to bring Israel and Egypt towards face to face peace negotiations. Perhaps Dulles and Eisenhower may have felt that peace between Egypt and Israel was an unlikely proposition.

Israelis disapproved of America's use of its foreign aid program to influence and direct Israel's foreign policy. As Eban said to Dulles, this American tactic used "our financial difficulties as a means of preventing us from maintaining our national and international rights by peaceful discussions." It might be that Israel found itself in some "financial difficulties, but national pride would prevail against economic pressures."[21]

Dulles objected to Israel's pursuit of an independent foreign policy. He thought Israel had made things difficult for both its friends and the United Nations "by creating *de facto* situations and then asserting that these situations can never be changed except by war." He illustrated this Israeli tendency by citing two instances of Israel's policy that seemed to disturb him: Israel's move in the North regarding the Jordan River water project and its move of the Israeli Foreign Office from Tel Aviv to Jerusalem. He claimed that those two measures had caused various representations from members of Congress who asked him "why he did not do anything about it." Dulles insisted that "the U.S. had to give a clear impression of even-handed policy in its relations to the Middle Eastern states."[22]

Foreign Minister Sharett observed that the "moral and intellectual level of senior policy-makers has declined." President Eisenhower fell "below his predecessors in terms of inner seriousness and the extent to which he let his decisions to be determined by his conscience." He "lacked the moral weight and rectitude that characterized Truman." Eisenhower was "only superficially familiar with Israel related issues." Dulles "gave the impression of being rather confused and still incapable of grasping the complexities of the matter." Dulles was "intellectually inferior to his predecessors," he was "groping in the dark," and this seemed to be the case with Secretary of Defense Charles Wilson. The Eisenhower administration's view was that Israel had "to make territorial concessions in return for peace."[23]

Assistant Secretary of State Henry A. Byroade insisted that Israel had to display "a willingness to give up territory." Sharett tried to make the Eisenhower people understand that a settlement based on Byroade's conditions would be "the antithesis of peace." When Byroade insisted that the United States "might well be compelled to stipulate what it considers to be suitable conditions of peace," Sharett warned against such a step, "only by force could the U.S. deprive Israel of territories under its control."[24]

Sharett noted that the United States seemed overly concerned with Soviet expansion in the Middle East.[25]

Eban complained that American leaders had failed to "affirm and assist" the American-Israeli friendship. Both states were "governed by their public opinion" and it was "important not only that friendly relations should exist but that friendly relations should seem to exist." Instead of displaying friendship, the Eisenhower administration made a point of publicly stressing Israeli-American differences. The Americans exhibited "every disassociation of the United States from Israel's hopes or requests." Moreover, the United States sold weapons to the Arab states that were at war with Israel, but it failed to sell arms to Israel. The Eisenhower administration did not seem to comprehend Israel's need for weapons with which to defend itself.[26]

Dulles insisted that the Eisenhower administration had remained loyal to Israel and to its needs. He insisted that even the Arab delegations at the United Nations complained that the United States had not altered its pro-Israel stand. "I wonder whether that does not reassure you?" asked Dulles.[27]

That did not reassure Israel. As Eban put it, the Arab complaints regarding U.S. policy proved that the "steps which the U.S. had taken and which had such a disquieting effect on Israeli and Jewish opinion had no compensating advantage on the Arab side. The question was whether there was any point in diluting or concealing the American-Israeli friendship in the hope of making an impression on the Arabs."[28]

Francis H. Russell, U.S. chargé d'affaires, could not understand why Israel had decided to go ahead with the Jordan River project. He seemed surprised by the fact that Israel moved its Foreign Office to Jerusalem. Russell claimed that the United States had "worked out practically 99.9 percent of a plan for Jerusalem which would have satisfied Israel completely—but now, by your action, you have put off a solution for at least two years. We cannot understand why you do these things."[29]

As Dulles talked with various American Jewish "leaders" like Senator Herbert H. Lehman, Rabbi Abba Hillel Silver, and Philip Klutznik, he reassured them of America's good intentions and that he planned to "allay Israel's apprehensions." But his words of reassurance were insufficient. Eban told him that United States and western leaders only delivered words of reassurance, but they armed and bolstered the Arabs and in that way condoned their aspirations to make war against Israel. There was an imbalance in the Middle East because of American and British military pacts and military aid programs. The Americans and the Western allies seemed unwilling to offer Israel military assistance or a defense treaty, "nor was there any disposition by the western powers to withhold aid from the Arab states until they would abandon their hostility. It was as if a pair of scissors had been taken and Israel had been cut out of existence in its region, while all forms of cooperation and reinforcement were offered the Arabs alone. "There is the grave and extraordinary fact that all the security arrangements of the Western Powers in the Middle East have been directed and oriented towards the Arab states and have been based upon Israel's exclusion." As the United States and Great Britain continue "their security activity in the Middle East solely upon strengthening the Arab states," Israel can conclude that its "survival and security" are in "dire peril and this sense of peril" may "inspire all her policies." The current U.S. and western plans to arm the Arabs left the "impression in the Arab countries of unconditional American indulgences of their collective hostility to Israel." In brief, American and British security policies created disadvantages for Israel and upset the balance of power against her. That was the situation as of 1953–1954.[30]

Israel found itself without U.S. or Soviet support. While the United States had claimed to be fair to the nations of the Middle East, Israel did not find this to be the case. The Russians promoted their friendship with Arab states such as Egypt, Syria, and Iraq, but the Americans failed to stem the tide of Russian expansionism. Whatever the United States tried to do in order to win over the Arabs, they did not succeed. The more concessions they received from the Americans and the so-called "West," the more the Arabs wanted. The end result was a greater imbalance and insecurity in the Middle East and Israel's sense of security declined. Israeli political leaders were unable to change the course of this inclination of American policy led by the American foreign policy establishment.

During the Eisenhower administration, American officials promised Israel equitable treatment, but it was not forthcoming. On a number of occasions Dulles would express his sympathy for Israel to such Israeli officials as Eban and Sharett. Dulles would even declare his concern for Israel's "sense of isolation and vulnerability," and he would promise to "cancel" any possible disadvantage that the United States might have created in the Middle East, but the Eisenhower administration would go no further than issue laudatory proclamations.[31]

At times, American officials asked Israel to share its military secrets. One of those officials was Congressman Prouty of the House National Security Committee. He advised Ambassador Walter Eytan that the United States knew Israel had an armed force that could be of "real value in a world war . . . and America desired to establish a relationship of mutual confidence and trust with Israel, similar to that which existed between the U.S. and all the NATO states." Therefore, the United States wanted Israel to share its military information. He advised that "if Israel were only willing to confide with the U.S. regarding its military forces it might be easier for the U.S. to help Israel militarily."[32]

The United States, Britain, France, and Turkey tried to encourage various Arab states to join them in a Middle East Defense Organization aimed to protect the area against possible Soviet expansionist moves. Both Israel and Egypt were wary of this alliance since it would include Iraq. Some U.S. officials observed that this "defensive" alliance never came into being because certain Middle Eastern states were too preoccupied by local quarrels and by existing disputes with the West.[33] Israel had been very concerned with the Eisenhower administration's support of the Baghdad Pact that allied such Arab states as Iraq with the West. Ambassador Eytan advised Prouty that Iraq had sent volunteers to fight Israel in 1947 and in May 1948 it had launched an invasion of Israel. "Iraqi troops came within a few miles of Tel Aviv and they cut Jerusalem's water supplies. Iraq had not signed an armistice with Israel. Israeli and Iraqi Jews were hanged in public and Iraq forced a mass exodus of Iraqi Jews." Israel had expected impartiality and fairness from the United States. If the Eisenhower administration were to sell and send arms to the Arabs it would be a signal to them that they should continue their hostility towards Israel. The "political and psychological effects of any military aid, however modest, would be little short of disastrous."[34]

Eban repeatedly tried to help Dulles understand Israel's difficult situation. Every Arab state had security arrangements with such powers as Britain, France, the Soviet Union, and even the United States. Israel had none. The Middle East security arrangements excluded Israel. Israelis were astonished and disappointed to see the United States encourage its "adversaries while excluding Israel from any process of parallel reinforcement." The United States, in effect, strengthened Israel's adversaries during the Eisenhower-Dulles years. Eban advised Dulles that the United States could help stabilize the Middle East situation if it provided Israel with "whatever military arrangements or relationship it offered the Arab states."[35] Moreover, the increased Soviet anti-Semitic campaigns and attacks against Israel for its ties with the West, said Eban, "merit and require the public reinforcement of the American-Israel friendship.[36]

Eban tried to help Dulles visualize Israel's difficult geopolitical situation. All of Israel was no "more than a few miles from a hostile frontier." The Arabs attacked ceaselessly and Israelis were killed. Israel's losses during its war of independence were proportionate to America's having lost six hundred thousand Americans during the Korean War. The Arabs pursued a policy to "embarrass," "infiltrate," and make life for Israel "as miserable as possible."[37]

Dulles said that he supported Israel's desire for peace and its tactical approach, but he explained that the United States had achieved an armistice in Korea only after "it had made it clear that there were other alternatives" and that the West was not going to go on its knees for an armistice. And for the same reasons, Dulles advised that it might be better for Israel to avoid giving the impression of "over-eagerness."[38]

Dulles would often philosophize regarding America's "special friendship" with Israel and he would ascribe that friendship to ties of blood, religion, and culture. He observed that there were a large number of Americans who were "bound by ties of blood and religion to the people of the State of Israel." Moreover, the American people had a "profound appreciation of what the Jewish people had contributed to the fundamental concepts of American culture and morality . . . The Judeo-Christian heritage." Dulles was fond of that phrase and according to Eban he used it during various sermons he had delivered before a church "founded by his father in a village on the border between Canada and New York." He believed that the American people admired Israel's political and economic accomplishments "recorded after 2,000 years." America's aim was to bring peace to the Middle East, but this could not be if it gave the "impression that it was prepared to support Israel blindly right or wrong, irrespective of the views of the American people and of world opinion as represented by the U.N." Peace between Israel and the Arabs could more easily be attained if it were understood that America was even-handed. He asked the Israelis to review their policies from the "viewpoint of international harmony" and to adopt "a temperate, moderate mood which would promote international goodwill." Eban assured Dulles of Israel's peaceful intentions and advised that peace would be more easily attained if the Arabs would know that the United States had "no intention of departing from its friendship with Israel," any uncertainty in this respect would delay the peace process.[39]

Promises were made by the United States during the Eisenhower-Dulles years, but no commitments were implemented. In October 1954, Eban advised Dulles that he had not made good on his promises and that no reassurances were provided regarding Israel's security nor was there "an offer made to include Israel in the U.S. military aid program."[40]

Ambassador Avraham Harman found Israel's growing economic dependency on the United States disturbing. He thought it would be far better if Israel would be more economically independent. "Our political position in the U.S. would also be very much stronger than it is if we were able to lessen the degree of our economic dependence even on income from Jewish sources in the United States."[41] Rather than provide Israel with any kind of political or moral support, the United States joined Britain in placing obstacles in the way of Israeli security which helped establish an unfavorable atmosphere against Israel. One such instance involved the Kibya affair.

The United States led the UN condemnation of Israel after Israeli forces retaliated against a Jordanian terrorist base. The position taken by Dulles left Israel with the impression that the United States tried to increase its influence in the Arab world at Israel's expense. As Eban put it, this "impression of excessive indulgence to the Arabs in matters relating to Israel had already done much damage and was partly responsible for the deterioration of the Middle Eastern situation."[42]

Israeli leaders had expected, at the very least, impartiality from the United States, but despite the many words of reassurance from Dulles and Eisenhower, the United States failed to be impartial. Directly or indirectly, it sent arms to the Arabs and this signaled the Arabs to continue their hostility towards Israel. The "political and psychological effects of any military aid to the Arabs however modest would be little short of disastrous," said Eban.[43]

But Dulles insisted that "any arms the U.S. would give the Arabs would be very meager."[44] Dulles reported to Eban that the prime minister of England thought Israel wanted to see the United States increase its influence in the Arab world and thereby be more effective in the Arab-Israeli peace process and regional security. Dulles considered this to be a most "remarkable and statesmanlike view" and asked Israel to consider the sentiments of the founders of the American republic to show a "decent respect for the opinion of Mankind." He called on Israel to review its policies from the "viewpoint of international harmony" and see if Israel might not adopt "a temperate, moderate mood which would promote international goodwill."[45]

Peace, Eban insisted, could more easily be achieved if the Arabs were sure that the United States had "no intention of departing from its friendship with Israel." If there were "any uncertainty on this matter in the Arab mind" a peace settlement would be delayed.[46]

The Middle East arms race accelerated and consumed the resources of the countries of that region. Prime Minister Sharett advised Eisenhower that the arms being shipped to such Arab states as Egypt and Iraq would only serve to encourage the Arab states to mischief and war and that Israel watched "with profound dismay and mounting anxiety the policy of the American government to arm the Arab states—Iraq today, Egypt maybe tomorrow and Syria the day after tomorrow." In order to counterbalance the weapons shipped to the Arabs, Israel was forced to use its meager resources to purchase arms. Israel was "at a loss to understand how the U.S. could reconcile that policy with its declared policy and concern to see Israel prosperous and secure." Israel had "repeatedly declared her readiness to do her share in defense of its democracy and of democracy generally." Israel stood by its declaration and it was up to the United States "to say whether it wanted an alliance with Israel." Both the United States and the Soviet Union courted Arab friendship and often at the expense of Israel. The United States was prepared to "woo the friendship of the Arab states, maybe not intentionally, against Israel, but in the actual result of it, to Israel's detriment."[47]

A good many members of Congress wanted to see both Israel and the Arab states treated with equity. Congressman Emanuel Celler observed that the United States had offered Egypt weapons and he wanted to know if the United States was prepared to "award a similar grant of arms to Israel, so that the balance of military power in the Middle East will not be disturbed to Israel's disadvantage." Celler observed that Israel had asked for arms back in 1952 and that it had been told that Israel's application would be granted "eventually." Two years had passed, but Israel had still not received those arms. Why did it take so long to remedy the imbalance? "Why not now?" It was the "historic moment to grant equality of arms." The Arabs would use their armaments to make war against Israel, and not against Russia as some of their supporters have maintained. Moreover, Egypt continued to blockade Israeli shipping and it was not "proper for the United States to arm Egypt as long as it continued such illegal blockade."[48]

More than fifty members of Congress had "failed to get assurances" from Acting Secretary of State Walter Bedell Smith and Assistant Secretary of State Byroade that the United States would withhold arms aid to Arab states who refused to make peace with Israel. The only response they got from the State Department was that the arms shipped to the Arabs were necessary "for the security" of the area.[49]

During his conversations with the secretary of state, Eban noticed that Dulles was an extremely nervous and jittery person. Dulles's lack of calm was "frightening" since he held such a pivotal and important position. "At times his left eye twitched, and at times his right. He runs his pencil down the parting of his hair and then sucks his pencil. . . . The man is scarcely still for a moment." And while Dulles testified before the Foreign Affairs Committee he doodled: "Dulles Must Go." Eban thought that Sigmund Freud might have had a good time figuring him out.[50]

Some western politicians did not have the slightest idea of Middle East conditions. One of those was Lester Pearson, prime minister of Canada. At one point in his conversations with Israeli diplomats, Pearson said that he understood "how many of our people, after all the persecutions they had been through would be emotionally unstable and ready to resort to reprisals." The Israeli representative who spoke with Pearson advised him that there were "many people in Israel . . . quite emotionally stable, but they still regarded self-defense as essential." The need for self-defense became more and more apparent as the Arabs refused to cooperate in keeping the peace and as the United Nations proved itself ineffective to promote peace.[51]

The attitude prevalent in U.S. State Department circles was reflected in the remarks of Byroade, one time assistant secretary of state for Near Eastern, South Asian, and African Affairs, when he addressed the Chicago branch of the Council on Foreign Relations and said that the Middle East was important to the United States because (1) of its strategic location, (2) it held one half of the world's proven oil reserves, and (3) they had "65 million souls whose desires we must take into account in our efforts to work in genuine harmony for a better world."[52]

Some officials like Byroade believed that Israel was "the major stumbling block to good relations between the U.S. and the Arab states." Moreover, they did not have much hope for Israel's future. They believed that Israel's "divergent elements" would eventually bring on Israel's downfall because they believed that they would be "unable to work together." The "most likely conflict would be between religious and secular elements of the population." And they observed that the country had no economic foundation, that it depended "almost entirely on outside sources of supplies."[53]

McCARTHY, THE RED SCARE, AND THE JEWS

Senator Joseph R. McCarthy and his colleagues had placed a scare into the American public during the Truman and Eisenhower years. American Jews had always been afraid of being accused of disloyalty. That may explain why they were silent, for the most part, as Franklin D. Roosevelt refused to help save the Jews of Europe. Israeli officials noted this phenomenon in their reports from America. One Israeli report of January 1955, noted a conversation with Reverend G. E. Hopkins who observed that U.S. policy to arm the Arabs had been an integral part of U.S. policy because it was in America's best interest. But "American Zionists in their frantic attempts to obstruct that policy were doing a distinct disservice both to the case of Israel and to the status of American Jews." American Jews who supported Israel raised "doubts as to their loyalty when they dared obstruct a policy established by America's highest policy makers."[54]

Writer Drew Pearson of the *Washington Post* observed in March 1954, that when Senator McCarthy visited Wall Street financier Bernard M. Baruch to win support, the senator had said that the City College of New York "specialized in graduating Communists." While McCarthy discounted accusations that he was an anti-Semite, he admitted that "some of his followers might well be described as anti-Semitic and that it would be difficult to restrain them if the big networks, whose executives were Jewish, would refuse him air time" to answer Democrat Adlai E. Stevenson.[55]

AMERICAN GUARANTEES TO ISRAEL

On May 25, 1950, the United States, Britain, and France had declared "their unalterable opposition to the use of force or threat of force between any of the states in the area." In July 1956, Dulles reiterated U.S. reassurances to Israel that "the U.S. would, within constitutional lines, oppose any aggression in the Near East and render assistance to the victim of aggression; and the U.S. foreign policy embraces the preservation of the independence of the State of Israel." Once again the U.S. expressed its concern for the preservation of the "independence and security of Israel and the other states in the area."[56]

After the Sinai War of October 1956, Dulles wrote Ben-Gurion "of the deep interest of the U.S. in preserving the independence and integrity of Israel." That was on September 12, 1957. The next day Baxter of the U.S. embassy in Israel said to Comay of Israel's Foreign Office that there was a "deep U.S. interest in preserving Israel's independence."[57] After American intervention in Lebanon, Eisenhower wrote Ben-Gurion on July 25, 1958, that U.S. intervention in Lebanon "reflected the assurances which had been given to the nations of the Middle East and notably the provision of the Middle East Resolution of the U.S. Congress that the independence and integrity of the nations of the Middle East are vital to world peace and to the national interest. Since the Middle East comprehends Israel, you can be confident of U.S. interest in the integrity and independence of Israel."[58]

Throughout his White House years, Eisenhower promised to consider Israel's defense needs. Dulles made these promises quite often. On August 1, 1958, Dulles wrote Ben-Gurion: "We believe that Israel should be in a position to deter an attempt at aggression by indigenous forces, and are prepared to examine the military implications of this problem with an open mind." A week later Dulles wrote to Ben-Gurion that the United States was concerned with Soviet intentions towards Israel: "I do not believe that the world at large and particularly the Soviet Union can have any doubt as to the reaction of the United States."[59]

Christian Herter, Dulles's successor, wrote to Ben-Gurion on August 4, 1960, to persuade him that "Israel could find assurance in the historic role our country has played in opposing aggression and championing the cause of freedom."[60]

Such were the assurances, but they were not backed up with arms sales.[61] Israel could not feel secure as huge arsenals of arms from the Soviet Union, Britain, and the United States were given to the Arabs. Paper promises of support could not match weapons.

By 1954 Israel found itself without U.S. and Soviet assistance. The United States had promised equity, but it did not deliver on that promise. The Russians sought and achieved the friendship of such Arab states as Egypt, Syria, and Iraq. America's effort to stem the tide of Soviet influence in the Middle East did not succeed. American efforts to appease the Arabs likewise failed. Western appeasement of the Arabs resulted in a decline of Israel's security. Israeli politicians and diplomats, American Jews, and friends of Israel were unable to change that historical development.

As a result, Israel was isolated. Some Israeli leaders like Ben-Gurion did not believe that the isolation would end. But then some of the Middle Eastern states, allied with the West, were not satisfied with the western commitments. The foreign minister of Turkey advised the Israelis that he favored neutrality and a closer affiliation with the Arab community. He complained bitterly that the western states had refused to grant Greece and Turkey the "slightest guarantee for practical help in case of aggression."[62]

He was furious that all his proposals for defense had been rejected by the Americans. Turkey had called for American guarantees; a partnership with the Atlantic Pact; a Turkish-Greek Pact connected with the Atlantic Alliance or the incorporation of America into a Turkish-British-French Alliance, but all those suggestions were not accepted by the Americans. The Turkish ambassadors to England and France had learned that the military situation of the western powers "was such that they were thoroughly unable to meet with Turkey's requests." Turkey felt abandoned, and it tried to find some sort of rapprochement with the Arab and Moslem states so as to pursue a policy independent of the United States and the West. It planned to use its armed forces only for the purpose of its self-defense. As far as Israeli diplomats were concerned, this new Turkish approach represented an additional danger to the Middle East condition. Turkey's possible rapprochement with the Arabs might turn into a "factual solid reality," which might induce Turkey to support the Arabs on all matters.[63]

In October 1954, Israeli representatives tried once again to explain Israel's situation to Dulles. Israel faced the "implacable hostility of her neighbors." There was an "enormous preponderance of Arab states in relation to Israel in area, population and financial resources." The West had concluded security arrangements with the Middle Eastern states, but there was a "grave and extraordinary fact that all the security arrangements of the western powers" had "been based upon Israel's exclusion." Israelis were astonished and disappointed as the United States encouraged its adversaries while it excluded it from any process of "parallel reinforcement." Eban reminded Dulles that in the past he had expressed sympathy with Israel's predicament and its "sense of isolation and vulnerability" and that he had promised to "cancel" any disadvantages that the United States might have created. Finally, he reminded Dulles that he had promised to send Israel a letter promising that the United States "would not place Israel in a disadvantageous position; specifying Israel's eligibility for military aid pacts; guaranteeing Israel's security; and promising U.S. efforts to help end the Egyptian Suez Canal blockade against Israel." All this had been promised, but had not been forthcoming. Israel did not receive security reassurances and no mention was made of Israel's "inclusion into the U.S. military aid program."[64]

KIBYA

Egypt and Transjordan encouraged terrorist incursions and attacks against Israel, who retaliated against those attacks. The United Nations condemned Israel's retaliations and the United States joined in those condemnations. When Israeli commandos attacked Arab terrorist bases Kibya, Jordan, the United Nations reproached Israel.

Ambassador Eban candidly told Dulles that the attitude of the United States made it appear as if the United States wished to increase its influence in the Arab world and it did not matter what it might cost Israel. This "excessive indulgence" of the Arabs had done much damage and was in part responsible for the deterioration of the Middle East situation. It would be much better if the United States would publicly declare its support of the armistice agreements, and its opposition to any act or expression of hostility would be most helpful.[65]

By 1955, Israel's military and diplomatic position was precarious. It did not have the military equipment to match that of the Arabs, nor did it have diplomatic backing. But the intrigues and complications of international diplomacy would soon change this situation. As French and British security interests in Africa would be challenged by Egypt and the Soviet Union, they concluded understandings with Israel and provided Israel with the arms it needed to meet the Russo-Egyptian challenges in the Middle East.

In October 1956, Israeli and Egyptian forces met in the Sinai and fought a war. Britain and France backed Israel, while the Soviets and to some extent the Eisenhower administration backed Egypt. It was to be Israel's second war of independence and as with its first war in 1947–1949, it received little help from the United States. On the contrary, the United States made every possible effort to impress the Arabs that America was their best friend.

Israel would win that war and the Eisenhower administration would force Israel to yield its successes in return for paper promises that the United States was unable to uphold.

NOTES

1. *Foreign Relations of the United States, 1952–1954*, Volume II, Part I (Washington, D.C., 1986), pp. 9, 14, 20.

2. Ibid., pp. 39, 70.

3. Ibid., pp. 75–78.

4. U.S. House of Representatives, Committee on Foreign Affairs, *Selected Executive Session Hearings of the Committee, 1951–1956*, Volume XVI, July 23, 1953, pp. 172–173; March 24, 1954, p. 230 (Washington, D.C., 1980).

5. Ibid., pp. 183–187, 188–189.

6. Undated Israel Foreign Office Papers, A.H. 00/107/6, Israel State Archives, Jerusalem.

7. Ibid.

8. Undated Israel Foreign Office Papers, A.H. 00/1962, Israel State Archives, Jerusalem.

9. Moshe Sharett's meeting with Adlai Stevenson, June 8, 1953, Israel Foreign Office Papers, A.H. 00, Israel State Archives, Jerusalem.

10. Ambassador's Report, February 25, 1953, Israel Foreign Office Papers, 2414/27B, Israel State Archives, Jerusalem.

11. William Epstein, conversation with Pavel F. Shakhov, January 1953 memo, Israel Foreign Office Papers, Eliav Files 2457/14, Israel State Archives, Jerusalem.

12. Foreign Office Memo dated February 12, 1953, Israel Foreign Office Papers, 2457/14 (Eliav Files), Israel State Archives, Jerusalem.

13. Foreign Office notation dated February 25, 1953, Israel Foreign Office Papers, 2457/14 (Eliav Files), Israel State Archives, Jerusalem.

14. Foreign Office Notation, 1954, Israel Foreign Office Papers, 2480/1B, Israel State Archives, Jerusalem.

15. Abba Eban-John F. Dulles talks, February 26, 1953, Israel Foreign Office Papers, 2412/27/B, Israel State Archives, Jerusalem.

16. Ibid.

17. Yehoshua Freundlich, *Documents on the Foreign Policy of Israel*, Volume 6 (Jerusalem 1991), pp. 8–13.

18. Notes on John F. Dulles, Moshe Sharett and David Ben-Gurion conversation, May 13, 1953, Israel Foreign Office Papers, 106/42, Israel State Archives, Jerusalem.

19. Ibid.

20. Memo on Abba Eban-John F. Dulles talks of September 25, 1953, Israel Foreign Office Papers, 2414/27/B, Israel State Archives, Jerusalem.

21. Ibid.

22. Ibid.

23. Moshe Sharett to Walter Eytan April 4, 1953; Moshe Sharett to David Ben-Gurion, April 17, 1953, Yehoshua Freundlich, ed., *Documents on the Foreign Policy of Israel*, Volume 8 (Jerusalem, 1995), pp. 146–147; 155–157.

24. Ibid.

25. Ibid.

26. Ibid.

27. Ibid.

28. Abba Eban meeting with John F. Dulles, January 15, 1954, Israel Foreign Office Papers, 2414/27/B; Abba Eban to John F. Dulles, October 8, 1954, Israel Foreign Office Papers, 2480/5, Israel State Archives, Jerusalem.

29. Memo of Walter Eytan's conversation with Francis H. Russell, September 24, 1953, Israel Foreign Office Papers, 2414/27/B, Israel State Archives, Jerusalem.

30. Abba Eban meeting with John F. Dulles, January 15, 1954, Israel Foreign Office Papers, 2414/27/B; Abba Eban to John F. Dulles, October 8, 1954, Israel Foreign Office Papers, 2480/5, Israel State Archives, Jerusalem.

31. Walter Eytan to Foreign Office, Israel Foreign Office Papers, 2414/27B, Israel State Archives, Jerusalem.

32. Statement by Assistant Secretary of State Jernegan on Middle East Defense, March 6, 1955, Israel Foreign Office Papers, 2475/4, Israel State Archives, Jerusalem.

33. Walter Eytan to Foreign Minister, Israel Foreign Office Papers, 2414/27B, 1953 (no date given on document), Israel State Archives, Jerusalem.

34. Abba Eban to John F. Dulles, October 8, 1954, Israel Foreign Office Papers, 2480/5, Israel State Archives, Jerusalem.

35. Ibid.

36. Ibid.

37. Conversation with John F. Dulles, October 8, 1953, Israel Foreign Office Papers, 2414/27B, Israel State Archives, Jerusalem.

38. Ibid.

39. Abba Eban-John F. Dulles conversation, October 8, 1954, Israel Foreign Office Papers, 2480/5, Israel State Archives.

40. Ibid.

41. Avraham Harman to Teddy Kollek, June 23, 1954, Israel Foreign Office Papers, A.H. OO, Israel State Archives, Jerusalem.

42. Memo of Abba Eban-John F. Dulles conversation, January 15, 1954, Israel Foreign Office Papers, 2414/27B, Israel State Archives, Jerusalem.

43. Ibid.

44. Ibid.

45. Ibid.

46. Ibid.

47. Ibid.

48. Emanuel Celler to John F. Dulles, August 4, 1954, Israel Foreign Office Papers, 2475/3, Israel State Archives, Jerusalem.

49. Foreign Office Notation dated March 7, 1954, Israel Foreign Office Papers (identification number missing), Israel State Archives, Jerusalem.

50. Abba Eban memo on an Abba Eban–John F. Dulles meeting, February 26, 1953, Israel Foreign Office Papers 2414/27/B, Israel State Archives, Jerusalem.

51. Foreign Office Notation dated April 13, 1954, Israel Foreign Office Papers, 2475/3, Israel State Archives, Jerusalem.

52. Foreign Office Notation, undated, Israel Foreign Office Papers, 2475/1, Israel State Papers, Jerusalem.

53. Foreign Office Notation on U.S. official views, November 1953, Israel Foreign Office Papers, 2472/7, Israel State Archives, Jerusalem.

54. Israel Embassy Report regarding conversation with the Reverend G. E. Hopkins, January 19, 1955, Israel Foreign Office Papers, 2475/4, Israel State Archives, Jerusalem.

55. Israel Embassy Report, March 27, 1954, Israel Foreign Office Papers, 2472/15, Israel State Archives, Jerusalem.

56. U.S. assurances to Israel found in Foreign Office Notation, September 20, 1962, Israel Foreign Office Papers, 3294/71, Israel State Archives, Jerusalem.

57. Ibid.

58. Ibid.

59. Ibid.

60. Ibid.

61. Ibid.

62. Eliahu Sasson to David Ben-Gurion May 14, 1951, David Ben-Gurion Letters, 1951, David Ben-Gurion Library, Sdeh/Boker, Israel.

63. Abba Eban-John F. Dulles talks, October 8, 1954, Israel Foreign Office Papers, 2480/5, Israel State Archives, Jerusalem.

64. Ibid.

65. Abba Eban-John F. Dulles talks, January 15, 1954, Israel Foreign Office Papers, 2414/27B, Israel State Archives, Jerusalem.

10

The 1956 Sinai War

After the armistices between Israel and its Arab neighbors were concluded in 1949, some believed that peace might be achieved in that part of the world. But there was no peace. The Arab states even refused to acknowledge the existence of Israel and they used Israel as a hate target to maintain unity within their own borders. Representatives of Arab states called on Israel to return to its 1947 boundaries and to repatriate 500,000 to 750,000 Arab "refugees." Moreover, they imposed economic boycotts against Israel and barred Israeli ships through the Suez and the Gulf of Eilat despite UN recommendations that Israeli shipping be permitted passage. Only days after truces were concluded, the Arabs inaugurated murderous attacks against Israeli civilian population centers. These terrorist bands, or Fedayeen—based, organized, and equipped by Egypt and Jordan—spread their terror throughout Israel by looting, bombing, and murdering men, women, and children.

From 1949 to 1953, 175 Jews were killed and 282 were wounded in 1,182 incursions from Jordan. Those attacks reached a climax during the first half of October 1953. On October 14, 1953, Israel retaliated by sending a paramilitary force into Jordan. The Mixed Armistice Commission reported to the Security Council that fifty-three Arab men, women, and children had been killed and that fifteen had been wounded in the village of Kibya. The Security Council took up the Kibya matter on November 24, 1953, and it approved a resolution sponsored by the United States, Britain, and France that censured Israel, adding the admonishment that Israel should "take effective measures to prevent all such actions in the future." The resolution included only slight reference to Jordanian crossings into Israel. It was a one-sided condemnation and the Security Council invariably refused to differentiate between cause and effect, provocation and reaction. The United States would repeatedly respond to Arab complaints by supporting the resolutions of censure condemning Israel; and Israeli complaints seldom received U.S. support.[1]

After the Kibya retaliatory raid, Israel proposed a review of the armistice agreement with Jordan. In accordance with Article XII of that understanding, which stipulated that if either party would ask the UN Secretary General to call a meeting with the other party to reconsider or revive the agreement, attendance was mandatory. Secretary General Dag Hammarskjold asked Jordan to meet with Israel, but Jordan refused. Thus, the Security Council was inhibited by Soviet vetoes; the Mixed Armistice Commission was impotent; and Jordan refused to permit any revisions. Israel had no alternative but to stop the Arabs through deterrent action.[2]

Foreign Minister Moshe Sharett witnessed "a most gruesome and revolting sight" on his return trip from Beersheba. A bus had been attacked, its driver and passengers had been killed. "The gang of killers had come from Transjordan." They broke into the bus and killed off the wounded. "Of the fifteen people only four survived by simulating death." "It was naked slaughter, carefully planned as a military operation, perpetrated in broad daylight with satanic ferocity."[3]

From the fall of 1954, the greatest number of Arab attacks on Israel came from the Egyptian-occupied Gaza Strip. Between 1954 and 1955, there were a total of 179 border incursions and some 429 armed clashes. Fifty-five Israelis were killed and 185 wounded. In retaliation for the Egyptian attacks, the Israelis hit hard against the Egyptian military camps at Gaza. Forty Egyptians were killed in February 1955. Israeli forces suffered eight dead. A special session of the Security Council was requested by Egypt. The American spokesman declared that Israel's action was "indefensible from any standpoint," and that the United States stood opposed to "any policy of reprisal or retaliation." President Dwight D. Eisenhower's ambassador to the United Nations, Henry Cabot Lodge Jr., went even further when he declared that "whatever the provocation might have been in this case, there was no justification for the Israeli military action at Gaza." Israel had retaliated against an Egyptian military base because of Egyptian attacks on Israeli civilian targets, but no mention was made of those Egyptian attacks. Israel was unanimously censured by the Security Council on March 29, 1955.

While the Security Council debated and condemned the Israeli action without considering the Egyptian provocations, the Egyptians and the Fedayeen threw grenades and fired at a village called Patish, where a wedding was taking place. A woman was killed and eighteen guests were wounded. The Arab attacks continued, but the United Nations and the world ignored Israel's sufferings, just as the world had ignored the Nazi extermination of six million European Jews only some ten years before.

To counteract Soviet expansionist ambitions, the United States inspired the development of a Middle East defense treaty known as the Baghdad Pact. This February 24, 1955, defense treaty between Iraq and Turkey was tied to an earlier treaty between Turkey and Pakistan. Iran and Britain joined, but the Americans declined, even though Secretary of State John F. Dulles had conceived of the idea and the United States agreed to provide some of the necessary arms and financial assistance. Egyptian president Abdel Nasser was offended by the pact, which he felt would deprive him of his position in the Arab world. He responded by seeking to overthrow the governments of Iraq and Jordan and building closer ties with the Kremlin. Nasser's arms deals with the Soviets in September 1955, were primarily a response to the Baghdad Pact, although some have claimed they were a reaction to Israel's retaliatory raid into Gaza. As Abba Eban put it, Nasser could never have forgiven the West for "taking over the leadership of Arab international policy."[4]

Israel likewise opposed the Baghdad Pact. The only difference was that it was alone. While Arab states were armed by the major powers, Israel still had neither a reliable source of supplies, nor any guarantee of security.

Added to Israel's increasing isolation, there were efforts to force the Jewish state into making territorial concessions to the Arabs. President Eisenhower wrote to David Ben-Gurion on April 10, 1956, and asked that Israel turn the other cheek: "I sincerely hope that in view of the terrible tragedy that general hostile actions will undoubtedly bring to this region, you will abstain, even under the pressure of extreme provocation, from any retaliatory acts which may result in very dangerous consequences."[5]

Ben-Gurion replied that if Eisenhower understood and appreciated the entire situation, he would never have restricted himself to "merely expressing the hope that we would abstain from military acts." Israel was grateful to the United States for its declaration that it would oppose any attack in this region, but such a statement did "not relieve our grave anxiety for Israel's security."[6]

A few days later, on the occasion of Israel's Independence Day celebration, Ben-Gurion recalled how the world had failed to respond when Adolf Hitler's armies were hunting down and killing the people of Israel. It seemed as if history was repeating itself. Egypt was arming itself and sending murder squads to kill Israelis while the world powers refused to sell arms to Israel and even to condemn the Arab atrocities. Ben-Gurion wondered: "The conscience of the great powers failed when Hitler sent six million Jews of Europe to the Slaughter. Will that conscience fail again . . . ?"[7]

One Israeli self-defense action against Jordan almost brought a direct military confrontation between Israel and Britain. On October 10, 1956,

Israeli forces retaliated for Jordanian incursions by decimating the Jordanian fort at Qalquilya. Jordan suffered many casualties and King Hussein I demanded that Britain's Royal Air Force (RAF) be brought into the fight according to the Anglo-Jordanian Treaty. In his memoirs, Anthony Eden recalled that the RAF was "on the point of going up," and the British minister in Israel told Ben-Gurion that if Israel attacked Jordan again, Britain would come to Jordan's assistance. But when he informed Ben-Gurion that an Iraqi division would enter Jordan, the Israeli prime minister replied that Israel would feel free to take whatever action it felt necessary.

The Suez Canal should have been kept open to all nations according to the principles of international law, but Egypt closed it to Israel and to any ship that was either leaving or bound for an Israeli port. In response to Israel's complaint that Egypt was preventing it from using the canal, a resolution was introduced into the Security Council that noted "with grave concern" that Egypt had not complied with a September 1, 1951, council resolution, which required Egypt to "terminate the restrictions." But while the resolution received eight votes, it did not pass because the Soviet Union vetoed it.

The indifference of the world organization to Israel's plight continued as Egypt occupied the island of Tiran at the mouth of the Gulf of Eilat and then prevented Israeli shipping from using the port of Eilat. Israel protested, but the world remained indifferent. In September 1954 the Israeli ship *Bat Galim* tried to pass through the Suez Canal in an effort to challenge Egypt's defiance of the 1951 UN resolution and to encourage the United Nations to take further steps. Egypt seized the ship and its cargo, but released the ten crew members. Israel lodged a complaint before the Security Council on September 24, 1954, but the council adjourned without passing any formal resolution or recommendation. There was no reference made to Israel's right of passage. The council's presiding officer merely said that he hoped the affair would be settled by the Mixed Armistice Commission.

In addition to the Fedayeen attacks and the Egyptian closure of Suez and the Gulf of Eilat, there were other violations of the armistice agreements. In disregard of the armistice agreements that provided for the orderly reactivation of the cultural and humanitarian institutions on Mount Scopus, free access to the holy places and cultural institutions, and the use of the cemetery on the Mount of Olives, the Jordanians kept the Old City of Jerusalem closed to Israelis.

SOVIET INFLUENCE SPREADS

As Soviet influence in the Middle East increased, peace prospects decreased. Encouraging Arab nationalism from Iraq to Algeria, the Soviets gained influence throughout the Arab world. When the United States rejected an Egyptian request for $27 million in arms, the Egyptians turned to the Soviet Union and in 1955, concluded an arms deal estimated at $200 million. The United States tried to prevent the Egyptians from consummating that deal by dispatching George Allen to Cairo, but he failed in his mission. On September 27, the arms agreement was publicly announced. During a foreign ministers conference in Geneva, Secretary of State Dulles advised Soviet foreign minister Vyacheslav Molotov that the arms deal with Egypt would make war in the Middle East more likely than ever.[8] But the Soviets were not about to change their minds.

In view of this growing threat to its security, Israel asked the United States for arms, but Eisenhower was opposed to providing Israel with arms because he felt that "would speed up a Middle East arms race." Influenced by Eden and Dulles, the president advised the Israelis to seek peace by ceding territory to Egypt.[9] Israeli foreign minister Moshe Sharett flew to Paris and later to Geneva to win help from the great powers, but all he got was a promise of a few planes from France. Israel was very much alone.

The U.S.–Israeli discussions regarding the arms imbalance in the Middle East was long and difficult. Neither Eisenhower, nor Dulles, nor any of the Eisenhower team seemed to appreciate Israel's peril. The U.S.–Israeli correspondence for the months prior to the 1956 Sinai War reflect a callous indifference to Israel's needs for security and defense. That indifference was a factor that brought on the 1956 war.

Foreign Minister Sharett advised the United States of the "tremendous disadvantage which Israel was facing. There was almost a complete lack of defensive facilities to meet the Egyptian jet air threats."[10]

On January 10, 1956, Ben-Gurion advised the Americans: "If we don't get quality arms in time it may be too late—there may be an explosion the consequences of which cannot be foreseen."[11] A few days later Sharett once again tried to get Dulles to understand how Israelis felt: "We cannot conceive that the U.S. Government should contemplate with equanimity the development of so ominous a crisis, with all of its incalculable consequences." Israel had pursued the path of negotiation and peace, but it "could not pin all of its hopes on that problematical chance." To suggest as Dulles suggested to Israel that "arms alone will not solve the problem [was] tantamount to telling a starving person that man does not live by bread alone." The United States needed to undertake a "sober appraisal of the peril" that Israel faced. "Time is of the essence."[12]

Dulles's response to Israel's repeated quests for arms was to advise Israel to "play the part of a good neighbor to the Arabs" and not seek to maintain itself by its own force and foreign backing. He insisted that unless Israel would realize this it was doomed.[13]

Ben-Gurion shared some of his great concerns with Robert B. Anderson, the U.S. special emissary to the Middle East. Egypt received arms from the Russians and British, and Egyptian soldiers were being trained by Russian and Polish officers. Russian-made bombers could reach Israeli locations within ten minutes and make ten trips per day carrying six-thousand-pound bombs. In this way they could destroy Israeli cities and population and industry centers. With all this power Nasser might very well believe that he did not have to make peace with Israel. But this was Israel's last stand. If the United States continued its embargo of weapons to Israel, the United States would be "Guilty of the greatest crime in its history."[14]

Sharett observed that Nasser "already had advantages that we cannot hope for or do not want to overtake quantitatively." Why should Nasser want to increase his armaments if his intent was not offensive? Time was running out against Israel.[15]

In a letter to the president, Ben-Gurion asked if Colonel Nasser sincerely desired peace or was he merely seeking to gain time until he could absorb Soviet arms into the Egyptian army and then be militarily capable of striking down Israel? America's "denial of defensive arms to Israel jeopardizes its very survival. In the absence of a positive response from the U.S. we find it well-neigh impossible to get arms from any other country in the free world." But if attacked, "we shall fight desperately and with our backs to the wall, for Israel today is the last refuge of our people even as at the dawn of history it was our first homeland." Ben-Gurion felt "bound to say in all earnestness that the U.S. is assuming a very grave moral responsibility. Every day that passes without our receiving from your country or her allies planes and tanks . . . brings the danger ever closer and deepens the feeling that we are being abandoned by our closest friends. No Arab country is ever likely to make peace with a defenseless Israel."[16]

Anger, resentment, and prejudice against Israel and Zionism could sometimes be seen in the correspondence of some American Middle Eastern envoys. This attitude was reflected in Ambassador Henry A. Byroade's February 23 letter to Dulles. He urged President Eisenhower to deliver a "fireside chat" and there present the facts about the Middle East to the American people. He could talk "in such a way as to practically break the back of zionism as a political force." Byroade recalled that when he had talked before the Council on Foreign Relations, "ninety-nine percent of those present would have voted against arms for Israel." He believed that this would have "included most of the Jewish people present." Byroade was consumed by a hatred toward such Israeli diplomats as Eban. He felt that Eban's behavior "clearly exceeded that of an accredited foreign diplomat." And as for individuals like Nahum Goldmann, they "have demonstratively violated the right to U.S. citizenship." He suggested that all this needed to be exposed, but "if we wait for what may happen in the Middle East—when the record will have to be exposed—this may not be possible."[17]

Dulles felt that progress for peace had been made "because we had not thus far supplied Israel with arms." He believed that "Israel should not jeopardize present prospects for a momentary respite which arms might give." Perhaps some "intermediate steps" might be found to strengthen Israel militarily without causing an Arab reaction which might hinder friendly relations. The U.S. might provide Israel with radar equipment.[18]

As of February 28, 1956, the U.S. National Intelligence estimate was that there would be a war between Israel and the Arabs. They estimated that the further introduction of Soviet arms to the Middle East had "substantially increased the chances of Arab-Israeli hostilities." Israel might very well "initiate such hostilities while it still enjoyed military superiority over the Arabs." On the other hand, increased Arab weaponry might increase their "militancy and the explosive potential of border clashes and stimulate Arab readiness for a second round."[19] But the American intelligence community believed that despite Soviet weaponry Israel was still able to defeat the Arabs. But by "late 1956 the Arabs would be able to use Soviet ground equipment effectively."[20]

With the arrival of new weapons, Egypt placed practically all of its army in the Sinai close to Israel's border. The same situation prevailed in Syria. Israel took precautions "short of substantial mobilization," but this was "extremely expensive and disruptive of her economy and daily life."[21]

There were times Ben-Gurion was furious with Dulles. Edward Lawson, the U.S. ambassador in Israel, reported on February 29, 1956, that he had "never seen Ben Gurion so emphatic, forceful or so emotionally upset and, on several occasions, so near to tears." Sharett "for the first time in my experience was unsmiling throughout . . . displaying an attitude of undisguised cold bitterness and foreboding criticisms." When Dulles testified before the Foreign Relations Committee, he spoke against arming Israel. Ben-Gurion found Dulles's testimony to be a "very bitter disappointment." Dulles insisted that "peace should not rest on arms alone," but he chose to ignore the fact that Egypt, Saudi Arabia, Syria, and Iraq were well supplied with arms. Ben-Gurion wanted to know how Dulles could suggest that Israel should rely upon the United Nations and the Tripartite Declaration. "None of us would be living," said Ben-Gurion, "if Israel had relied on the U.N. in 1948." Britain was a member of the Tripartite Declaration; but it continued to ship guns to the Arabs. Israel did not rely on the United Nations, nor could it rely on the Tripartite Declaration and it did not intend to. He was furious at Dulles's assertion that Israeli frontiers could not be guaranteed until they were defined by agreement. From Israel's standpoint, Dulles's suggestions would only bring about a change for the worse, but this would not happen as long as "we are alive." "Our girls and boys will fight to the death." Israel would not rely on Dulles's advice when the lives of the people of Israel were at stake.[22]

Sharett could not endure Eisenhower's inability to make up his mind. The Eisenhower-Dulles team had issued many statements of reassurance for many months, but nothing came of them. Israel still had not obtained weaponry it needed from the United States. There was "no dignity for Israel in continuing to beg for arms. However, it is not only undignified but dangerous to feed our people for so many months on false hopes."[23]

President Eisenhower confided with Undersecretary of State Herbert Hoover Jr., that he was "a little worried that perhaps we were being too tough with the Israelis with respect to arms." He thought of selling Israel some jet interceptors. He also considered sending Israel a battalion of Nike's "if for nothing else, but to see if they would work!" President Eisenhower also considered publicly declaring that the United States was making "a really sympathetic study" of Israel's situation because "we understood the position the Israelis were getting into."[24]

A few days later on March 6, President Eisenhower noted that the Soviets continued to send arms to the Arabs and he thought that "if this activity was kept up for very much longer, it might be necessary to give defensive arms to the Israelis—particularly those for ground forces, since air and naval support in the event of aggression against them could come from outside sources."[25]

As one reads Eisenhower's diary notations, it seems that he was much more sympathetic than Dulles towards Israel. Eisenhower recalled that after World War II he had a visit of "a couple of young Israelites who were anxious to secure arms for Israel." He talked with them about the future of the Middle East and he remembered how confident they were of the future. He was concerned that Nasser was not going to make any "move whatsoever to meet the Israelites in an effort to settle outstanding differences. Moreover, the Arabs, absorbing major consignments of arms from the Soviets, are daily growing more arrogant and disregarding the interests of Western Europe and the United States in the Middle East region." He even thought that it might be a good idea to conclude a treaty with Israel protecting its territory. "I know of no reason why we should not make such a treaty with Israel and make similar ones with the surrounding countries."[26]

Eisenhower was not impressed by the huge military forces and resources possessed by the Arabs. He observed that the "Arabs had certainly laid themselves open to a quick thrust by the Israelis" and that he did not have much confidence in Arab military planning.[27]

But during his press conference of March 7, President Eisenhower did not indicate that the United States would provide Israel with weapons.[28] Ben-Gurion was greatly disappointed and irritated.[29]

By February 1956 Israel Defense Force chiefs advised Ben-Gurion that "only a very short time remained before the balance of power would shift to the Arab side and they urged action before it became too late."[30]

As Foreign Minister Sharett explained it to Ambassador Lawson, the Arabs had tremendous advantage over Israel: "We are not asking for 200 jets to meet the 200 MIGs Egypt is receiving—we are asking for 24 F86's from the US. We are going to ask France for another 12 Mysteres."[31]

Ambassador Lawson agreed with Ben-Gurion's evaluation that Israelis would rather fight than agree to a truncation of Israel's territory. Lawson reported that Ben-Gurion was of the "firm belief that surrender of Israeli territory would constitute the first of a series of weakening measures designed to culminate in Israel's eventual termination."[32]

U.S.–Israeli relations continued to fade. Dulles blamed Israel for the deterioration of relations. He complained that "there was not the close working relationship which ought to exist between Israel and the United States"; that Israel appeared to be carrying on a form of political warfare against the Eisenhower administration; and that Israel had seemed to be "entirely self-centered, there being no evidence that the Israel Government had given any consideration whatsoever to the vital interests of the NATO countries in maintaining accessibility to the oil and other resources of the Middle East." The Arabs had always said that they could not rely on the United States and they moved closer to the Soviets. The more the "friends of Israel" tried to exert pressures against the administration, the more difficult it would be to persuade the Arabs not to turn to the Soviet Union. "All the activities that friends of Israel customarily resort to in whipping up pressures—the paid advertisements, the mass meetings, the resolutions, the demands of Zionist organizations, the veiled threats of domestic political reprisals—do not help to create a basis for understanding cooperation between our two Governments." Dulles insisted that it was not a wise way for Israel to "operate."[33]

Eban responded to Dulles's charges. Israel felt that the United States did not understand its problems and it did not seem to realize how Nasser had become an ally of the communists. Nasser had agreed to house the communist bloc labor organization; Cairo radio was pro-Soviet. But worst of all, Nasser had helped the Russians penetrate the Middle East and Africa. And then Eban returned to Israel's real difficulties: The Arab states received arms from the United States, Britain, and Russia, while Israel got none.

Dulles insisted that he had taken no position in his Senate Foreign Relations Committee testimony that was different from what he had said previously to Ambassador Eban or to Foreign Minister Sharett. He claimed to have said on previous occasions that he did not favor the

United States giving Israel a security pact until the frontiers had been fixed. As for arms, if the United States had supplied Israel the weapons it requested then America's relations with the Arabs would have been damaged and that would ultimately damage Israel.

Anderson returned empty handed from the Middle East where he had tried to bring about an understanding between Egypt and Israel. Eisenhower observed that Anderson had "made no progress whatsoever in our basic purpose of arranging some kind of meeting between Egyptian officials and the Israelites." "Nasser proved to be a complete stumbling block." He wanted to be recognized as the chief political leader of the Arab world. The Israelis, while anxious to talk with the Egyptians, were "adamant in their attitude of making no concessions whatsoever in order to obtain a peace." Their general slogan was "not one inch of ground," and their "incessant demand is for arms." Eisenhower felt that Israel could get arms at lower prices from almost any European nation; but they wanted the arms from the United States because they felt that in this way they could accomplish an alliance for "any trouble they might get into in the region."[34]

Eisenhower observed that there was "no easy answer." Arab oil grew "increasingly important to all of Europe" and European economies would collapse if the oil supplies were cut off. If the European economies would collapse then the United States "would be in a situation of which the difficulty could scarcely be exaggerated." Israel has "a very strong position in the heart and emotions of the Western world because of the tragic suffering of the Jews throughout twenty-five hundred years of history." The president thought that perhaps Saudi Arabia and Libya could become friends of the West and then Egypt would no longer be regarded as a leader of the Arab world.[35]

Ben-Gurion wrote to Eisenhower of how Egypt had opened up the African continent to Soviet penetration. "It would be presumptuous on our part to suggest to the U.S.A. how to safeguard the vital interests of world democracy in the Middle East and Africa," but Israel must seek to defend itself. There was an arms race, but it was a "one-sided" arms race with Egypt receiving arms from Russia and Great Britain and Saudi Arabia and Iraq receiving arms from the United States. Iraq and Jordan also got arms from Great Britain. Israel was denied the essential means for self-defence. All this was contrary to international justice and morality and incompatible with the intent of the Tripartite Declaration and various statements made to Israel by the Eisenhower administration.[36]

Dulles chose to ignore Israel's difficult circumstances and the United States still refused to provide Israel with weapons. Its prime concern was to maintain its influence within the Arab world. Dulles advised Eisenhower on April 1, 1956, that if they could go through the present U.S. political campaign without giving in to the "Zionist pressures for substantial arms to Israel, this would encourage the Arabs and have a very good effect on them."[37]

Eisenhower asked Israel to desist from retaliation against Egyptian-trained Fedayeen attacks. Ben-Gurion's response to Eisenhower's advice was to say that the president's "denunciation of acts of hostility and war evoke a deep echo in our hearts," but why were the words not "accompanied by a positive response to our application for arms for self defense." A stronger Israel would be "the only effective way of deterring Egyptian aggression" and to save the area from war.[38]

The Arab terrorist or Fedayeen attacks against Israelis continued. On April 11, 1956—within a fifteen kilometer radius of Tel Aviv—three schoolboys and one teacher were killed; five Israelis were wounded while at evening prayers in their synagogue; a family of three were wounded in their house; and six passengers were wounded while riding in a bus. The terrorists also shot up the main gate of Israel Defense Force headquarters at Tserifin. Total casualties for that day were: four killed and fourteen wounded.[39]

When Rabbi Abba Hillel Silver visited the White House, he tried to persuade Eisenhower to sell Israel some of the weapons it needed. Dulles presented the oft repeated Eisenhower administration viewpoint: the United States worked to secure a peace for the Middle East and that it would not serve the interests of peace for the United States to provide Israel with arms. Dulles said that the administration did not want "our policy to seem to be made by the Zionists" and that he did not think that "the mass meetings and public appeals helped the situation."[40]

Eisenhower said that he was not going to be influenced at all by political considerations and that "if doing what he thought right resulted in his not being elected, that would be quite agreeable to him."[41]

In a further effort to forestall the Soviet arms deal, Secretary of State Dulles called for fixed permanent boundaries between Israel and her neighbors, and he suggested that Israel give up the Negev. At the same time, he spoke of possible U.S. boundary guarantees and the resettlement of Arab refugees where feasible. Eden went much further when he called for a compromise between the boundaries of the 1947 UN resolution and the 1949 armistice lines. He asked Israel to give up territories to both Egypt and Jordan.

Ben-Gurion rejected Eden's suggestions. They lacked "legal, moral and logical foundation." Sharett, in reply to Dulles, agreed to some mutual adjustments of the 1949 lines for security and communications purposes, but he refused to agree to the 1947 lines as a basis for negotiations. While Israel agreed to provide the Arab states with transit rights and port facilities, it would not agree to the creation of any extra territorial corridor. Nor would Israel agree to unilateral concessions such as the surrender of Eilat or the internationalization of Jerusalem.[42] Unashamedly, they called for appeasement. American officials were prepared to reward Egypt, Syria, Lebanon, and Jordan for their invasion of Israel. They suggested that aggressors and violators of international treaties should be rewarded. The Anglo-American position of the 1950s was similar to what it had been towards free Europe in the 1930s. But unlike the abdicators and appeasers of the 1930s, Israel refused to surrender its freedom. Except for France, whose empire was threatened by Algerian rebels supported by Soviet weapons received via Egypt, the Israelis had no friends. And France was a questionable ally.[43] France was willing to sell Egypt all the arms it wanted to destroy Israel, if only Nasser would refrain from supporting the Algerian rebels. Nasser refused. Soviet foreign minister Dimitri I. Shepilov went to Egypt while the Egyptians celebrated the British withdrawal from Suez with a display of Soviet arms. Shepilov was rumored to have offered Egypt an interest-free loan for a hydroelectric dam. To some, like Secretary of the Treasury George Humphrey, it seemed that Egypt was shopping around for the best offer.[44]

Nasser's recognition of Red China, his trade with communist countries, and his intervention in Yemen, Iraq, Jordan, and Saudi Arabia contributed to the decline of his popularity in America and the West. According to Raymond A. Hare, former head of the State Department's Middle East Division, "southern cotton growers were in fact opposed to the Aswan deal for fear that it would increase competition with Egyptian cotton and their views were reflected in Congress, which had singled out the Aswan deal for criticism, and had demanded that there should be special consultation if it were included in the aid bill, which was then under consideration and having its usual difficulties."[45] Eisenhower concluded that America should not participate in the Aswan Dam project.[46]

Dulles revealed on July 10 that the loan to Egypt was "improbable." On July 13 he informed the Egyptians that he could not deal with the Aswan Dam question because he could not predict what action Congress might take, and that U.S. views had changed "on the merits of the matter."[47] On July 19 Egypt's ambassador asked Dulles not to say that America would withdraw the loan because he had a Soviet offer to finance the dam. Dulles shot back, "Well, as you have the money already, you don't need any from us! My offer is withdrawn!"[48]

As the U.S. withdrew from the project so did Britain and the International Bank. That brief exchange between Dulles and the Egyptian ambassador represented the nadir point in the deteriorating relations between the United States and Egypt.

President Eisenhower felt that the cancellation of the loan was handled in a rather undiplomatic and abrupt manner, and he told Dulles how he felt. Dulles explained that there had been increasing congressional opposition to the loan,[49] and he publicly announced the reasons for U.S.

withdrawal from the Aswan Dam project: "Do nations which play both sides get better treatment than nations which are stalwart and work with us? That question was posed by the manner in which the Egyptians presented their final request to us, and stalwart allies were watching very carefully to see what the answer would be—stalwart allies which included some in the area."[50]

Once the Americans said no, the Russians did not appear very willing to build the Aswan Dam. On July 22, Foreign Minister Shepilov denied that he had made any firm commitment to build the dam. This may have encouraged President Nasser to publicly denounce the United States and later proclaim the nationalization of the Suez Canal Company with all of its assets in order to finance the construction of the Aswan Dam. Nasser expected some $100 million per year from that canal.

Their empires threatened with extinction by the growing Soviet influence in the Middle East and Africa, the British and French prepared to destroy Nasser, Russia's newly found ally. But Eisenhower tried to discourage his North Atlantic Treaty Organization (NATO) allies from intervening militarily against Egypt. For three months he fathered various efforts to negotiate an agreement that would internationalize the canal while protecting "the sovereign rights of Egypt."

On July 27, 1956, Prime Minister Eden wrote the following appeal to President Eisenhower: "We cannot afford to allow Nasser to seize control of the Canal in this way.... If we take a firm stand over this now, we shall have the support of all the maritime powers. If we do not, our influence and yours throughout the Middle East will ... be finally destroyed.... I am convinced that we must be ready, in the last resort, to use force to bring Nasser to his senses."[51] Eisenhower was concerned that if Britain and France would intervene militarily in Egypt, Russia's influence might increase in the Third World. Eisenhower did not approve of France's plan to send additional jets to Israel. He thought it a mistake to "link" the canal problems with "the Arab-Israeli borders."[52]

Deputy Undersecretary of State Robert Murphy reported on July 29 that, for the time being, Britain and France would not use force, "pending the outcome of a conference of affected nations." The next day, Prime Minister Eden announced that Britain had cut off all aid to Egypt and that no arrangement for the Suez Canal would be acceptable if complete control was left in the hands of any single state.

Throughout his communications with Britain and France, Eisenhower argued that force would not work. The history of India, Indochina, and Algeria revealed that occupying forces could not succeed unless they resorted to the brutalities of dictatorships and "we of the West, who believe in freedom and human dignity, could not descend to the use of Communist methods."[53]

During the morning of July 31, Dulles returned from a trip to South

America and he brought Eisenhower a message he had received from London that described Britain's firm decision to "break Nasser" at the earliest possible opportunity.[54] On that very day, Eisenhower sent Dulles to London with a message advising Eden that if England chose war, "the American reaction would be severe and that the great areas of the world would share that reaction."[55]

At his news conference in early September, President Eisenhower declared that the United States was "committed to a peaceful solution of this problem, and one that will insure to all nations the free use of the canal for the shipping of the world." A week later, Eisenhower implied that America would not back Britain and France in case of war. America will "not got to war ever, while I am occupying my present post, unless the Congress is called into session, and Congress declares such a war." Dulles added that we would not "try to shoot" our way through the canal.[56]

THE SINAI WAR

In the midst of the Suez confrontations, there were many battles between Israeli and Arab forces along the Israeli frontiers. On October 23, a three-way military pact was signed by Egypt, Syria, and Jordan. Abdul Hakim Amer, the Egyptian minister of war, was placed at its head. Ali Abu Nawar, commander of Jordan's Legion, proclaimed that the "time has come when the Arabs will be able to choose the time for an offensive to liquidate Israel."

At about the same time a temporary military alliance was concluded between France, Israel, and Great Britain. French aircraft arrived in Israel between October 22 and October 29. These planes were to help protect Israeli population centers from possible Egyptian attacks.[57] While the French wanted to end Nasser's support of rebels in the French North African empire and the British sought to regain control over Suez, the Israelis wanted to remove the Egyptian threat from Sinai and Gaza and to secure freedom of the seas through Sharm el-Sheikh and the Straits of Tiran.

Israel mobilized on October 27. President Eisenhower warned Premier Ben-Gurion not to start a war. Ben-Gurion reminded Eisenhower that Israel had supported his efforts for peace, but Egypt had repeatedly called for Israel's destruction. While he reviewed the military situation that Israel faced,[58] Ben-Gurion advised Eisenhower that Israel would not submit to subjugation at the hands of the Arabs. If Israel did not "take all possible measures to thwart the declared aim of the Arab rulers to destroy Israel" then it would not be "fulfilling its elementary responsibilities."[59]

Ben-Gurion anticipated trouble from many sources, but mainly from the United States. On October 28, as he reviewed the need to destroy Fedayeen bases in Gaza, and to secure unhampered passage through the Straits of Tiran, he advised his cabinet that he did not expect Jordan or Syria to intervene on behalf of Egypt. India, Africa, and the Soviet Union might intervene against Israel, but what worried Ben-Gurion most of all was what the United States might do. The Soviets would have to use military force to impose their will, but the United States would not have to send a single soldier to the Middle East in order to harm Israel. The United States held economic and political weapons with which it could intimidate Israel. But whatever the cost might be, Israel would have to take measures to defend itself.[60] If Israel failed to safeguard its existence, no one else would.

Hostilities began on October 29.

Israel penetrated Sinai and Gaza and within one hundred hours defeated the Egyptians.[61] Britain and France informed the Security Council that they called on the belligerents to withdraw their forces to a distance of ten miles from Suez. If the combatants would not meet those conditions within twelve hours, Britain and France would intervene to safeguard the canal and restore peace. Israel agreed to the cease-fire. Egypt refused and the Anglo-French forces attacked Egyptian military installations along the Suez Canal area. Egypt sank ships in the canal and thereby closed it to all.

The anticipated British and French action was slow in coming as far as Israel was concerned. It was to have begun at dawn on October 31, with an air attack on Egyptian airfields and other strategic targets, but it was delayed by some eight hours. When Ben-Gurion contacted the British and French allies, he was told that they were waiting for the evacuation of diplomats from Egypt and that weather conditions had not permitted their launching the attack. Failure on the part of the British and French to launch their attack endangered Israeli cities and it jeopardized Israeli forward positions in such Sinai locations as the Mitla and Gidi passes. After the initial delay the French and British fulfilled their part of the agreement.[62]

As British and French troops landed in the Port Said area on November 5, the Soviets threatened to send volunteers against Israel and to bombard Britain and France with its missiles. When Soviet Premier Nikolai Bulganin proposed that America join him against Britain, France, and Israel, Eisenhower responded by calling the Soviet idea "unthinkable" and he placed United States forces on alert. Eisenhower made it clear to Bulganin that any entry of new troops into the Middle East would force UN members to take effective countermeasures.

President Eisenhower took the initiative to condemn Israel, Britain, and France. On the day the war began, he informed the Security Council that Israeli forces had invaded the Sinai in violation of the armistice agreement, and he called for an immediate meeting to consider the "Palestine question: steps for the immediate cessation of military action of Israel in Egypt." The Soviet ambassador "warmly welcomed" the Eisenhower position. Perhaps Russian and American spokesmen differed in tone, but the substance of their position was the same. Disregarding Egyptian violations, the Eisenhower administration charged Israel with violating the armistice, and called on Israel to withdraw. The Americans insisted that all UN members "refrain from giving any military, economic or financial assistance to Israel as long as it had not complied with the resolution." From October 30 until November 1, the Security Council considered the question, but it could not act because of British and French vetoes. The U.S. delegation then engineered an emergency session of the General Assembly to deal with the situation.

The General Assembly adopted a resolution on November 2 that called for a cease-fire and the reopening of the Suez Canal.[63] The parties to the armistice agreements of 1949 were urged to promptly "withdraw all forces behind armistice lines . . . desist from raids across the armistice lines to neighboring territory, and observe scrupulously the provisions of the Armistice Agreements." The next day, Lodge expressed his regret that the resolution had not been complied with, but he added that the United States was convinced that the problems that had given rise to the situation could and had to be "solved by peaceful and just means." This time the American delegation observed that "the problems and conditions" that had created the situation should not be disregarded, and he introduced resolutions to help resolve those problems.

The first resolution concerned the issue of "Palestine" and suggested that a five-member committee be established to prepare recommendations for the General Assembly after consulting the interested parties. The second resolution concerned Suez and adhered to the draft resolution of October 12, 1956, which provided for a three-member committee with responsibilities to take measures necessary for the immediate reopening of the canal; to draw up a plan, in consultation with the three nations most directly concerned, for the purpose of operating and maintaining the canal; and to put such a plan into effect. This committee was to report to the General Assembly and the Security Council.

On November 5, the United States supported a Canadian resolution that authorized the Secretary General to establish a UN Emergency Force to supervise the cessation of hostilities. Although President Eisenhower expressed America's readiness to assist the UN forces with supplies and transportation, the United States would not contribute troops.

Despite Eisenhower's efforts at even-handedness, the Arab states remained suspicious of American intentions. They seemed to believe that Washington had tried to find a settlement favorable to the West and to Israel. Their suspicions seemed to have been confirmed as President Eisenhower rejected a Soviet suggestion that American and Soviet forces unite to halt hostilities.

RUSSIAN AND AMERICAN THREATS

Both American and Soviet leaders threatened Israel. On November 5, 1956, Premier Bulganin wrote Ben-Gurion that Israel was "acting according to instructions from abroad" and "toying with the fate of peace, with the fate of its own people, in a criminal and irresponsible manner. It is sowing such hatred for the State of Israel among the peoples of the East as cannot but affect the future of Israel and which will place in jeopardy the very existence of Israel as a state." A few days later, President Eisenhower wrote Ben-Gurion of his "deep concern" with Israel's unwillingness to withdraw: "I need not assure you of the deep interest which the United States has in your country, nor recall the various elements of our policy of support to Israel in so many ways. It is in this context that I urge you to comply with the resolutions of the United Nations General Assembly . . . and to make your decision known immediately."

Herbert Hoover Jr., on behalf of Secretary Dulles (who was hospitalized), summoned Israeli ambassador Reuven Shiloah to present him with an oral supplement to the Eisenhower letter of November 7. Once again Israel was told that its actions threatened the peace since the Soviets were creating a menacing and disastrous situation and that Israel would be the first to perish since it refused to withdraw as the UN resolutions had commanded. Hoover concluded that the consequences of the Israeli position would be the discontinuance of all U.S. assistance—from governmental as well as private sources. The State Department likewise threatened Israel with UN sanctions and expulsion from that international organization. That was the communication from a diplomat whose nation was presumably on good terms with Israel.[64]

On November 7, the secretary general reported that a cease-fire had been achieved, but that peace was still a distant prospect.

Thus, by November 7 Israel had been threatened with Soviet military intervention, and American and UN economic and political sanctions as well as expulsion from the United Nations. Ben-Gurion said that Israel would not permit foreign troops to set foot on any of the occupied areas, but the combined Soviet-American pressure seemed to be too much and he backed down. Israel made its withdrawal from Sharm el-Sheikh and Gaza conditional on the deployment of a UN Emergency Force (UNEF) in those areas. Ultimately, the United States and the United Nations accepted those conditions.

On November 8, Israeli foreign minister Golda Meir informed the United Nations that Israel would withdraw its troops from Sinai with the understanding that the United Nations would "call upon Egypt . . .

to abandon its policy of boycott and blockade, to cease the sending into Israel of murder gangs, and in accordance with its obligations under the U.N. Charter to live in peace with Member States, to enter into direct peace negotiations with Israel." From December 1956 to January 1957, Israeli forces withdrew from all captured territories except Sharm el-Sheikh and the Gaza Strip.

After meeting with his cabinet on the issues confronting Israel, the prime minister drafted and sent the following response to Bulganin and Eisenhower on November 8, 1956:

> The action that we carried out at the end of October was necessitated by self-defense and was not an action dictated by foreign wishes as you were told. In response to the appeal of the special emergency Assembly of the UN, we ceased fire, and for several days past there has been no armed conflict between us and Egypt.
>
> . . . we are willing to enter immediately into direct negotiations with Egypt to achieve a stable peace without prior conditions and without any compulsion, and we hope that all peace-loving states and especially those that maintain friendly relations with Egypt will use all their influence in Egypt to bring about peace talks without further delay.
>
> I am constrained in conclusion to express my surprise and sorrow at the threat against Israel's existence and well-being contained in your note. Our foreign policy is dictated by our essential needs and by our yearning for peace. It is not and will not be decided by any foreign factor.[65]

And to Eisenhower he wrote:

> We will, upon conclusion of satisfactory arrangements with the UN in connection with this international force entering the Suez Canal area, willingly withdraw our forces. . . . we must repeat our urgent request to the UN to call upon Egypt, which has consistently maintained that it is in a state of war with Israel, to renounce this position, to abandon its policy of boycott and blockade, to cease the incursion into Israel territory of murder gangs and, in accordance with its obligations under the UN charter to live at peace . . . to enter into direct peace negotiations with Israel.[66]

The combined Soviet and American pressures on Britain, France, and Israel were too much for them to bear. In addition to the harsh diplomatic correspondences from Bulganin, Russian intelligence services spread rumors that Soviet submarines, planes, and volunteers were on their way to the Middle East. U.S. representatives went along with the Soviets. American diplomats even refused to speak to British and French diplomats at the United Nations and for a time Eisenhower refused to receive Prime Minister Eden at the White House. Eisenhower added economic pressures to his tough stance. He refused to supply Britain with oil and this brought Britain closer to a currency collapse. Eisenhower and Bulganin forced Britain and France to suffer a humiliating retreat and they helped perpetuate Israeli-Arab tensions.

On November 21, Britain and France notified the United Nations that they would execute a phased withdrawal of their forces from Egypt as the UNEF would be strong enough to take over. Apparently dissatisfied with this response, various Asian states led by India introduced a resolution in the General Assembly on November 22 that called for the "forthwith" withdrawal of all foreign troops from Egypt. The United States refused to support a Belgium-sponsored amendment that provided for the withdrawal of foreign troops only after the UNEF had effective powers. The U.S. position may have won some prestige for America among some neutralists, but it did NATO little good.

By December 3 Britain and France agreed to "complete withdrawal" and by December 22 they completed their evacuation. Foreign Minister Meir met with Secretary Dulles towards the end of December and assured him that Israel wanted to live on good terms with the United States and the United Nations; but she asked the United States to support freedom of passage through the Straits of Tiran, and the nonreturn of Gaza to Egypt. She also asked Dulles to persuade Secretary General Hammarskjold to postpone introducing any changes in the Sinai and Gaza area until after a settlement could be achieved.

Dulles was willing to support freedom of navigation through the Straits of Tiran and he admitted that Gaza had never been under Egyptian domain, but he reminded Meir that the armistice agreement had not made Gaza Israeli territory. He advised Israel to work things out through the United Nations.

On January 14, 1957, Israel agreed to evacuate Sinai by January 22, but it refused to leave Sharm el-Sheikh until some concrete guarantees could be worked out for freedom of navigation through the straits. The United Nations did not attend to Israel's request. On February 2, the General Assembly, by a vote of 74 to 2, called upon Israel to withdraw from Gaza and Sharm el-Sheikh with the understanding that UNEF would be placed there. This was followed by further American pressures on Israel.

On February 4, President Eisenhower warned that Israel's disregard of international opinion would "almost certainly lead to further U.N. action which will seriously damage relations between Israel and U.N. members, including the U.S."[67] A day later, he declared that the United States was seriously considering the application of economic sanctions against Israel. Despite all this pressure, Israel did not withdraw from Sharm el-Sheikh or Gaza without guarantees for freedom of passage through the Gulf of Eilat and the placement of UN troops in Gaza to help prevent further terrorist attacks on Israel. Eisenhower warned that unless Israel were to withdraw "forthwith," he could not "predict the consequences." As Eisenhower seemed prepared to support sanctions, Ben-Gurion tried to help him understand in a letter dated February 8, 1957, that Israel would not accept the United Nations's double standards:

The law we received over three thousand years ago at Mount Sinai, and which has since become the heritage of mankind, forbids discrimination between one man and another, or between one people and another. Despite thousands of years of persecution, we have never lost our faith in the ultimate triumph of justice, peace and human brotherhood. It is inconceivable that now, after we have regained our independence in our ancient homeland, we should submit to discrimination. Whatever the consequences, our people will never agree to do so.[68]

On February 11, the United States promised Israel that UN troops would be installed in Gaza and that there would be freedom of navigation through the straits if Israel would withdraw. For Israel, the February 11 promises were not enough since it was expected to withdraw from Gaza and Sharm el-Sheikh prior to a settlement. Israel was concerned lest the UNEF might suddenly be withdrawn, the passage through the Gulf of Eilat obstructed, and the fighting renewed.

Israelis were not the only ones disappointed with the Eisenhower administration's approach. Various members of Congress were likewise disappointed. Republican senator William Knowland advised Eisenhower that if sanctions were to be imposed they had first to be imposed against the Russians for their invasion of Hungary. Senate majority leader Lyndon B. Johnson was altogether opposed to Eisenhower's approach and he called for guarantees to protect Israel against Egyptian incursions and threats in the Gulf of Eilat. The Senate Democratic Policy Committee approved Johnson's statement unanimously and called upon Eisenhower to resist UN efforts to impose sanctions against Israel. As Johnson said in his February 19, 1957, letter to Eisenhower, the United Nations could not "apply one rule for the strong and another for the weak." There had been no UN sanctions against Russia for its invasion of Hungary. Israel "complied with the directives of the U.N. Russia has not even pretended to be polite."[69]

Eisenhower insisted that things go his way: "I do not believe that Israel's default should be ignored because the U.N. has not been able effectively to carry out its resolutions condemning the Soviet Union for its armed suppression of the people of Hungary. Perhaps this is a case where the proverb applies that two wrongs do not make a right."[70]

On February 24, 1957, Senator John F. Kennedy challenged Eisenhower's Middle East diplomacy and presented his own peace plan:

let no one be deceived into believing that the Middle East crisis will be over once Israeli troops are pulled back and the Suez Canal cleared. Little is to be accomplished by merely restoring the muddled and frictional situation out of which the present crisis came.

What we clearly need in the Middle East, and need quickly, in my opinion, is a final entente, a permanent settlement of all major problems which reasonable men and nations can accept—a settlement, in short, based not on armed truce but on comity, accepted not out of fear but out of civic friendship.

We have the responsibility now to approach the problem as a whole, not on a piecemeal basis—to let Israel, Egypt, and all the world know that we look for a solution ending all outstanding differences, not simply Egypt's current grievances against Israel. I respectfully urge that the Government of the United States—through the Department of State, its United Nations delegation, and perhaps through a Presidential declaration of a status equal to the less long-range declarations on the Gulf of Aqaba and Communist aggression—promptly set forth, after consultation with Arab, Israel and other world leaders, a specific and comprehensive formula for a permanent . . . settlement based not upon force of arms or fear of men, but upon common sense and comity.

First, let us consider the problem of the Suez Canal. In our concern over its obstruction we have very nearly forgotten what started the dispute in the first place. Whether Egypt's rights flow from sovereignty, suzerainty, or dominion is not as crucial as an accommodation by Egypt and all user nations, by which the canal will be in full operation, benefiting Egypt through the revenues it provides and benefiting the world by offering free and open transit to the ships of all nations without discrimination or political interference. The canal can be enlarged and deepened to make its continued operation even more profitable to Egypt.

Second . . . permanent boundaries must be fixed . . . I would recommend consideration in this regard of the familiar device of an International Boundary Commission, staffed by impartial experts in geography, economics and history as well as diplomacy and international law, men who can draw reasonable, practical lines that both sides can live with, ignoring sentimental claims and giving neither side all it seeks.

Once such boundaries are determined, the United Nations and the United States could sponsor a security guarantee or exchange of treaties formally fixing those lines and preventing their alternation by force. Such a solution would immediately reduce not only tensions by the need for armaments expenditures both in Israel and the Arab states. The same treaties fixing boundaries could renounce the use or threat of force for aggressive purposes and provide for progressive limitations of armaments. A Special UN Commission on Arms Traffic could be established to prevent outside nations, Communist or otherwise, from renewing the Middle East arms race; and a more permanent United Nations force could police the area, much as it is now, until all threats to peace have vanished.

I would propose, therefore, a Middle East Regional Resources Fund, under the auspices of the United Nations and the World Bank for assisting in the stimulation, initiation, and financing through loans and grants of resource development and other projects in the area. Soil projects could include harnessing the waters of the Nile for the benefit of the Sudan, Ethiopia, and Uganda as well as Egypt; coordinated development of the resources of the Jordan River Valley for the benefit of Israel and the three Arab states through which it flows; the development of arable land and irrigation projects for the settlement of refugees; and a Middle Eastern Nuclear Center, similar to the Asian Nuclear Center already proposed, which could bring untold benefits in energy utilization to former deserts and wastelands.

These projects would be developed and administrated under the auspices and control of the nations in the region, who would also participate in their financing wherever feasible (and many of these nations are not poor), much as our states participate in Federal grant programs which assist and stimulate them to great action.[71]

After further negotiations, Secretary General Hammarskjold issued a memorandum on February 26, that assured Israel that any proposal for the withdrawal of the UNEF would have to be first submitted to the Advisory Committee of the General Assembly. As the General Assembly debate resumed, Foreign Minister Meir announced on March 1 that Israel agreed to a "full and complete withdrawal" on the basis of the secretary general's February 26 report.

Israel agreed to withdraw on condition that the UNEF would be installed in Gaza and that the United Nations would take responsibility for the area until a peace treaty were signed or a definitive agreement on the future of Gaza would be reached. Moreover, Israel asserted that it would reserve its freedom of action if it were threatened by a return to October 1956 conditions. As for the Gulf of Eilat and the Straits of Tiran, Meir declared that Israel was prepared to withdraw from Sharm el-Sheikh "in the confidence that there will be continued freedom of navigation for international and Israeli shipping in the Gulf and the Straits of Tiran." Israel declared that it would regard any interference with her rights of passage as an "attack entitling her to exercise her inherent right of self-defense."[72]

Meir's March 1 speech had been "drafted in consultation with the United States" and with the endorsement of the "French, British and all the major maritime nations." The United States and France had provided Israel with what it had requested. Eban recalled that the United States "in clear terms and France, in even more vigorous language, stated that they would support Israel as she exercised her right of self-defense against any renewal of the blockade in the Straits of Tiran or any resumption of Fedayeen raids from Gaza."[73]

When Ambassador Lodge Jr., spoke before the General Assembly on March 1, his remarks were in complete accord with Meir's statement, but he omitted the understanding on Gaza. Israel delayed her withdrawal until the Gaza matter would be cleared up. Only after Eisenhower sent Ben-Gurion the following letter in support of Meir's speech was Israel prepared to withdraw:

> It has always been the view of this Government that after the withdrawal there should be a united effort by all of the nations to bring about conditions in the area more stable, more tranquil. . . . Already the U.N. General Assembly had adopted resolutions which presage such a better future. Hopes and expectations based thereon were voiced by your Foreign Minister and others. I believe that it is reasonable to entertain such hopes and expectations and I want you to know that the United States, as a friend of all the countries of the area . . . will strive that such hopes prove not to be vain.[74]

Thus, after President Eisenhower assured Ben-Gurion that he supported Meir's statement, Israel agreed to withdraw.[75]

But Ben-Gurion still believed that Israel should not have withdrawn from any of the territories. In a letter he sent to Eisenhower, Ben-Gurion said that the only reason Israel did withdraw was because of the president's March 2 letter, which had reassured Israel that it "would have no cause to regret" and that its "hopes and expectations" would "not prove groundless." There were careful and detailed agreements to ensure that Eisenhower's commitments to Israel would manifest themselves concretely. But the Egyptians were not stopped when they sent their personnel back into Gaza in violation of the understandings. Despite all the documents and agreements, Israel was very much alone. Within a few short years, Israel's future was again threatened by the Arabs and their Soviet friends. Israel found that the 1957 commitments of the United States, Western Europe, and the United Nations could not help save her.

As a result of Eisenhower's 1956 diplomacy, Soviet influence greatly increased, while the influence of the West declined in the Middle East and throughout the underdeveloped world. The West, especially the United States, was singled out as interventionist and imperialistic, while the Soviet Union and Egypt were considered emancipators. The Suez remained in Egyptian hands, and after continued Soviet and Egyptian support of the rebels in Algeria, the French were forced to withdraw from Algeria in 1958. The Israeli victory of 1956 had enabled the state to survive, but because of Great Power intervention, there was still no peace in the Middle East, and by 1967 Israel's fears regarding the worthlessness of the February 1957 guarantees would be substantiated. Furthermore, the U.S. attempt to restore the moral position and influence of the West in Asia and Africa was a blow to NATO from which it would never recover. Charles de Gaulle would drive NATO out of France.

Once more, there had been a great deal of talk and diplomacy, but little rescue. Major power intervention only resulted in greater confusion. If the major powers would have left the nations of the Middle East alone they might have come to some mutual understanding. Their intervention not only prevented a settlement, but it ultimately resulted in greater major power intervention in the Middle East in order to uphold their positions. The Soviets would pour greater quantities of military hardware into Egypt, Syria, and Iraq, while Eisenhower would come forward with a proclamation against further communist intervention, which he would have to support with American troops in Lebanon.

The Eisenhower Doctrine, approved by Congress on March 9, 1957, provided economic as well as military assistance and the deployment of American troops should any nation in the Middle East request assistance to stop an armed aggression from a state controlled by international communism. Israel welcomed Eisenhower's statement, although it was most cautious in its response. Israel did not wish to endanger immigration of Jews from Poland and the lives of Jews living within the Soviet orbit. On May 21, 1957, Israel issued a carefully worded official response to the Eisenhower Doctrine. Israel's statement did not mention communism, but it clearly stated its opposition to "aggression against the territorial integrity and political independence of any country," and declared that Israel held "no aggressive intent against any other people or nation anywhere."[76]

Ben-Gurion tried to obtain concrete security guarantees from Eisenhower, but failed to do so. His efforts to purchase weaponry likewise failed for the most part. Ben-Gurion met with Eisenhower in March 1960 and the president promised to review Israel's arms requests. Late in May 1960, Eisenhower agreed that Israel could purchase some $10 million worth of radar and other electronic equipment.[77] Eisenhower turned down Ben-Gurion's request for arms.

As in 1948–1949, so in 1956, Israel had been very much alone. If not for the ability of its people to defend Israel there would have been no state of Israel. But instead of helping her in 1956–1957, the United Nations and the Eisenhower administration, in particular, put Israel in greater danger and indirectly encouraged the Soviet Union to expand its influence in Egypt. Israel's isolation would be evident once again in 1967, and again in 1973, when the Arabs and their Kremlin backers would again conspire to destroy the Jewish state.

NOTES

1. During this time, the United States discontinued its assistance to the development of Israel's water project at B'not Ya'akov. The aid to the water project would not be renewed until after a great deal of public pressure was exerted in the United States.

2. Abba Eban, *My Country* (New York, 1972), pp. 122–123.

3. Moshe Sharett Memorandum, March 19, 1954, Israel Foreign Office Papers (Eliav Files), Israel State Archives, Jerusalem.

4. Eban, *My Country*, pp. 125–136; Kenneth Love, *Suez: Twice Fought War* (New York, 1969).

5. David Ben-Gurion, *Israel: A Personal History* (New York, 1972), pp. 474–476.
6. Ibid.
7. Ibid.
8. Hugh Thomas, *Suez* (New York, 1967), pp. 15–16.
9. Dwight D. Eisenhower, *The White House Years: Waging Peace* (New York, 1965), p. 25.
10. Ambassador Edward Lawson (Tel Aviv) to Department of State, U.S. Department of State, *Foreign Relations of the United States, 1955–1957*, Volume XV (Washington, D.C., 1989), January 2, 1956, p. 5.
11. Ambassador Edward Lawson to Department of State, *Foreign Relations, 1955–1957*, Volume XV, January 10, 1956, p. 18.
12. Foreign Minister Moshe Sharett to Secretary John F. Dulles, *Foreign Relations, 1955–1957*, Volume XV, January 16, 1956, pp. 26–27.
13. Memo of Conversation at White House, *Foreign Relations, 1955–1957*, Volume XV, January 11, 1956, pp. 20–22.
14. Ibid., pp. 55–56.
15. U.S. Embassy in Tel Aviv to Department of State, *Foreign Relations, 1955–1957*, Volume XV, p. 73.
16. David Ben-Gurion to Dwight D. Eisenhower, *Foreign Relations, 1955–1957*, Volume XV, February 14, 1956, pp. 185–187.
17. Henry Byroade to John F. Dulles, *Foreign Relations, 1955–1957*, Volume XV, February 23, 1956, pp. 210–212.
18. Memo of Abba Eban-John F. Dulles conversation, *Foreign Relations, 1955–1957*, Volume XV, February 10, 1956, p. 165.
19. Special National Intelligence Estimate, *Foreign Relations, 1955–1957*, Volume XV, February 28, 1956, p. 248.
20. Ibid.
21. Ibid., p. 255.
22. Edward Lawson, U.S. Embassy in Israel to Department of State, *Foreign Relations, 1955–1957*, Volume XV, February 29, 1956, pp. 257–259.
23. Ibid.
24. Memo from Undersecretary of State Herbert Hoover Jr. to John F. Dulles, *Foreign Relations, 1955–1957*, Volume XV March 1, 1956, pp. 260–261.
25. Colonel Goodpaster Memo of Conversation with the President March 6, 1956, *Foreign Relations, 1955–1957*, Volume XV, pp. 307–308.
26. Diary Entry by President Dwight D. Eisenhower dated March 8, 1956, *Foreign Relations, 1955–1957*, Volume XV, pp. 326–327.
27. Memo from Acting Secretary of State to Dulles, *Foreign Relations, 1955–1957*, Volume XV, March 12, 1956, pp. 340–341.
28. Robert Anderson to Secretary of State, *Foreign Relations, 1955–1957*, Volume XV, March 9, 1956, p. 334.
29. Ibid.
30. Ambassador Edward Lawson to Department of State, *Foreign Relations, 1955–1957*, Volume XV, March 1, 1956, p. 270.
31. Ambassador Edward Lawson to Department of State, *Foreign Relations, 1955–1957*, Volume XV, March 6, 1956, pp. 318–319.
32. Ibid., pp. 271–272.

33. Memo of a Conversation, Department of State, *Foreign Relations, 1955–1957*, Volume XV, March 2, 1956, pp. 276–281.

34. Diary Entry by the President, *Foreign Relations, 1955–1957*, Volume XV, March 13, 1956, pp. 342–343.

35. Ibid.

36. David Ben-Gurion to President Dwight D. Eisenhower, *Foreign Relations, 1955–1957*, Volume XV, March 16, 1956, pp. 372–374.

37. Memo of a Conversation, Department of State, *Foreign Relations, 1955–1957*, Volume XV, April 1, 1956, pp. 435–445.

38. Embassy in Israel to Department of State, *Foreign Relations, 1955–1957*, Volume XV, April 11, 1956, pp. 520–521.

39. Embassy in Israel to Department of State, *Foreign Relations, 1955–1957*, Volume XV, April 12, 1956, p. 524.

40. Memo of Conversation, White House, *Foreign Relations, 1955–1957*, Volume XV, April 26, 1956, p. 585.

41. Ibid.

42. Eban, *My Country*, pp. 129–130.

43. During World War II, when Syria was under Vichy rule, the Yishuv helped Charles de Gaulle maintain contact with the French underground in Syria and Lebanon. Both the French high command and the people of France appreciated the heroism of the Haganah before the state of Israel was proclaimed, but it took France several months after Israel's declaration of independence before it extended recognition.

When Guy Mollet came to power in early 1956, the deal to supply Israel with arms was undertaken not with the knowledge of the French Foreign Ministry, but with Foreign Minister Christian Pineau's personal and active participation. The French equipment helped rescue Israel's "military strength" according to Abba Eban. By the time Abdel Nasser announced his nationalization of the Suez Canal, the idea that France might help Israel resist Egyptian pressure was already familiar to some parts of both the Israeli and French governments.

On June 20, 1956, two destroyers, the *Eilat* and the *Yafo*, arrived in Israel. They were brought in by an Israeli crew that had spent several months training with the British navy. From July to September 1956, the Middle East balance of arms was improved with the arrival of tanks, guns, planes, and ammunition from France. Without this equipment, Israel would have been at the mercy of the Arab arsenals, which had been filled mainly by the Soviet Union and the United States. For more information, see Eban, *My Country*, pp. 132–133.

44. Thomas, *Suez*, p. 17.

45. Interview with Raymond A. Hare, January 27, 1970.

46. In its deliberations on the Aswan Dam funds, the Senate Appropriations Committee declared that money for the Aswan Dam could not be used for that project "without prior approval of the Committee of Appropriations." Eisenhower refused to accept that codicil because it would have cut into the president's constitutional powers. See Eisenhower, *Waging Peace*, p. 32.

47. Ibid.

48. Herman Finer, *Dulles over Suez: The Theory and Practice of His Diplomacy* (Chicago, 1964), pp. 47–48.

49. Ibid., p. 33.

50. Ibid.
51. Anthony Eden, *Full Circle* (London, 1960), p. 428.
52. Eisenhower, *Waging Peace*, pp. 36–38.
53. Ibid., p. 40.
54. Ibid.
55. Ibid., pp. 41, 664–665.
56. Eban, *My Country*, pp. 131–132.
57. Zach Levey, *Israel and the Western Powers, 1952–1960* (Durham, N.C., 1997), pp. 75–76.
58. The Arabs were fully equipped and they once again made ready to destroy Israel. In jet planes alone, Egypt outnumbered Israel 305 to 79.
59. Ben-Gurion, *A Personal History*, p. 514.
60. Ibid., p. 504–505.
61. The casualty figures differ from source to source. Ben-Gurion reported that 171 Israelis were killed and that one pilot was wounded and taken prisoner. Eban reported that 180 were killed and four taken prisoner. The Egyptians lost more than one thousand killed and six thousand were taken prisoner.
62. Mordecai Bar-On, *The Gates of Gaza: Israel's Road to Suez and Back, 1955–1957* (New York, 1994), p. 309.
63. The five opposed were Australia, Britain, France, Israel, and New Zealand. There were also six abstentions.
64. Ben-Gurion, A *Personal History*, pp. 532–533.
65. Ibid., p. 511.
66. Ibid.
67. Ibid., pp. 524–526.
68. Ibid., p. 526; Herman Finer, *Dulles over Suez: The Theory and Practice of His Diplomacy* (Chicago, 1964), pp. 472–473.
69. Ibid., pp. 476–477.
70. Ibid., p. 482.
71. Senate Papers, John F. Kennedy Library, Boston; *Congressional Record*, 1957, pp. 3178–3180.
72. Eban, *My Country*, pp. 148–149.
73. Ibid.; Ben-Gurion, *A Personal History*, pp. 532–533; interview with Abba Eban, June 17, 1986.
74. Ibid.
75. Ibid.
76. Levey, *Israel and the Western Powers*, p. 88.
77. Ibid., p. 97.

11

Dwight D. Eisenhower and Israel, 1958–1960

Throughout Dwight D. Eisenhower's years in the White House, Israel had little if any assistance from the United States. The relationship between Israel and the United States during the last two years of the Eisenhower years were filled with frustration, strife, and difficulty. Israel found itself struggling with an Eisenhower administration that refused to sell it defensive weapons and often interfered with its basic right to defend itself.

In 1958 the Eisenhower administration tried to intervene with Israel's right to maintain naval craft in the Eilat–Gulf of Aqaba area. When Arab states like Egypt wanted Israeli vessels out of the Gulf of Aqaba, the Eisenhower administration supported the Arab wishes and on April 8, 1958, they asked Israel to take the ships out of Aqaba waters. Foreign Minister Golda Meir asked John F. Dulles: "How much could reasonably be asked of Israel in an effort to appease these states?"[1]

Meir tried to help the Eisenhower administration understand that the removal of the vessels in any case offered practical difficulties for Israel. Could they be removed through the Suez Canal, or had they to go half way around the world? If they were removed, "was there a United States guarantee to Israel that no attack on Israel in the Eilat and the Tiranian Straits area would occur?" She explained that the ships were there "solely for defensive purposes" and they "would not be used unless Israel were attacked." The Port of Eilat and freedom of passage through the Tiranian Straits were of vital interest to Israel and it had the right to protect those interests.[2]

In 1956 Israel had fought and won its "second war of independence" against overwhelming odds. The United States held to its contention that it could not provide arms to Israel because it might undermine America's influence in the Arab world: "While we recognize Israel's need to maintain its defense establishment at an appropriate level, we frankly would prefer to defer action on the Israeli requests for military vehicles and shooting weapons for the present."[3]

After the Sinai War, the Eisenhower administration continued to maintain that the sale of arms to Israel would undermine American interests, but it added that American weapons might "be used as a means of undermining the position of friendly Arab states." They advised Israel to seek such weapons elsewhere.[4] The State Department advised Ambassador Abba Eban: "We have never been a major supplier of arms to Israel and have no desire to become one." State Department officials suggested that since Israel was about to get one hundred half-tracks from Great Britain it should get another one hundred from there as well.[5]

In 1958, the United States and Great Britain trooped into Lebanon and Jordan in order to protect those countries from a Russian-backed United Arab Republic (UAR) intervention. Allied planes flew over Israeli territory. When the Russians objected and accused Israel of aggression David Ben-Gurion insisted that the United States and Britain discontinue those flights over Israel.

On August 2, 1958, Ben-Gurion sent a most urgent message calling upon the British and the Americans to discontinue those flights over Israel. Ambassador Edward Lawson promised that the flights would be discontinued by August 6, and he tried to persuade the Israelis to permit the flights to continue until that time. Ben-Gurion insisted that they had to be stopped immediately. Lawson explained that U.S. planes were poised to fly that night and he doubted whether they could be stopped in view of communication and technical difficulties. Ben-Gurion insisted that they had to be stopped immediately, from the receipt of his message. The Russian notes had been firm and threatening.[6]

Once again a crisis overshadowed U.S.–Israeli relations. Dulles was outraged by Israel's demand. He conveyed his and the president's shock that as soon as Israel had received a Soviet protest regarding American and British flights over Israel to Jordan, it had yielded to the Russians. Dulles complained that "it was particularly shocking that Israel would do this without consulting the U.S." Did not Israel fully agree with American and British goals in Lebanon and Jordan in showing the Russians and Nasser that there was a point beyond which they could not go?" Dulles wanted to know if Israel had changed its mind. "There were wide political implications in giving the USSR a sense of power in the Middle East by such subservient action as Israel seemed prepared to take."[7]

Eban tried to help Dulles understand that Israel was "deeply concerned over the malevolent power of the Soviet Union which could destroy Israel in five minutes." Since Israel had "no formal security guarantee from the U.S." it felt itself in a most difficult position.[8]

Dulles claimed that the Eisenhower Doctrine made it clear that the United States would aid Israel should it be attacked by a communist power. "For future guidance" we want to know whether Israel feels "so menaced by the USSR that it would do whatever the Soviet Union requested."[9]

Eban responded "Israeli general fortitude could not be questioned."[10]

Two days later Ben-Gurion wrote to Secretary Dulles to remind him that the United States had never given Israel security guarantees. In its ten years of existence, Israel had "incurred more risks, defied more threats, displayed greater resolution in grave hours than most other nations in the world." "Although we have no doubt of the sincere interest of the United States in the independence and integrity of Israel . . . we have never been granted a guarantee of our integrity. Moreover, we have not heard that the Soviet Union has ever been told concerning Israel what it has been told about the consequences of an attack on Turkey. . . . We are surrounded by foes who received abundant arms from the Soviet Union and who receive Western arms as well, and yet we are not intimidated. I must admit however that we are concerned because up to now we have not been successful in receiving arms assistance from the United States."[11] "In the days immediately following the American and British actions in Lebanon and Jordan, at a time when the air was full of tension and the possibility of world conflict, I did not object to flights over Israel territory in connection with the American air demonstration over Jordan; to an airlift of British troops to Jordan; to an American oil airlift; and to a continuation of British and American supplies to British troops in Jordan for a number of days." But from July 16, Ben-Gurion had urged the Americans and the British to find "an alternative route."[12]

As a consequence of those overflights, Israel became "involved in serious embarrassments and dangers." Ben-Gurion could not understand why after three weeks of initial landings, an alternative route had not been "brought into full use." It would be best for all concerned, said Ben-Gurion, if the United States and Israel would "strengthen mutual ties, albeit for the time being without publicity."[13]

That strengthening of mutual ties did not take place during the Eisenhower administration.

Israel continued to request military equipment from the United States. On August 22, 1958, Israel asked for antitank rifles, submarines, tanks, and guided missiles. The sachems of the State and Defense Departments agreed to provide Israel with antitank recoilless rifles, but no submarines, no tanks, and no antiaircraft missiles.[14] While U.S. officials said no to most of Israel's military requests, they agreed to send weapons to Iraq in order to keep Iraq from going to the Russians.

Eban reminded the Americans that Israel needed tanks, submarines, and guided missiles. Moreover, the one hundred antitank rifles that the

United States had agreed to send Israel were operationally insufficient. Israel needed many more. Jordan's difficulties with such extremist Arab states as Egypt could be resolved if Transjordan cooperated with Israel. Israel could even provide Transjordan with an outlet to the sea via the port of Haifa.[15]

Dulles was proud of the American action that helped save Lebanon and Jordan from the Soviet-backed Egyptians and Syrians. Dulles insisted that this was proof that Israel could depend upon the United States.

Foreign Minister Meir felt that a public statement by the United States reflecting its determination to defend the territorial integrity of all nations in the Middle East would help a great deal. But again the American response was that Israel could not expect to match the Arabs gun for gun and tank for tank. After all, the Arabs were greater in number and wealth.

Meir agreed that Israel could not match the Arabs tank for tank or plane for plane. But its policy was "to match quality for quality." If the Arabs had one thousand heavy tanks, Israel should have two hundred. If the Arabs had six submarines, Israel should have two."[16]

On April 11, 1960, the Americans responded to Israel's request for antiaircraft missiles. Undersecretary Douglas Dillon advised Ambassador Avraham Harman that the Hawk missile could not be made available to Israel because it was needed by American forces and that they would "absorb the supply for several years to come." And there was the question of whether training facilities for missile operators would be available. If Israel were to receive the missiles after 1963 or 1964, another year would have to pass before training slots could be provided for Israeli personnel. Moreover, the missiles had technical limitations: they were effective within a small radius and at a height of thirty-five thousand feet. They were "useless for aircraft flying above that ceiling." Eisenhower was willing to provide Israel with electronic warning equipment—some immediately from existing stockpiles. This could be done within eighteen months or two years. This equipment would expand Israel's air defense capability and increase the range of Israel's interception capability.[17]

Ben-Gurion was greatly disappointed that missiles were not yet on the list of items to be provided. "The plain fact is that our air defense today depends exclusively on fighter aircraft operating from three or four airfields." But the UAR had more than twenty-seven airfields. In the absence of geographic depth, Israel could not rely on fighter aircraft alone to meet an air attack. The Hawk missile, which was designed to provide local air defense against low-flying aircraft, was the only effective and reliable defensive shield against air attack. Electronics or radar might give Israel an improved alert system but as such they were no protection against attack. Ben-Gurion asked if "a way will be found, with due regard to existing commitments and availabilities, to make possible the initiation of a program by which the Israel Defense Forces could acquire, over a period of time, a Hawk missile system and the necessary training for its operation." "We face a possible attack of Soviet origin and manufacture. I am sure that we will not be left to face it alone."[18]

Israeli ambassador Harman reported that by 1960, the Russians had not only replaced all of Egypt's equipment, but Egypt had increased the number of troops in its armed forces. Russia sent more advisors to train the Egyptians in how to use Russian equipment. Harman "credited the UAR with great improvement in its paratroop outfits, under water or 'frogmen' units, and submarine crews." What mostly concerned Israel was to find itself in a situation that "could not be remedied after it became aware that the danger was imminent." The principal danger was an air attack since it did not require long preparations if the enemy had the aircraft.[19]

Israel had a whole shopping list of supplies that it needed to purchase from the United States: one hundred of the latest model aircraft; five hundred tanks; three hundred armored cars, sixty howitzers, two hundred fifty recoilless rifles, six hundred Sidewinder and Hawk type missiles, two small submarines, and a large quantity of electronic equipment.[20]

Ben-Gurion observed that President Abdel Nasser had asked for more MiG squadrons, and that Nikita Khrushchev said "no" and commented that what Nasser needed was not "more squadrons, but better squadrons." The real danger, said Ben-Gurion, was when Nasser addressed himself to quality rather than quantity. What Israel needed was defensive missiles that could intercept planes flying at thirty thousand to forty thousand feet and over.[21]

On March 10, 1960, Ben-Gurion met with Eisenhower. The last time they had met was in Europe, at the end of World War II. During the 1960 meeting, Ben-Gurion spent much of the time analyzing the world communist threat and global politics. It was as if Ben-Gurion had come to give Eisenhower a lecture on world politics. When Ben-Gurion finally got to dangers facing Israel, he said that it came right down to "whether we were to remain a free, independent nation or whether we are going to be exterminated." If ever Nasser would defeat the Israeli army he would then seek to "exterminate the Jews just as Hitler had exterminated them in Germany." The Jewish people had been fighting for survival for some four thousand years, "the Israeli Republic" is "our last stand." It "represented the fulfillment of the prayers of Jews over thousands of years." Egyptian bombers were capable of carrying three tons of bombs, but the new bombers they were about to get from the Soviet bloc could carry ten tons of bombs. Ben-Gurion then went over the list of military equipment that the UAR had received: they had 1000 more tanks than Israel, 450 more armored vehicle than Israel, 450 more heavy mortars, 2500 more antitank guns, 350 more antiaircraft guns, 280 more jets, 80 more bombers, 30 more helicopters, and 30 more torpedo boats. Egypt also had eight submarines.[22]

Ben-Gurion quoted from a letter Eisenhower had once sent him: "The independence and integrity of the nations of the Middle East are vital to peace." And then he quoted four points from a letter Dulles had written:

1. The United States favors legitimate Arab national goals
2. There was a real and urgent necessity to strengthen international organizations to protect those nations that are determined to be free
3. The world community must preserve the independence of these nations
4. Israel must be brought to a position where it is able to resist attack from indigenous local forces[23]

He urged that at the forthcoming U.S.–Soviet summit both agree to keep the status quo in the Middle East and that the independence and integrity of all states in that part of the world should be guaranteed. This would be a most important contribution to peace.

Israel has a "right to exist," said Ben-Gurion, and Israel will fight to the last. It would be a grave responsibility for the world if it would permit war to come to this area.

Eisenhower repeated the American approach to the sale of arms to Israel. He hoped that the United States would keep out of the Middle East arms race and he believed that France and Britain could better supply Israel than the United States. This would enable the United States to keep on working for peace in the Middle East. The United States "would not stand for the destruction of any nation in the Middle East." And finally he concluded the recitation by saying that in the long run security did not lie in arms and that the United States "had no lack of admiration for the accomplishments of the Israeli nation and for its sturdiness. The United States is not indifferent to the future of Israel and the U.S. certainly agrees that Israel has a right to exist." He did promise that the State Department would study Ben-Gurion's requests for arms, but again said that the United States "did not wish to establish itself as a partisan supporter of any nation in the Middle East."[24]

From that meeting of March 10, 1960, Ben-Gurion had somehow gotten the impression that the United States would be forthcoming with the Hawks.

Ben-Gurion had proposed that the United States and the Soviet Union issue a joint appeal to the states of the Middle East to reach a mutually acceptable agreement to preserve the independence and integrity of all the countries of the region. Eisenhower seemed to like that proposition and he asked his State Department to study it.[25] But nothing came of Ben-Gurion's suggestion.

Ben-Gurion spoke with State Department officials that same day and repeated his request for antiaircraft missiles. The UAR had some twenty-seven airfields and it was impossible for Israeli planes to prevent an attack. Some six hundred thousand people lived in Tel Aviv. The city could be destroyed in two or three days of bombing. A successful surprise attack would make it impossible for Israel to mobilize its ground forces for defense.[26]

On March 16, Ben-Gurion wrote Eisenhower: "Grave indeed are the difficulties and dangers which still face us. We find confidence in the pioneering spirit of our people and in the goodwill and friendship of the American people and of other peoples devoted to freedom, justice and peace. I return to Israel confident that the aid required to sustain our deterrent capacity and thus to ensure that the peace of the area will not be disrupted, will indeed be forthcoming."[27]

Israel did not get the Hawks from Eisenhower. State Department officials advised that they knew this was a disappointment to Israel, but they could not give Israel hope that they would be provided in the near future.[28]

Foreign Minister Meir expressed her great disappointment that the Americans had not agreed to provide Israel with the Hawk missiles:

> The plain fact is our defense today depends exclusively on fighter aircraft operating from three or four airfields. Without protection of anti-aircraft missiles an air attack against us could put our bases out of action and thus endanger our entire defense capacity. In the absence of geographic depth one cannot rely on fighter aircraft alone to meet air attack. The Hawk missile which is designed to protect local air defense against low flying aircraft is the only effective shield against air attack on which we can rely in our situation.
>
> It was for this reason that in my presentation to you I invariably linked our electronic needs to our need for missiles, giving the latter priority. Electronics would give us an improved alert system but by themselves are no protection against attack. However it is my confident hope that a way will be found with due regard to existing commitments and availabilities to make possible the initiation of a program, by which Israel defence forces could acquire over a period of time a Hawk missile system and the necessary training for its operation. We face a defense problem of Soviet origin and manufacture. I am sure we will not be left to face it alone.[29]

Israeli diplomats did not give up their efforts to persuade the Eisenhower administration to make the Hawk missiles available, but to no avail. Minister Mordechai Gazit was advised on July 26, 1960, by the

State Department that the Hawk missile request had been given "sympathetic" and "thorough" study, but it could not be provided to Israel.[30]

The State Department pressed Ben-Gurion on the issue of the readmission of Arab refugees to Israel. Ben-Gurion insisted that there was no possibility for repatriation. Since the Arabs had fled on their own volition, Israel was not responsible for them, not to mention the fact that Israel had to take in three hundred thousand European Jewish displaced persons, one hundred thousand Iraqi Jews, fifty thousand Yemeni Jews, and others. It was a physical impossibility to take in the Arab refugees. All the states surrounding Israel were in a virtual state of war against Israel, and for Israel to take in the refugees from those states would be like an "injection of poison." It would be suicidal for Israel to accept the refugees. They would enter Israel with the mission of seeking to destroy Israel. It was a tragedy that the Arab leaders were using the refugees as a political weapon. The Arabs were good at making deserts out of prosperous areas, but they were not capable of "unmaking deserts." But Ben-Gurion revealed that on a most secret basis Jordan and Israel were working toward the relocation of the refugees.[31]

While the Eisenhower administration continued to press Israel on the Arab refugee question, Israel's position was that it was a matter to be settled by Israel and the Arabs. As Gazit put it, "Israel opposed mediation" and believed that the powers should help bring the parties to the negotiating table. There were also Israel's counterclaims that had to be taken into account.[32]

On March 13, 1960, Ben-Gurion met with Vice President Richard Nixon, a few days after meeting with President Eisenhower. Again Ben-Gurion spoke of Israel's need for antiaircraft missiles and electronic air warning equipment.

On the refugee matter Ben-Gurion came up with a new approach. He suggested that once a peace treaty would be reached, "Israel would be prepared to accept the repatriation of a reasonable number of Arabs who might be prepared to resettle in Israel." They would be resettled in the desert area that was being rehabilitated by Israel.

Nixon advised that the Arabs were effectively using the refugee issue and that Israel should find some means to offset this by making clear Israel's willingness to accept the Arab refugees once a peace agreement had been reached. The United States was not asking Israel to accept refugees before a peace treaty would be concluded.

The vice president then asked what Israel's population growth rate might be. Ben-Gurion said that besides normal population increases he expected two million more immigrants. He believed that the time would come when Russia would permit its Russian Jews to leave and then at least one million more Jews would come from Russia. The other million would come from the satellite and Moslem states. All these people could be settled in the newly developing desert areas. Once more the prime minister stressed the need for a joint statement from Eisenhower and Nikita Khrushchev on the Middle East.[33]

American officials still insisted that the United States could not provide Israel with the missiles or other advanced equipment it needed because this might damage America's relations with the Arabs. They also stated that the missiles were unavailable in terms of the immediacy with which Israel had "asserted its requirements."

Christian Herter replaced Dulles when Dulles became ill. During a State Department meeting, Herter observed on July 27, 1960, that the Hawk missiles could be made available by the end of 1961.[34]

Herter "found it difficult to understand" why the United States refused to allow the Israelis to buy the Hawk missiles especially since they were of a "purely defensive character." He had asked Admiral Arlie Burke as to the importance of security considerations and the admiral did not consider the security element to be a "major problem."

Secretary Herter noted that the United States had informed the Israeli government that the Hawks were unavailable and he was concerned with the "dishonesty" since reports indicated that U.S. production would be completed by the end of 1961, and "presumably the Hawks could then be produced for the Israelis." He felt that unless some "better arguments could be presented than he had thus far heard the Israelis should have the missiles."[35]

Herter was new to the State Department establishment and his new associates were surprised by Herter's statement. Undersecretary Douglas Dillon advised him that if the United States would introduce such "spectacular weaponry" into the Middle East, it would increase the arms race there. Another official maintained that it was neither in U.S. interest nor in Israel's interest to sell them the missiles. Deputy Assistant Secretary Parker Hart introduced a fresh element into the State Department's formula against Israel: "Many Israelis have relatives behind the Iron Curtain and the Defense Department has grave reservations about entrusting classified material to the Israelis." Dillon favored continuing the stalling tactics—"delay of several months before closing the door completely."[36]

Herter soon fell in line with State Department thinking. On August 4, 1960, he wrote to Ben-Gurion that in "today's world the task of maintaining an appropriate defensive posture is assuming Herculean proportions. Each new advance seems to exceed its predecessor in death-dealing capability. In modern warfare there can be no victor; there may even be no survival." He thought that the Hawk missiles could stimulate an arms race. The Arabs might even get surface-to-surface missiles from Russia. He recognized "the vital importance of adequate levels of self-defense, for Israel as well as ourselves," and was gratified that Israel was able to obtain tanks and aircraft from France and Britain.[37]

Undersecretary of State for Political Affairs Livingston T. Merchant had advised the secretary of state on July 15, 1960, that the Hawk posed a declassification problem. It could also produce some problems with NATO allies whose needs could not be met until the Israelis had their missiles. Moreover, Nasser would regard it as a change of U.S. policy and he would become a closer ally of the Soviet Union. Merchant claimed that Ben-Gurion was trying to promote the deterioration of the U.S.–UAR relationship. "Ben Gurion's request, while openly based on a persuasive military rationale, has nevertheless concealed in it a desire to change our relations with the UAR to Israel's benefit."[38]

Ben-Gurion had reported that the MiG 19s would be delivered to Egypt by October 1960, and that this would present a great danger to Israel, through 1962. The delivery of French Mirages would begin in December 1961. Four aircraft arrived and were followed by two each month, altogether totalling forty aircraft. The UAR had some one hundred Il-28 bombers—each capabable of carrying ten-ton loads—and after they finished their bombing runs there would not be much left of Israeli cities. Nasser would be in a position to bomb Israel's airfields and immobilize Israel's fighter aircraft. But whatever the situation, Israel "would fight to the death." Israel "might win" but at what cost? "Israel could not afford to lose its best youth, particularly since the flower of European Jewry was already destroyed by the Nazis." Israel's "prime concern, therefore, was to prevent war." The only answer for Israel was to deter conflict.[39]

Prime Minister Ben-Gurion did not have much confidence in anyone other than Israel to protect Israel. He believed that Egypt would attack Israeli shipping and block the Straits of Tiran. But then if such a thing would happen, said U.S. ambassador Ogden Reid, the United States would "query this most seriously" and so would the United Nations. In the event of an attack the United Nations and "the U.S. would take action."[40]

"But that action would be too late," said Ben-Gurion. Any possible UN action could be stopped by a Soviet veto. All this would take too long and in the meantime much of Israel would be destroyed. Then the United Nations could "pass a pious resolution after the fact. This would not save Israel's best youth." Other means were needed. Israel needed the Hawk.[41]

On July 22, 1960, both Egypt and Israel mobilized. Israel engaged in large-scale maneuvers against a simulated "Soviet-type blitzkrieg attack." There were reports that Egypt moved some of its troops back into the Sinai.[42]

It was one of many Middle Eastern brinkmanship exercises.

It was about this time that Israel asked for loans and aid to help build more housing. Minister of Finance Levi Eshkol suggested that the financing of private housing might be a useful channel for making substantial aid available to Israel. There were tens of thousands of Israelis who lived in slums and substandard housing facilities. Perhaps it might also be possible for Israel to purchase some two thousand milk cows as agricultural surplus.[43]

Meanwhile, the Americans became concerned with Israel's atomic research. Unable to obtain weapons necessary to secure its survival, Israel cast about for weaponry that might contribute to its survival.

During a National Security Council Meeting on December 8, 1960, Dulles reported that Israel was constructing with "French assistance, a nuclear complex in the Negev." That complex "probably included a reactor capable of producing weapons-grade plutonium." France supplied the equipment and training as well as fuel elements. Dulles anticipated that the Arab reaction would be "particularly severe," and he felt there were "serious implications of this development." The Americans estimated that the cost was somewhere between $40 million and $80 million. This "when we were providing aid to Israel raises serious questions."[44]

Nixon wanted to know which other states had similar nuclear facilities. Dulles said that the Chinese Communists, France, and Germany were making efforts. Herter said India was contemplating a large-scale reactor. It was pointed out that Israel might have built this with funds from Jewish charitable organizations in the United States. Dulles observed that the United States had known that Israel was building a facility, but apparently it did not know that it was a nuclear facility.[45]

The Eisenhower administration grew increasingly concerned about Israel's atomic research. Israel's response was that it was part of its scientific research.[46] Ambassador Harman reported on December 20, 1960, that Israel was building a research reactor of twenty-four megawatts, not of industrial importance. It was twenty-four megawatts, not one hundred to three hundred megawatts. Israel sought to develop "scientific knowledge for eventual industrial, agricultural, medical and other scientific purposes." It was part of a general program to develop the Negev.[47]

KENNEDY DEFEATED NIXON

The 1960 Democratic platform promised to encourage direct talks between Israel and the Arab states. It called for the relocation of the Arab refugees, an end to the Arab boycott and blockade of Israel, and freedom of passage through the Suez Canal for all states.

Meanwhile, the Republicans promised to help resolve the issues between Arab states and Israel. They promised to help resolve the Arab refugee problem, help end restrictions on free trade and passage, and abolish discrimination in Arab countries against Americans on the basis of religion. Their platform promised progress towards the establishment of peaceful relations between Israel and its neighbors, which would render the arms race redundant.

John F. Kennedy defeated Nixon and became symbolic of a New Frontier and a new generation of Americans; and for Israel the young president represented a hope for better relations with the United States.

On December 6, 1960, and January 19, 1961, President-elect Kennedy met with President Eisenhower and some of the members of his administration. There were a variety of issues that they talked about including Laos, the Congo, Latin America and Cuba, Algeria, Sudan, Berlin, nuclear disarmament, and nuclear warfare.

It was Kennedy who apparently introduced the question of Israel. He said that an atomic development in Israel was highly distressing. He believed that through this project Israel would have by 1963 some ninety kilograms of plutonium that could be made available for weapons. Secretary Herter said that "the Arab reaction to this would be very bad, indeed explosive." That was why the State Department was "so anxious for international inspection and control—so that plutonium could be kept out of the manufacture of weapons."[48]

Kennedy found it disturbing that the Sudan decided to buy some ten thousand tons of wheat from the Russians in preference to a purchase from the United States. Secretary Herter pointed out that cotton crops in the Sudan were also involved in this matter. The Sudanese sold cotton to the Russians, while the United States competes with the Sudan in the sale of cotton. Secretary Herter added that "the Egyptians were playing foul ball and were furnishing the real brains for these Sudanese decisions, and are acting in the interest of the Soviets."[49]

The Eisenhower years had been some of the most difficult years in the area of U.S.–Israeli relations. During those eight years, Israel could not penetrate through the wall of the American foreign policy establishment. The Eisenhower administration was persuaded that Israel should not be the recipient of military assistance from the United States. Israel fought and defeated Egypt in October 1956. When the war was over, Eisenhower joined France, Britain, and the United Nations in guaranteeing that the Sinai and Gaza would be demilitarized and that there would be freedom of passage in the Gulf of Aqaba. After the Sinai War, the Russians accelerated their arms delivery to Egypt, but the Eisenhower administration still refused to provide Israel with weapons to counterbalance the rearmed Arab armies. The Eisenhower administration still held the view that if it would become a supplier of weapons to Israel its position in the Arab world would be handicapped.

By the 1956 Sinai War, Israel won its "second war of independence," but it did not win its security. The threat of extinction at the hands of the Arabs and their new friends, the Russians, was very real. As the

Arabs acquired a greater arsenal of weapons Ben-Gurion repeatedly expressed his concern that the Arabs would seek to exterminate Israel as the Germans had almost completely eliminated the Jews of Europe. Israel was pushed against the wall. Another war seemed inevitable. Israel sought to develop its water resources, but the Eisenhower administration cautioned Israel not to deprive neighboring Arab states of their waters. Eisenhower sent Robert Anderson on a peace-finding mission that inevitably failed. Eisenhower learned that such Arab leaders as President Nasser of Egypt did not want peace. For a time Eisenhower joined Prime Minister Eden of England in trying to pressure Ben-Gurion into making territorial concessions in the Negev so as to persuade the Arabs that Israel was prepared to make every possible sacrifice for peace. Ben-Gurion would not yield to that pressure. Nor would he yield to American demands that Israel should repatriate "Palestinian Arab refugees."

Israel's independence had been a hard-won struggle in 1947–1949. Israel's struggle for survival as a sovereign, independent state was never ending. The Soviet bloc and such countries as the United States of the Western Alliance were unwilling to sell weapons to Israel and risk losing the friendship of the oil-rich Arab states. Israel had no alliances with any state, while Arab neighbors sought its elimination. The United States, although friendly, was not very helpful in such matters as the acquisition of weapons.

Eisenhower had been shocked when Israel undertook a preemptive war against Egypt in 1956. The Eisenhower team was likewise shocked when they discovered that Israel pursued atomic research as part of its struggle for survival. For the Eisenhower administration, it seemed all right for the United States to develop its knowledge of atomic energy, but it was another matter altogether if Israel worked in that area of research and development. They did not seem to appreciate the fact that it was a basic matter of survival. Israel had to seek every possible means of defense.

Kennedy was to inherit a troubled world situation from Eisenhower. The area of the Middle East was turbulent and war seemed imminent. U.S.–Soviet relations were troubled over the arms race, nuclear weapons, Berlin, Laos, Cambodia, Vietnam, the Congo, Cuba, and the Middle East. Young President Kennedy would have to learn how to deal with each of these areas of difficulty. He would have to seek courageous, imaginative, and innovative approaches, something that Eisenhower and his foreign policy establishment headed by Dulles had been unable to achieve.

NOTES

1. U.S. Department of State, *Foreign Relations of the United States, 1958–1960,* Volume XIII (Washington, D.C. 1992), pp. 39–40.

2. Ibid.

3. Memo from Assistant Secretary of State William Rountree to Secretary of State, *Foreign Relations, 1958–1960,* June 28, 1958, Volume XIII, pp. 57–58.

4. Ibid.

5. Memo of Conversation between Israeli representatives and the Secretary of State, *Foreign Relations, 1958–1960,* Volume XIII, June 30, 1958, p. 62.

6. Edward Lawson to Department of State, *Foreign Relations, 1958–1960,* Volume XIII, August 2, 1958, pp. 80–81.

7. Memo of Conversation between John F. Dulles and Abba Eban, *Foreign Relations, 1958–1960,* Volume XIII, August 3, 1958, pp. 82–83.

8. Ibid.

9. Ibid.

10. Ibid.

11. David Ben-Gurion to John F. Dulles, *Foreign Relations, 1958–1960,* Volume XIII, August 5, 1958, pp. 85–87.

12. Ibid.

13. Ibid.

14. Memo from William Rountree to John F. Dulles, *Foreign Relations, 1958–1960,* Volume XIII, August 22, 1958, pp. 88–91.

15. Memo of Conversation, Department of State, *Foreign Relations, 1958–1960,* Volume XIII, September 10, 1958, pp. 91–95.

16. Memo of Conversation, Department of State, *Foreign Relations, 1958–1960,* Volume XIII, October 2, 1958, pp. 95–97.

17. Memo of Conversation, Department of State, *Foreign Relations, 1958–1960,* Volume XIII, April 11, 1960, pp. 306–307.

18. Letter from Ambassador Avraham Harman to the Secretary of State, *Foreign Relations, 1958–1960,* Volume XIII, June 9, 1960, pp. 333–334.

19. Memo of Conversation, Department of State, *Foreign Relations, 1958–1960,* Volume XIII, February 16, 1960, pp. 265–267.

20. Memo from Assistant Secretary of State for Near Eastern and South Asian Affairs to the Secretary of State, *Foreign Relations, 1958–1960,* Volume XIII, February 12, 1960, pp. 263–264.

21. U.S. Embassy in Israel to Department of State, *Foreign Relations, 1958–1960,* Volume XIII, March 5, 1960, pp. 275–277.

22. Memo of Conversation between David Ben-Gurion and Dwight D. Eisenhower, *Foreign Relations, 1958–1960,* Volume XIII, March 10, 1960, pp. 280–288.

23. Ibid.

24. Ibid.

25. Avraham Harman to Minister of Foreign Affairs, March 11, 1960, Baruch Gilead, ed., *Documents on the Foreign Policy of Israel,* Volume 14 (Jerusalem, 1997), pp. 111–112.

26. Memo of Conversation, Department of State, *Foreign Relations, 1958–1960,* Volume XIII, March 10, 1960, pp. 289–290.

27. Ibid., pp. 214–215.
28. Ibid., p. 121.
29. Golda Meir to Ministry of Foreign Affairs, June 4, 1960, *Israel Documents*, Volume 14, pp. 258–260.
30. Mordechai Gazit to Ministry of Foreign Affairs, July 26, 1960, *Israel Documents*, Volume 14, pp. 160–161.
31. Memo of Conversation, Department of State, *Foreign Relations, 1958–1960*, Volume XIII, March 10, 1960, pp. 291–292.
32. Mordechai Gazit to G. Rafael, September 16, 1960, *Israel Documents*, Volume 14, pp. 168–170.
33. Memo of Conversation between Richard Nixon and David Ben-Gurion, *Foreign Relations, 1958–1960*, Volume XIII, March 13, 1960, pp. 295–296.
34. Memo for the files of a meeting, Department of State, *Foreign Relations, 1958–1960*, Volume XIII, July 27, 1960, p. 356.
35. Ibid., p. 356–357.
36. Ibid.
37. Christian Herter to David Ben-Gurion, *Foreign Relations, 1958–1960*, Volume XIII, August 4, 1960, pp. 358–361.
38. Livingston T. Merchant to Secretary of State, *Foreign Relations, 1958–1960*, Volume XIII, July 15, 1960, pp. 349–350.
39. Ambassador Ogden Reid to Department of State, *Foreign Relations, 1958–1960*, Volume XIII, July 18, 1960, pp. 350–353.
40. Ibid.
41. Ibid.
42. Christian Herter to Mission at United Nations, *Foreign Relations, 1958–1960*, Volume XIII, July 22, 1960, p. 355.
43. Memo of Conversation, Department of State, *Foreign Relations, 1958–1960*, Volume XIII, September 20, 1960, pp. 372–375.
44. Memo of discussion at the 470th meeting of the National Security Council, *Foreign Relations, 1958–1960*, Volume XIII, December 8, 1960, pp. 391–392.
45. Ibid.
46. *Israel Documents*, Volume 14, pp. 174–175.
47. Memo of Conversation, Department of State, *Foreign Relations, 1958–1960*, Volume XIII, December 20, 1960, pp. 396–399.
48. Memo by Wilton D. Persons, December 6, 1960, Dwight Eisenhower as President (Ann Whitman File 16), Presidential Transition Series Box 1, Dwight D. Eisenhower Library, Abilene, Kansas.
49. Ibid.

12

John F. Kennedy and Israel, 1939–1962

John F. Kennedy and Israel represent a history of an American president, who, like Harry S Truman, sympathized and supported Israel, but at the same time was concerned with what was in the best interest of the United States and in the furtherance of freedom throughout the world. He wanted to do his best to avoid the mistakes of the Dwight D. Eisenhower administration. The "history of failure in that area and about the possibility of something like the (1958) Lebanon crisis that attended Eisenhower" was of great concern to President Kennedy and he had made a commitment "to bring peace in that area" of the world.[1]

Kennedy sought to establish a balanced policy. He tried to persuade both the Israelis and the Arabs that he was fair to them all. He wrote to the Israelis and to the heads of the Arab governments that he wanted to see good relationships established with Israel and with all the Arab governments. The texts went through some ten drafts before President Kennedy was satisfied with them because, as Myer Feldman recalled, President Kennedy "wanted to give the impression that he was seeking a dialogue with them, a continuing dialogue and that they should feel free to write to him personally and not even through regular State Department channels."[2] He also wanted to show them that he "was sympathetic to all their legitimate aspirations and he did not want to give the impression that he was siding with them in their conflict with Israel."[3] He discussed the variations in text of each letter with advisors including Feldman, so that "they would feel that this was a personal interest, and that this would then get them involved in the discussions with us."[4]

The letters were supposed to be private and secret, but President Abdel Nasser of Egypt published a portion of the letter that President Kennedy had sent him. "The President was fit to be tied at that because there had been no prior consultation with him regarding the publication of these letters; he felt the publication was being used as a propaganda move by Nasser, and he considered it a breach of faith." While this made Kennedy "a lot more cautious in his dealings with Nasser," it did not change his feeling that Nasser was "the key to the settlement of this whole problem."[5]

What did young Kennedy know about Israel and the Jews? His contacts with Jews and Israel had been sparse. His father, Joseph P. Kennedy, did not love Jews. Even so, he had tried to help save some during the destruction of European Jewry.

Did President Kennedy try to make up for his father's reported anti-Semitism? That is pure speculation.

Feldman, a pro-Israel Jew who was one of the president's closest advisors on the Middle East, recalled that "one of the major handicaps that we had to overcome, in the Jewish community, was the feeling that Kennedy's father had never been a friend of the Jews."[6] This changed when Richard Nixon became the Republican standard bearer. Thereafter, liberals then rallied to Kennedy. "No liberal could support Nixon."[7]

As a young man, Kennedy had traveled to the Holy Land in 1939 and reported back to his father some rather penetrating observations regarding Palestine, the Jews, and the Arabs. As he reviewed the history of British policies and the various claims to the desert of Palestine, Kennedy observed that the "important thing is to try to work out a solution that will work, not to try to present a solution based on two vague, indefinite and conflicting promises" such as the Sir Henry MacMahon letter[8] to the Arabs and the Balfour Declaration to the Jews. "This is my objection to the White Paper of May 1939. It theoretically presents a good solution, but it just won't work."[9]

He noted that

> on the Jewish side there is the desire for complete domination, with Jerusalem as the capital of their new land of milk and honey, with the right to colonize in Trans-Jordan. They feel that given sufficient opportunity they can cultivate the land and develop it as they have done in the Western portion. The Arab answer to this is incidentally, that the Jews have had the benefit of capital, which had the Arabs possessed, equal miracles could have been performed by them. Though this is partly true, the economic set up of Arabic agricultural progress with its absentee landlords and primitive methods of cultivation, could not under any circumstances probably have competed with the Jews. However, this very fact lies in the background of the Arabic objection to the Jews. They realize their superiority and fear it.[10]

According to Hirsh Freed, a Boston politician, when John Kennedy entered politics he "did not know any Jews." Freed claimed that he may have been the "only Jew Kennedy knew, at that particular time; at least politically or personally, in the sense of asking, who's this and what's that. Although he had taken trips through Europe or traveled in the Near East or something of that sort, he knew it in a very academic way." He never had come to grips with the issues confronting "Italians or the Negroes or Jews or for that matter, Irish, in any specific or immediate way as a politician or as a statesman." "I used to receive phone calls from him from Washington as to who was this guy and who was that organization and should I associate myself publicly with this and so on."[11] Freed arranged for Kennedy to meet Jewish leaders of Boston in April 1947, so that he could ask them questions regarding Zionism and Israel. The people at that gathering "were people who were devoted to a cause. They knew they were right and they couldn't help but speak the truth as they saw it."[12]

In 1957, Senator Kennedy joined Senator Lyndon B. Johnson and other senators, in persuading Eisenhower and the United Nations not to impose sanctions against Israel: "Israel asks only that she be given a guarantee of no future raids or of blockading of Israeli shipping."[13]

When Kennedy became president, he wanted to separate from the ineffective foreign and domestic policies of his predecessor—Dwight D. Eisenhower. His was a New Frontier. He envisioned taking the lead in making the world a better place in which to live. He had high hopes and ideals. Israel represented hope and progress to him, to Jews and to all of mankind. He believed that it would be easier to live with an Israel that was getting weapons and was secure than an Israel that might undertake unpredictable adventures such as the 1956 Sinai War. Israel might even become an effective arm against Soviet expansionist ambitions.

The State Department Kennedy inherited held the same harsh views towards Israel as State Department officials of previous decades. Officials there were very much concerned with Arab views and feelings. They wanted Israel to absorb some three hundred thousand Arabs who claimed to be refugees from the Holy Land. State Department officials were opposed to Israel's strong retaliatory measures against Arab infiltrators and terrorists; they opposed Israel's divergence of the Jordan River waters for its own agricultural programs; and they did not support Israel's desire to make Jerusalem the capital of Israel. Perhaps most of all they did not wish to see Israel become stronger militarily. Throughout the years 1948 to 1960, some elements of the State Department suspected Israel of being more sympathetic to Russia than to the United States. On July 12, 1962, Secretary of State Dean Rusk stated that the "United States does not recognize Israel's rights in Jerusalem as paramount nor does the United States accept Jerusalem as Israel's national capital."[14] It had been "Dean Rusk of the State Department's U.N. desk who had pushed for the establishment of Palestine as a trusteeship." Foreign Minister Moshe Sharett (Shertok) felt that Rusk had not changed much since 1947–1948 "even though so many years had passed. Nothing seemed to have changed in Rusk's heart."[15]

President Kennedy had an open mind and would listen to various advisers. When Feldman had said quite frankly that he "had an emotional sympathy with Israel" and that this would "color" the advice he might give the president, and that perhaps the president might want somebody else, President Kennedy said "no." Kennedy observed that he would expect that Feldman would have those sympathies and that "he would think less of him" if he did not and to keep him advised of "anything that was happening."[16]

President Kennedy would often turn to Feldman for advice on "anything dealing with the Middle East." The secretary of state at times resented this. Feldman recalled that on one occasion President Kennedy asked him to call Rusk and to advise him of his discussion and what position the United States was taking on a particular matter. Rusk was upset and told Feldman: "I want it clearly understood that I'm running the State Department and not somebody in the White House, and if there's any doubt about that I want to go to the President." The president then told Feldman that Rusk had to be kept fully advised and that Rusk had to be "kept happy." From then on President Kennedy carried messages to Rusk himself, rather than through Feldman.[17]

DIRECT ISRAELI-ARAB NEGOTIATIONS

Israel wanted to have direct, face-to-face negotiations with the Arabs. It had tried to persuade the Eisenhower administration to encourage the Egyptians to negotiate directly. The Israelis believed that if Egypt would negotiate and make peace then the other Arab states would likewise make peace. They tried to get Kennedy's support for direct peace negotiations. The Congo Republic in Brazzaville came up with a resolution, which some twenty-one UN members supported, calling upon the Arabs and Israel to enter into direct peace negotiations. Feldman knew that this "was not just the idea of the Congo, that this had been generated by Israel." The Israelis believed that they had a "good chance of getting the Brazzaville resolution passed if the United States would support it." But when Feldman inquired of the State Department and the UN "people," they informed him that it would not be possible to get sufficient support to pass the resolution.[18] While Kennedy had no objection to calling for direct negotiations between Israel and the Arab states, he felt "it would be a rather futile gesture" and if the United States "took the position that there should be direct negotiations, all the Arab states would feel that the United States was siding with Israel and that it would be a rather futile thing, so why do it."[19] But after "considerable soul-searching" the Kennedy administration came up with a "compromise" that "didn't satisfy anybody."[20]

ISRAEL, KENNEDY, AND THE PALESTINIAN REFUGEES

According to the State Department's plan, Palestinian Arabs would be repatriated to Israel. If this were to happen, estimates were that the United States would assume sixty percent of the costs, which would be about $1 billion. President Kennedy preferred to have a trial run of a few rather than many thousands. "Wouldn't we say that we would run a trial for a few rather than push the whole 1,100,000?" To limit the number might reassure Israel. Otherwise it will be hard to get Israel's acquiescence fearing that all would come. Such a "trial might show that only a few would come."[21]

Feldman felt that if the United States could link the delivery of the Hawk antiaircraft missiles to the Palestinian repatriation issue it might work.[22] Kennedy was concerned with the domestic political consequences of an Israeli-Arab deal. "We should find out what Israel will do. I don't want to get into a costly fight without getting something. I'm still living with residue of the December vote. I don't want to live with the residue of another fight for years and years."[23]

Feldman advised that the refugee plan should be connected with security guarantees to Israel and that David Ben-Gurion should be notified ahead of time that he would get the Hawk missiles. Kennedy was seeking to establish good relations with Egypt and he felt that "we must talk to Nasser first on the Hawks. All of this must be carried out with utmost secrecy."[24] Kennedy sent Feldman to Ben-Gurion to reassure him that the United States would "use its influence only in support of those proposals which do not involve serious risks for Israel."[25]

Feldman met with Ben-Gurion, Foreign Minister Golda Meir, and Teddy Kollek of Israel's Foreign Office American Desk. "I began by informing them that the President had determined that the Hawk missile should be made available to Israel." But Feldman cautioned that this would have to be worked out in later conversations and through other channels. Moreover, Nasser would be informed in the hope that there would be no escalation of the arms race. Ben-Gurion said he preferred no weapons and no escalation of the arms race. He agreed to the repatriation of some Arab refugees, if Nasser would agree to resettle Arab refugees in the UAR and to not direct propaganda to the refugees accepting repatriation. Feldman estimated that not more than one in ten would seek resettlement.

Rusk rejected Ben-Gurion's reservations regarding the Palestinian

Arab resettlement and observed that "it would be most unfortunate if the Israelis would end up with the Hawks and strengthened security assurances while being responsible for derailing the Johnson Plan[26] before it could even be given a good try."[27]

Meir advised Feldman that the United States should first see if the Arab governments would accept the Johnson Plan for it would be most embarrassing to the United States to offer a proposal, establish an administrator, and find that the Arab states would continue their propaganda so that Israel could not accept the refugees and the whole project would have to be abandoned. And then Meir revealed that "she had received concrete evidence that the Egyptians have guided missiles which they had purchased from West German sources at a cost of 250,000,000 pounds sterling. This, she said, indicated their real intentions." Feldman recommended that under the circumstances "we defer final decision on the Johnson plan until I return Thursday night."[28]

Rusk urged that Nasser be advised that the United States agreed to sell the Hawk missiles to Israel "in the light of U.A.R.'s acquisition of new types of equipment and in the absence of any limitation on the arms race in the area." Moreover, Nasser should be advised that the Hawks are purely defensive in nature and that the United States still wanted to limit the arms race.[29]

On August 24 Feldman reported that Israel had received an offer from Britain to purchase Bloodhound missiles, but Israel would not purchase them because they were inferior to the Hawks and "for other reasons."[30] By September 14 Feldman reported that the Johnson Plan did not stand a chance since Johnson included a provision that the United Nations would have authority to arbitrate any conflict over the admissibility of refugees. The Israelis rejected this as interfering with their sovereignty. Some administration officials like Robert W. Komer of the NSC thought that Israel should not be the one to turn down the American idea, but that Israel should wait until the Arabs turned it down.[31]

President Kennedy did not wish to press Israel on the Johnson Plan, especially since there was an off-year election coming up. McGeorge Bundy advised that the State Department "should not shower the Middle East with telegrams in praise of the Johnson plan."[32] As far as the Israeli government was concerned, the Johnson Plan lacked "integrity and realism." It offered contradictory things to each side—free choice to the Arabs and a final say to Israel. Once the Syrians rejected the Johnson Plan, it came to an end. Lebanon, Transjordan, and Egypt had been ready to go with the plan, but they would not as Syria rejected it.

Foreign Minister Meir spoke with Secretary of State Rusk on a variety of issues involving the Middle East, the Far East, and the world in general. Rusk expressed concern about the security of Israel and the signs of a buildup of armaments in the Arab countries. The buildup of Egyptian armaments was as much against some of its neighbors as it was against Israel. "The President is very concerned about the security of Israel, as is the whole country and we have to be for a variety of reasons." "We are very concerned about the arms race in the Middle East but we know that you are not responsible for it and that is why we have taken this new look," said Rusk.[33]

Meir said that Israel was prepared for disarmament and that it did not wish to "spend all this money on defense."[34]

Rusk asked Meir if Israel had its own villa in Geneva. "We have some little hole in the wall that we use as an office," said Meir.

Rusk replied, "Well, I put my eye on a villa there which I thought we should buy but when I cabled over to the State Department, I received a reply that there was just no money for it. Just a day or two later, an announcement was made of the U.S. Aid Program to India in the amount of about one billion dollars and shortly thereafter India bought the villa."

Gideon Raphael suggested that Rusk ask the Indians if the United States could "rent it."[35]

Mordechai Gazit observed that the State Department might have been regarded as a "Fortress of Evil" by those who favored Israel, but "it was possible to change that situation" and that it was even possible to "neutralize" some of those who were opposed to Israel. Mordechai Gazit held more than ten lunch meetings each week in order to provide American officials with information and guidance about Israel. When he was once asked by a State Department official as to what he thought of State Department officials, he said: "The State Department officials are doing their job and a good diplomat has to be even-handed." Gazit's response was very much appreciated by that official.[36]

President Kennedy established a new and "special relationship" with Israel. He was the first president to sell arms to Israel and the first to guarantee Israel's security, not just once, but on at least three different occasions. During Kennedy's May 1961 meeting with Ben-Gurion, he said: "I was elected by the Jews. You know . . . I have to do something for them."[37]

When on December 27, 1962, the president met with Foreign Minister Meir, he said that "the United States has a special relationship with Israel in the Middle East really comparable only to that which it has with Britain over a wide range of world affairs." But at the same time he advised her that the United States had to maintain its friendship and ties with Arab countries throughout the world and if the United States "pulled out of the Arab Middle East and maintained our ties only with Israel this would not be in Israel's interest."[38] Kennedy reminded Meir of America's worldwide responsibilities and obligations. Israel was only one of those responsibilities. No other country carried the same sort of responsibilities for so many distant areas such as "Korea, South Vietnam, India, Pakistan, the Middle East, Africa, Latin America and elsewhere. Our concern is in maintaining the balance of power in the interest of the free world. This is why we find ourselves involved in issues between the Somalis and Ethiopians, Indians and Pakistanis, Cambodians and Thais, and so many other disputes which are not part of what we see as the central struggle, the struggle of free peoples against the Communist Bloc." Kennedy realized that Israel had security problems, but so did the United States. The United States "came almost to a direct confrontation with the Soviet Union last spring and again recently in Cuba." There had been almost four direct collisions with the Soviet Union and China during that time period.[39]

Meir praised Kennedy for the way he had handled the Cuban crisis. Israel had regarded the Cuban crisis not just as a Cuban-American issue, but as a big problem facing the world and it was "delighted at the way it came out." She advised Kennedy that Israel considered itself as part of the free world and it appreciated U.S. policies and actions. Israel gained much encouragement from America's concern with Israel's security and from American friendship. As for the Arabs, Israel was not anti-Arab and from the start it sought to live in peace with the Arabs. While Israel had always been prepared to have direct talks with the Arabs, there had been no reciprocation on their part. Egypt had been provided with great quantities of arms from the Soviet Union, especially since Egypt's intervention in Yemen. Israel observed that "Soviet-supplied TU-16s had been able to fly from Egypt to Yemen, drop bombs and fly back to Egypt. If they accomplished that, what could they do to Israel?" Israel knew that Egypt built missile systems with the help of German scientists since 1960 and now it had a considerable problem along its sea frontiers since Egypt acquired a considerable number of submarines. The "Egyptians say that Israel breathes through only one border—the sea border—since the land borders are taken care of. Maybe this is only Arab talk, but that talk could mean something."[40]

Meir tried to help Kennedy appreciate more fully what Nasser's ambitions were. It was Egypt that forced Syria into a union and since Nasser's intervention in the war in Yemen, he had gotten more weapons from the Russians. According to Israel's information, Egypt initiated a four-year $220 million to $250 million program for radiological warfare.[41] Egypt likewise intervened in the Congo and Ghana.

As for the Arab refugees, Meir informed Kennedy that Israel had tried to help solve this problem. In 1949 it had said that it would "take up to 100,000 refugees back" and even though there was no peace, "close to 40,000 did come back." Moreover there are some "230,000 to 240,000

Arabs living in Israel, and that constitutes about 11 percent of the population. Not all of them are peaceful citizens."[42]

President Kennedy conceded that "obviously Israel cannot accept a flood of refugees," and that the Arabs had their troubles, too. Perhaps no compromises were possible. But he did not think Israel should give up on the refugees. Moreover, the Arab refugees were costing the United States money and the issue was causing a great damage to the prospects of peace. In the judgment of U.S. officials, it seemed that the great majority of refugees would prefer to be resettled outside of Israel. No progress was made on the Johnson plan and "that is gone." But the president thought that "we should keep trying" and he was not convinced that it was impossible. He thought it was like the dispute involving Kashmir. He believed that it was not possible "to let this dispute run on and blow up."[43]

President Kennedy noted that the United States was interested in Israel as he was personally. "We are interested that Israel should keep up its sensitive, tremendous, historic task. What we want from Israel arises because our relationship is a two-way street. Israel's security in the long run depends, in part, on what it does with the Arabs, but also on us." He asked that Israel would consider "our problems on this atomic reactor. We are opposed to nuclear proliferation. Our interest here is not in prying into Israel's affairs but we have to be concerned because of the over-all situation in the Middle East."[44]

Meir tried to reassure Kennedy that there would be "no difficulty between Israel and the United States on the Israeli nuclear reactor."[45]

Kennedy expressed his concern regarding Israel's retaliatory raids. "Whether right or wrong, those actions involved not just Israel, but also the United States."[46]

JORDAN

As Egypt expanded its activities in Yemen and the Arabian Peninsula towards the latter part of April, it seemed to Israel that Egypt would also seek to gain control over Jordan. Israel regarded Egypt's move into Jordan as most dangerous to its security and future. The United States kept a close eye on those developments. President Kennedy advised the British to move into Jordan in case of war and prepared to send a U.S. air squadron to Saudi Arabia as an indirect warning to Nasser.[47]

George W. Ball advised the American embassy in Israel that a coup in Jordan was very likely and that it was "being planned by the Army and other groups in Jordan, probably with Nasser's assistance." If the coup succeeded, then there was a strong possibility that the UAR would have predominant influence there. In that case Israel might decide to undertake military intervention in Jordan, Egypt, or both. The American ambassador in Israel was advised that if the coup did take place "you should at once strongly advise Ben Gurion to take no military action," and that the United States would use its full weight and influence to make sure that the situation on the Jordan-Israel border would remain unchanged. The United States likewise advised the Syrians and the Iraqis to stay out of the conflict and Egypt was warned not to risk war.[48]

Feldman recalled that President Kennedy kept close touch with these developments. He met with such advisors as Bundy, Feldman, and Robert McNamara. He also received "the best intelligence reports from Israel" to find out whether Israel would move into the West Bank if King Hussein were overthrown. It appeared as if Israel would take over the West Bank and that presented the United States with a difficult predicament. What were the choices for the United States at that time? To send troops into the area and drive Israel away from the West Bank? Or would the United States help carve up Jordan? Feldman recalled, "we never decided that issue." But Kennedy did move the Sixth Fleet towards Israel. "It was on its way to Israel when we got word that Hussein was reasonably secure, and they didn't have to go all the way. Instead of going to Haifa the Fleet was ordered to put in at Malta." It had been a tense time and "the President devoted full attention to that because it looked like the beginning of the possibility of a real war."[49] Only the president "knew what action he would have taken if Hussein had been assassinated or had fled the country."[50]

Acting Secretary of State James P. Grant advised Israeli Ambassador Avraham Harman and Minister Gazit that indications were that "something might happen in Jordan," and that there was "a chance of something happening within a few hours or days." It was likely that if Israel moved militarily the UAR would not sit still and neither would the Soviet Union.[51]

The anticipated coup in Jordan did not materialize and the UAR did not try to take over Jordan.

AID TO ISRAEL

For the 1962 budget, State Department officials felt that Israel should not get any development loan money since Israel had attained self-sufficiency and did not need any more development loan money. Fowler Hamilton, the Agency for International Development (AID) administrator, recommended that Israel should not get anything. The ambassador from Israel advised Feldman that Israel had been promised $30 million in development money, but received only $15 million. Undersecretary of State Douglas Dillon of the Eisenhower administration had promised that the additional $15 million would be forthcoming. Israel required $45 million and the basis for the request were the benefits that Israel had provided the United States: good Israeli relations in Africa and Latin America would be useful to the United States. If Israel would not receive some assistance it would have to discontinue such overseas programs. Moreover, Israel did not receive any U.S. grant money for military assistance, while Jordan and other states did. It had always been understood that some of the development loan money was a substitute for such assistance.

The State Department finally recommended that no more than $10 million be given in aid to Israel.

Feldman went to see President Kennedy about this situation. President Kennedy said that he knew that $10 million was what the State Department and the AID administrator had recommended. "What do you think they ought to have?"

"Forty-five million dollars," said Feldman. And he presented Kennedy with a viewpoint other than that presented by the American foreign policy establishment. When Feldman finished he added that it was worthy of the United States to support Israel. The conversation lasted no more than ten minutes and at the end of it the president said, "Okay, forty-five million dollars. You tell them." That was how the decision was made. Feldman recalled that he telephoned Hamilton, the AID administrator, and told him, "The President said it's forty-five million for Israel." Hamilton responded, "Where are we going to get it?" Feldman replied, "That's not my problem."[52]

Egypt and Syria joined to form the UAR and then declared their intention to "liberate Palestine." Ben-Gurion felt that this action would adversely effect the stability of the Middle East and the security of Israel. But he advised the Americans that Israel was "not helpless." In a "test of strength it can defeat all three but was not eager for such a victory." Ben-Gurion found it difficult to believe that the U.S. government would acquiesce in an attempted "liberation." The fact that the United States and the West provided financial assistance to the UAR enabled them to buy Russian arms that they intended to use against Israel. This attempted "liberation" could be forestalled by a U.S.–Soviet joint declaration that would seek to guarantee the territorial integrity and security of all the Middle Eastern states. Peace would be furthered if the United States would cut off "all assistance to any state" that threatened or refused to recognize the existence of its neighbor. Ben-Gurion was willing to fly to Washington to discuss these matters with President Kennedy. He voiced his appreciation for the Hawk missiles, but since Israel's neighbors were gathering new offensive weapons, the Hawk alone was not a deterrent.[53]

The Kennedy administration did not think that such a visit by Ben-Gurion was advisable at that time, nor did they think that a joint Soviet-American statement would be forthcoming.[54]

CONCLUSION

Kennedy supported Israel, but that did not satisfy such Israeli leaders as Ben-Gurion, Levi Eshkol, Meir, and Yitzhak Rabin. In early October 1963, President Kennedy once again reassured Israel of his support. Said Kennedy: "The Arabs know full well that the United States would support Israel and the United States would come to Israel's assistance in case of aggression." These reassurances were not good enough for Israeli leaders. They wanted more specific commitments. But President Kennedy was not quite ready to provide those commitments, nor would President Lyndon B. Johnson—although they were sympathetic and supportive. Israel did not appreciate U.S. even-handed efforts to secure the balance of power in the Middle East. For Israel it was a matter of survival and not a matter of theoretical diplomatic or military games.

While President Kennedy could appreciate Israel's desire and need for security, such members of his administration and staff as Rusk neither appreciated nor condoned its nuclear and other military-scientific research. Like their predecessors in the Eisenhower administration, they believed that such endeavors not only endangered the balance of power, but also the future of the planet. Some in the Kennedy administration believed that Israel's possession of such weapons might ultimately bring about a Soviet-American nuclear showdown. While some members of the State Department, CIA and NSC sought to keep Israel in harness, President Kennedy had a greater understanding and appreciation for Israel's position. But he still continued to work to maintain a friendship with such Arab states as Egypt in order to keep the Russians out of the region.

NOTES

1. Oral History of Myer Feldman Transcript, p. 399, John F. Kennedy Library, Boston.
2. Ibid., p. 461.
3. Ibid.
4. Ibid., p. 462.
5. Ibid., p. 463.
6. Ibid., p. 482.
7. Ibid.
8. High Commissioner Sir Henry McMahon wrote to Sharif Jusayn Ali, Amir of Mecca, a rather ambiguous letter in 1916 suggesting that Great Britain was

"prepared to recognize and uphold the independence of the Arabs" in the areas lying within the frontiers proposed by the Sharif of Mecca. This he wrote in the hope that Husayn's followers would join in the fight against the Turkish Empire.

9. Jack Kennedy to Joseph P. Kennedy, 1939 (no other date is given to the letter), President's Office Files, #135, John F. Kennedy Library, Boston.

10. Ibid.

11. Recollections of Hirsh Freed, Oral History Collection, John F. Kennedy Library, Boston.

12. Ibid.

13. *Congressional Record*, 1957, pp. 3178–3180.

14. Dean Rusk statement of July 12, 1962, President's Office Files, #118, John F. Kennedy Library, Boston.

15. Interview with Mordechai Gazit, August 3, 1997, Jerusalem.

16. Myer Feldman transcript, p. 476.

17. Ibid., pp. 474–475.

18. Ibid., p. 469.

19. Ibid., p. 470.

20. Ibid.

21. U.S. Department of State, *Foreign Relations of the United States, 1961–1963*, Volume XVIII (Washington, D.C., 1995), pp. 56–58.

22. Ibid.

23. Ibid., pp. 56–57.

24. Ibid., p. 58.

25. Letter from President John F. Kennedy to Prime Minister David Ben-Gurion, *Foreign Relations, 1961–1963*, Volume XVIII, August 14, 1962, pp. 60–61.

26. It was a U.S.-sponsored plan for the resettlement of Palestinian refugees.

27. Ibid., pp. 66–67.

28. Myer Feldman to President Kennedy, *Foreign Relations 1961–1963*, Volume XVIII, August 21, 1962, pp. 69–70.

29. Letter from Dean Rusk to U.S. Embassy in UAR, *Foreign Relations, 1961–1963*, Volume XVIII, August 22, 1962, p. 71.

30. Letter from Myer Feldman to President John F. Kennedy, *Foreign Relations, 1961–1963*, Volume XVIII, August 24, 1962, p. 63.

31. Memo from Robert W. Komer to President's Special Assistant for National Security Affairs (McGeorge Bundy), *Foreign Relations, 1961–1963*, Volume XVIII, September 14, 1962, pp. 96–97.

32. McGeorge Bundy to Robert W. Komer, *Foreign Relations, 1961–1963*, Volume XVIII, September 20, 1962, p. 111.

33. Golda Meir's talk with Dean Rusk, September 26, 1962, Israel Foreign Office Papers, 3377/5 II, Israel State Archives, Jerusalem.

34. Ibid.

35. Ibid.

36. Interview with Mordechai Gazit, August 3, 1997, Jerusalem.

37. David Ben-Gurion interview, John F. Kennedy Library, Boston.

38. State Department Memo of Conversation with Foreign Minister Golda Meir, President's Office Files, December 27, 1962, 119A, John F. Kennedy Library, Boston.

39. Ibid.

40. Ibid.

41. State Department Circular 1168 re President Kennedy's December 27, 1963, meeting with Foreign Minister Golda Meir, President's Office Files, 119A, John F. Kennedy Library, Boston.

42. Ibid.

43. *Foreign Relations, 1961–1963,* Volume XVIII, pp. 282–283.

44. Ibid.

45. Ibid.

46. Ibid.

47. *Foreign Relations, 1961–1963,* Volume XVIII, April 27, 1963, pp. 485–486.

48. George Ball to U.S. Embassy in Israel, *Foreign Relations, 1961–1963,* Volume XVIII, April 27, 1963, p. 487.

49. Myer Feldman transcript, pp. 479–481.

50. Ibid.

51. Minutes of meeting with Minister Mordechai Gazit, Ambassador Avraham Harman, and Acting Secretary of State James P. Grant, *Foreign Relations, 1961–1963,* Volume XVIII, p. 489.

52. Myer Feldman transcript, pp. 578–580.

53. Dean Rusk to U.S. Ambassador to Israel, President's Office Files, April 26, 1963, 119A, John F. Kennedy Library, Boston.

54. Memorandum on reply to David Ben-Gurion May 1, 1963, NSF 119, John F. Kennedy Library, Boston.

Bibliography

GOVERNMENT ARCHIVES AND PAPERS

Dwight D. Eisenhower Papers, Abilene, Kansas.
Israel Foreign Office Papers, Israel State Archives, Jerusalem.
Lyndon B. Johnson Papers, Austin, Texas.
John F. Kennedy Papers, John F. Kennedy Library, Boston.
Office of Strategic Services Papers, National Archives.
Franklin D. Roosevelt Papers, Franklin D. Roosevelt Library, Hyde Park, New York.
Harry S Truman Papers, Harry S Truman Library, Independence, Missouri.
U.S. Department of State Papers, National Archives, Washington, D.C.

PAPERS AND PRIVATE COLLECTIONS

Dean Acheson Papers, Yale University, New Haven, Connecticut.
All Zionist Archives Materials were transferred to Zionist Central Archives, Jerusalem. When I examined them they were in the Jewish Agency building at 515 Park Avenue, New York.
American Jewish Committee Papers, Zionist Archives, New York.
American Zionist Emergency Committee Papers, Zionist Archives, New York.
Benjamin Akzin Papers, Zionist Archives, New York.
Louis D. Brandeis Papers, Zionist Archives, New York.
Clark Clifford Papers, Harry S Truman Library, Independence, Missouri.
Benjamin V. Cohen Papers, Zionist Archives, New York.
H. Druks Family Papers, New York.
Nahum Goldmann Papers, Zionist Archives, Jerusalem.
Jewish Agency Papers, Zionist Archives, New York.
Admiral William D. Leahy Papers, Library of Congress, Washington, D.C.
Breckinridge Long Papers, Library of Congress, Washington, D.C.
James G. McDonald Papers, Columbia University, New York.

Julian W. Mack Papers, Zionist Archives, New York.
Henry Morgenthau Jr. Papers, Yale University, New Haven, Connecticut.
Samuel I. Rosenman Papers, Harry S Truman Library, Independence, Missouri.
Charles Ross Papers, Harry S Truman Library, Independence, Missouri.
Henry L. Stimson Papers, Yale University, New Haven, Connecticut.
Robert Szold Papers, Zionist Archives, New York, and the Robert Szold Home, Westchester, New York.
Stephen S. Wise Papers, Brandeis University Archives, Waltham, Massachusetts.
Zionist Archives, Individual Files, New York: Benjamin Akzin Papers; David Ben-Gurion Papers; Jacob DeHaas Papers; Abba Eban Papers; Albert Einstein Papers; Nahum Goldmann Papers; Rose Jacob Papers; Eddie Jacobson Papers; Julian W. Mack Papers; George C. Marshall Papers; Robert Szold Papers.
Zionist Organization of America Files, Zionist Archives, New York.

AUTOBIOGRAPHIES AND PERSONAL DOCUMENTARIES

Aaronsohn, Alexander. *With the Turks in Palestine*. Boston, 1916.
Abdullah, King of Jordan. *Memoirs*. New York, 1950.
Allon, Yigal. *The Making of Israel's Army*. New York, 1971.
Arlosoroff, Chaim. *K'tavin*. Tel Aviv, 1934.
Barkley, Alben W. *That Reminds Me*. New York, 1951.
Begin, Menachem. *The Revolt*. New York, 1951.
Ben-Gurion, David. *Recollections*. London, 1970.
———. *Israel: A Personal History*. New York, 1972.
Bernadotte, Count Folke. *To Jerusalem*. London, 1951.
Bush, George. *All the Best, George Bush: My Life in Letters and Other Writings*. New York, 1999.
Byrnes, James F. *Speaking Frankly*. New York, 1947.
Crossman, Richard. *Palestine Mission*. New York, 1947.
Dayan, Moshe. *Story of My Life: An Autobiography*. New York, 1976.
Eban, Abba. *My Country*. New York, 1972.
Eden, Anthony. *Full Circle*. London, 1960.
Eisenhower, Dwight D. *The White House Years: Mandate for Change, 1953–1956*. New York, 1963.
———. *The White House Years: Waging Peace, 1956–1961*. New York, 1965.
Elath, Eliahu. *Israel and Elath: The Political Struggle for the Inclusion of Elath in the Jewish State*. London, 1966.
———. *Yoman San Francisco*. Tel Aviv, 1971.
Freundlich, Yehoshua, ed. *Documents on the Foreign Policy of Israel*, vols. 5, 6, 8. Jerusalem, 1988, 1991, 1995.
Gilead, Baruch, ed. *Documents on the Foreign Policy of Israel*, vol. 14. Jerusalem, 1997.
Goldmann, Nahum. *The Autobiography of Nahum Goldmann: Sixty Years of Jewish Life*. New York, 1969.
Granados, Garcia. *The Birth of Israel: The Drama as I Saw It*. New York, 1948.
Jabotinsky, Vladimir. *The Story of the Jewish Legion*. New York, 1945.

Johnson, Lyndon B. *Vantage Point*. New York, 1971.
Joseph, Bernard. *British Rule in Palestine*. Washington, D.C., 1948.
Kissinger, Henry A. *White House Years*. Boston, 1979.
———. *Years of Upheaval*. Boston, 1982.
———. *Diplomacy*. New York, 1994.
———. *Years of Renewal*. New York, 1999.
Kollek, Teddy. *For Jerusalem: A Life*. New York, 1978.
McDonald, James G. *My Mission in Israel*. New York, 1951.
Meir, Golda. *A Land of Our Own*. Philadelphia, 1973.
———. *My Life*. New York, 1975.
Neumann, Emanuel. *In the Arena: An Autobiographical Memoir*. New York, 1976.
Nixon, Richard M. *RN: The Memoirs of Richard Nixon*. New York, 1978.
Peres, Shimon. *Battling for Peace: Memoirs*. New York, 1995.
Philby, Harry St. John. *Arabian Jubilee*. London, 1953.
Powell, Colin L. *My American Journey: An autobiography*. New York, 1995.
Rabin, Yitzhak. *The Rabin Memoirs*. Tel Aviv, 1994.
Rafael, Gideon. *Destination Peace: Three Decades of Israeli Foreign Policy*. London, 1981.
Reagan, Ronald. *An American Life: The Autobiography*. New York, 1990.
Roosevelt, Eleanor. *This I Remember*. New York, 1949.
Rosenman, Samuel. *Working with Roosevelt*. New York, 1952.
Sharon, Ariel. *Warrior*. New York, 1989.
Stettinius, Edward. *Roosevelt and the Russians*. New York, 1949.
Truman, Harry S. *Memoirs*, 2 vol. New York, 1953–1955.
———. *Years of Trial and Hope*. New York, 1956.
Truman, Margaret. *Harry S Truman*. New York, 1973.
Vance, Cyrus R. *Hard Choices: Critical Years in America's Foreign Policy*. New York, 1983.
Waldman, Morris D. *Nor by Power*. New York, 1953.
Weizman, Ezer. *The Battle for Peace*. New York, 1981.
Weizmann, Chaim. *Trial and Error*. New York, 1949.
Welles, Sumner. *We Need Not Fail*. Boston, 1948.
Wise, Stephen S. *Challenging Years*. New York, 1949.

SECONDARY WORKS CONSULTED

Abu-Lughod, Ibrahim, ed. *The Arab-Israeli Confrontation of June 1967: An Arab Perspective*. Evanston, Ill., 1970.
Allon, Yigal. *The Making of Israel's Army*. London, 1970.
Alroy, Gil Carl. *The Kissinger Experience: American Policy in the Middle East*. New York, 1975.
Avriel, Ehud. *Open the Gates! A Personal Story of "Illegal" Immigration to Israel*. London, 1975.
Barnard, Harry. *The Forging of an American Jew: The Life and Times of Judge Julian Mack*. New York, 1974.
Bar-On, Mordecai, ed. *Israel Defense Forces: The Six-Day War*. Philadelphia, 1969.
———. *The Gates of Gaza: Israel's Road to Suez and Back, 1955–1957*. New York, 1994.

Bar-Zohar, Michael. *Ben Gurion: The Armed Prophet*. Englewood Cliffs, N.J., 1968.

———. *Embassies in Crisis: Diplomats and Demagogues behind the Six-Day War*. Englewood Cliffs, N.J., 1970.

Ben-Porat, Eitan Haber, and Zeev Schiff. *Entebbe Rescue*. New York, 1976.

Bober, Arie, ed. *The other Israel*. New York, 1972.

Brecher, Michael. *Decisions in Israel's Foreign Policy*. New Haven, Conn., 1975.

Christman, Henry M., ed. *The State Papers of Levi Eshkol*. New York, 1969.

Churchill, Randolph S., and Winston Churchill. *The Six-Day War*. New York, 1967.

Congressional Record. Various years. Washington, D.C.

Dagan, Avigdor. *Moscow and Jerusalem: Twenty Years of Relations between Israel and the Soviet Union*. London, 1970.

Daniels, Jonathan. *The Man of Independence*. New York, 1950.

Dayan, Moshe. *Diary of the Sinai Campaign*. New York, 1966.

Druks, Herbert. *Harry S Truman and the Russians*. New York, 1981.

Eddy, William A. *F.D.R. Meets Ibn Saud*. New York, 1954.

Feinberg, Nathan. *The Arab-Israeli Conflict in International Law*. Jerusalem, 1970.

Finer, Herman. *Dulles over Suez: The Theory and Practice of His Diplomacy*. Chicago, 1964.

Freedman, Max. *Roosevelt and Frankfurter: Their Correspondence*. Boston, 1967.

Freundlich, Yehoshua, and Balluch Gilead, eds. *Documents on the Foreign Policy of Israel*, various years. Jerusalem, 1988.

Friedman, Isaiah. *The Question of Palestine, 1914–1918*. New York, 1973.

Friedman, Saul S. *No Haven for the Oppressed*. Detroit, 1973.

Gazit, Mordechai. *President Kennedy's Policy Toward the Arab States and Israel: Analysis and Documents*. Tel Aviv, 1983.

Gilbert, Martin. *Israel: A History*. New York, 1998.

Golan, Matti. *The Secret Conversations of Henry Kissinger*. New York, 1976.

Habas, Bracha. *The Gate Breakers*. New York, 1963.

Haber, Julius. *The Odyssey of an American Zionist: A Half-Century of Zionist History*. New York, 1958.

Halpern, Ben. *The Idea of the Jewish State*. Cambridge, Mass. 1961.

Harkabi, Yehoshafat. *Arab Attitudes to Israel*. Jerusalem, 1972.

Henriques, Robert. *100 Hours to Suez*. New York, 1957.

Hertzberg, Arthur, ed. *The Zionist Idea*. New York, 1959.

Herzog, Chaim. *The War of Atonement*. London, 1975.

Holly, David C. *Exodus 1947*. Boston, 1969.

Horowitz, David. *State in the Making*. New York, 1953.

Hyamson, Albert. *Palestine under the Mandate*. London, 1950.

Kalb, Marvin, and Bernard Kalb, *Kissinger*. Boston, 1974.

Katz, Samuel. *Days of Fire*. New York, 1966.

Kimche, Jon. *There Could Have Been Peace*. New York, 1973.

Kimche, Jon, and David Kimche. *The Secret Roads: The "Illegal" Migration of a People, 1938–1948*. London, 1954.

———. *A Clash of Destinies: The Arab-Jewish War and the Founding of the State of Israel*. New York, 1960.

Kohler, Foy D. *The Soviet Union and the other 1973 Middle East War: The Implications for Detente*. Miami, 1974.

Kurzman, Dan. *Genesis 1948: The First Arab-Israeli War*. New York, 1970.
Lacqueur, Walter Z. *The Struggle for the Middle East: The Soviet Union in the Mediterranean, 1958–1968*. New York, 1969.
———. *A History of Zionism*. New York, 1972.
Lash, Joseph P. *Eleanor:The Years Alone*. New York, 1972.
Learsi, Rufus. *Fulfillment: The Epic Story of Zionism*. Cleveland, 1951.
Levey, Zach. *Israel and the Western Powers, 1952–1960*. Durham, N.C., 1997.
Livneh, Eliezer. *Yahadut Amerika*. Ramat Gan, Israel, 1967.
London Sunday Times. Yom Kippur War. New York, 1969.
Lorch, Netanel. *The Edge of the Sword: Israel's War of Independence*. New York, 1961.
Love, Kenneth. *Suez: Twice Fought War*. New York, 1969.
Manuel, Frank E. *The Realities of American-Palestine Relations*. Washington, D.C., 1949.
Mardor, Manya. *Haganah*. New York, 1957.
Marshall, S. L. A. *Sinai Victory*. New York, 1958.
Mason, Alpheus T. *Brandeis: A Free Man's Life*. New York, 1946.
Morse, Arthur D. *While Six Million Died: A Chronicle of American Apathy*. New York, 1967.
Nadich, Judah. *Eisenhower and the Jews*. New York, 1953.
O'Ballance, Edgar. *The Third Arab-Israeli War*. London, 1972.
Parkes, James. *A History of Palestine from 135 A.D. to Modern Times*. London, 1949.
Pearlman, Moshe. *Ben Gurion Looks Back*. London, 1965.
Prittie, Terrence. *Eshkol: The Man and the Nation*. New York, 1969.
Rabinovich, Abraham. *The Battle for Jerusalem, June 5–7, 1967*. Philadelphia, 1972.
Rabinowitz, Ezekiel. *Justice Louis D. Brandeis: The Zionist Chapter of His Life*. New York, 1968.
Rosenne, Shabtai. *Israel's Armistice Agreement with the Arab States*. Tel Aviv, 1951.
Sachar, Howard M. *A History of Israel: From the Rise of Zionism to Our Time*. New York, 1996.
Safran, Nadav. *The United States and Israel*. Cambridge, Mass., 1963.
———. *From War to War: The Arab-Israeli Confrontation, 1948–1967*. Indianapolis, 1969.
Samuel, Viscount Herbert L. S. *Memoirs*. London, 1955.
Schechtman, Joseph B. *The U.S. and the Jewish State Movement: The Crucial Decade: 1939–1949*. New York, 1966.
Schiff, Ze'ev, and Raphael Rothstein. *Fedayeen: The Story of the Palestinian Guerillas*. London, 1972.
———. *October Earthquake: Yom Kippur 1973*. Tel Aviv, 1974.
Smith, Charles D. *Palestine and the Arab-Israeli Conflict*. New York, 1996.
Snetsinger, John. *Truman, the Jewish Vote and the Creation of Israel*. Stanford, 1974.
Sobel, Lester A. ed. *Israel and the Arabs: The October 1973 War*. New York, 1974.
Stein, Leonard. *The Balfour Declaration*. London, 1961.
Steinberg, Alfred. *The Man from Missouri*. New York, 1962.
St. John, Robert. *Eban*. New York, 1972.
Sunday Times Correspondents. Insight on the Middle East War. London, 1974.
Thomas, Abel. *Comment Israel Fut Sauve, Les Secrets de L'Expedition de Suez*. Paris, 1978.

Thomas, Hugh. *Suez*. New York, 1967.

Tsur, Ya'akov. *Prelude a Suez: Journal d'une ambassade, 1953–1956*. Paris, 1968.

U.S. Department of State. *Foreign Relations of the United States, 1933–1960*. Washington, D.C., various years.

Urofsky, Melvin. *American Zionism from Herzl to the Holocaust*. New York, 1975.

———. *We Are One*. New York, 1978.

Urofsky, Melvin, and David W. Levy, eds. *Letters of Louis D. Brandeis*. New York, 1971.

Wyman, David. *The Abandonment of the Jews: America and the Holocaust, 1941–1945*. New York, 1984.

Index

About the Author

HERBERT DRUKS is Professor of History and Politics in the Department of Judaic Studies at Brooklyn College and a member of the Humanities Department of the School of Visual Arts.